REACHING FOR THE STARS

REACHING FOR THE STARS THE MAKING OF CONSTELLATION BRANDS BY RICHARD AND ROB SANDS

with Paul Chutkow

 Val de Grâce Books   Napa, California

Published by Val de Grâce Books
Napa, California

© 2008, CONSTELLATION BRANDS

ISBN 978-0-9817425-0-2

Cover and book design: Milton Glaser, Inc.
Original photography: Matthew Klein

This book was produced and printed in keeping with the highest standards of environmental protection and sustainability.

It is printed on Satin Kinfuji paper from the Oji Paper Company, Ltd., Japan, a company committed to procuring certified wood raw materials from sources that practice sustainable forest management.

It was printed at Toppan Printing Co., Ltd. in Japan, named one of the "100 Most Sustainable Corporations in the World" in 2007 and 2008 for its standards and high level of performance regarding the environment, society, and corporate governance.

Part I: Fighting for Survival

Part II: Learning the Hard Way

Part III: Building to Last

Part IV: Leaping to the Top

Richard Sands

Rob Sands

A Note From the Authors

My brother Rob and I feel very blessed.

For more than 70 years, our family has been intertwined with the history of American wine. In 1936, when the wine industry was struggling back to its feet after the lifting of Prohibition, our grandfather, Mack Sands, packed up his family, said good-bye to Brooklyn, and started a wine-bottling business down in Greensboro, North Carolina. Mack made a good start. Then in 1946, when his son Marvin was coming out of wartime service in the U.S. Navy, Mack talked him into moving north to Canandaigua, New York, to take over a struggling little wine company, Canandaigua Industries. Dad was only 22 years old at the time and he had no experience in business. Still, after the lean wartime years, the American wine industry seemed poised for a comeback and Dad decided to give it a try.

Dad's operation was modest. His "corporate headquarters" was one tiny building, and his "executive suite" was nothing more than an old adding machine and a scarred wooden desk. Behind his office, though, was the production facility, and day and night it was filled with the romance and the mystery of wine. There were huge wooden fermenting tanks where freshly-picked grapes from New York and juice from California would be turned into wine, by means of an ancient alchemy of art and science. There was a small lab, filled with instruments and glassware, where the winemakers worked their magic. And everywhere Dad looked there was heavy machinery, a constant reminder that the art and science of wine must always be under-girded by a strong business and financial foundation. As Dad learned right away, to make Canandaigua Industries successful, he had to fuse the romance of wine with the power of business.

That proved to be a daunting task. Within weeks of settling into the job, Dad was hit by a series of crises, and for the next five years Dad and our mom, Mickey Sands, struggled to keep the business afloat. The American wine industry was in chaos, competition was fierce, profit margins were paper-thin, and Dad and Mom labored against a mountain of debt. With so few in his pocket, Dad learned how to manage every penny and every dime. What our parents had, though, was something more precious than silver or gold: they had strength of character and clear, time-tested values regarding business and life.

Today every PR-savvy CEO maintains that his or her company "puts people first." Dad lived that credo every single day. Morning to night he talked with his winemakers, his sales people, his bottling crews, his truckers, and his customers. If anyone had problems or ideas to suggest, Marvin encouraged them to come straight to him. Likewise, in the early years Mom helped out at the winery, entertained customers at home, and helped put together the gift baskets at holiday time. They took good care of their people. Dad made sure that every one of his employees had both medical insurance and a retirement savings plan – and this was long before either benefit had become standard in the American workplace. Dad's personal manner was equally caring and respectful. With his staff or his customers, Dad was always a patient listener, and he had a gift for making everyone feel like a valued member of our extended family.

For Rob and me, Marvin was not only a father; he was a patient and inspiring mentor. He taught us the wine business from the ground up, from the grapevines and bottling lines to the banks and the corporate boardroom. He taught us the power of money and the importance of maintaining rigorous financial dis-cipline in every aspect of our operations. But Dad also taught us that success in business is about far more than costs, sales, and profit margins. It's about values. It's about people. It's about creativity, about balancing risk and opportunity, and always nurturing the entrepreneurial spirit. The key to long-term success in the wine business, Dad showed us, was building a rock-solid foundation of personal and business relationships,

Mickey and Marvin Sands

and the bedrock essentials here are integrity, loyalty, and trust. Your word is your bond, Dad used to tell us; make sure it's as good as gold.

For Rob and me, these were lessons to be treasured and enshrined in stone. And Marvin and Mickey also taught us something else. Through their work with the local hospital and their active support for the arts, they showed us the joy of serving our communities, and they helped us understand that true wealth is never measured in dollars and cents; it is measured in richness of character and generosity of spirit.

In the coming pages, Rob and I are going to tell you the story of how that struggling little family business grew into a diversified global giant, Constellation Brands, today the biggest wine company in the world. We will discuss the business strategies and decisions that propelled our growth, and we will show you how we brought into our portfolio many of the world's preeminent brands and companies in the realms of wine, beer, and spirits.

Still, this book is about far more than business. It's about the history of wine. It's about the evolution of American taste. And it's about how the art and science of modern winemaking have now found new expression in places like Australia, New Zealand, Canada, Chile, Argentina, South Africa, and beyond. Our most important message, though, is about character and values. Rob and I want to share with you the rich human stories behind our success and we want to show you how the values that Marvin and Mickey instilled in us continue to guide us today at Constellation Brands. In the early days, Dad could communicate those values just through his own demeanor and leadership style, by treating our staff and our suppliers and customers with dignity and respect. Today our Constellation family numbers nearly 10,000 people, and we have partners and operations around the globe, managing more brands in wine, spirits, and beer than our parents could ever dream of. Rob and I try our best to communicate our values and ideals to the general public and to every corner of our extended family, but it is not an easy task. We hope this book will help you understand who we are, what we seek to accomplish, and what we hold most dear.

Rob and I have one other purpose too. While much of our story focuses on our family history, we want to make clear that the real heroes of our company's story are not named Sands. They have last names like Meenan. Silk. Lanier. Selig. Read. Hetterich. Summer. Finkle. Rockwell. Jacobson. Fernandez. Moramarco. Berk. And thousands more. These are the men and women who do the heavy lifting, who secure the grapes, make the wines, control quality and costs, get our products to market, drive sales, and who always keep open the gates to fresh ideas and new opportunities. If Rob and I have learned anything along the way, it is how blessed we are to work with such gifted and dedicated men and women. Over the past two decades, Rob and I have led the company through a period of unprecedented growth and diversification, and we're proud of that. But we never forget who deserves our deepest thanks and our biggest salute: it is all the men and women we work with, the people who day in and day out honor our mission and keep us all "reaching for the stars." It is to each of you that Rob and I dedicate this book, and we do so with a grateful bow.

Richard Sands and Rob Sands

PART I

Fighting for Survival

The original office of Canandaigua Industries, above, was so cramped that during the day everyone had to squeeze past Marvin's desk to get to the bathroom.

CHAPTER 1

Grandpa Mack

One day, in the course of gathering material for this book, Rob and I came across an unexpected treasure. Stored away in several long, dusty cardboard boxes we found hundreds of old wine labels, small, rectangular labels that had never found their way onto the side of a bottle. Many of the labels were faded or yellowed with age, and some were badly frayed around the edges. To my eyes, though, these were precious jewels, and I immediately saw what a fascinating story they tell.

The labels featured names like "Old Maude," "Old Duke," and "Captain Jack," names that carry us back to an earlier, more rambunctious era in the history of American wine. I marveled, too, at the names of the grape varietals listed on those labels, varietals that many wine lovers today have never even heard of: varietals such as Scuppernong, Catawba, Dutchess, and Isabella. Examining those labels, smelling the musty paper, I felt I was holding in my hands miniature pieces of American history.

For Rob and me, those labels also held a deeper meaning. You see, we grew up with "Old Maude," "Old Duke," and "Captain Jack" – those were flagship brands of the old Car-Cal Winery, the wine bottling business that our grandfather, Mack Sands, ran down in Greensboro, North Carolina. Mack had started up in 1936, just three years after the lifting of Prohibition, an important benchmark in the histories of both America and American wine. A decade later, Mack urged his son Marvin – our father – to get started in the wine business and make a home here in Canandaigua, in New York's fabled Finger Lakes region outside of Rochester. So for Rob and me, poring through those musty old Car-Cal labels, marveling at their look and feel, was like reaching back in time and placing the tips of our fingers down on the roots of our family's own history in American wine.

In gathering material for this book, our mom presented us with another treasure: a stack of love letters that she and Dad wrote to each other during the early 1940s, the agonizing years of World War II, the time when they were courting. Many of the letters cover the period when Dad was an ensign in the Navy, serving in Tunisia, then Italy, and, near the end of the war, San Francisco. There were also later letters from when Dad was starting out in the wine business and struggling every inch of the way. By the time Mom shared those letters with us, Dad was gone – he had died of cancer in 1999 – and Rob and I could readily see why they held so much meaning and importance for her. They were like timeless whispers in her ear, permanent reminders of the first soaring joys – and difficult life decisions – that she and Dad were experiencing together.

Today, those letters sit on a worktable beside my writing desk, to guide me as I write and to remind me that the story of Constellation Brands is not driven solely by bold strategies or opportune mergers and acquisitions. It is driven by the vision, talent, commitment, and hard work of many exceptional people, starting with our father. In the course of our story, I will be returning to Mom and Dad's letters for they shine light deep into the crevices of our family history and they illuminate those two qualities that I will be returning to over and over: character and values.

Let me make a small confession here: when it comes to exploring human character, I am by no means a novice. Before joining my father in the family business, I did research and earned a Ph.D. in social psychology – essentially the study of what makes people tick

Labels such as these take us back to the colorful roots of the American wine industry.

Experience is the best teacher, and the rougher the experience, the deeper the learning.

and behave the way they do. That training has been invaluable to me at Constellation Brands, and it has given me a unique window into how companies work, especially family companies like ours. In essence, what I saw very early on was this: in any company, having high-quality, well-targeted products and services is essential. So is having rigorous financial discipline and good people working at every level inside your company. Ultimately, though, every company – and especially a family-run company – has its own set of intangible assets, its own way of leadership, its own specific DNA, and those are usually a far better indicator of strength and future success than any momentary share price or earnings report.

Throughout my career in business, I have seen time and again that the real secrets to business success are not to be found in any textbook or even the finest MBA program. They are to be found in the men and women who run companies that face the toughest challenges and go through the hottest fires – then emerge smarter, tougher, and more nimble, always ready and able to shift gears, to seize opportunity, and to innovate and pioneer. In sum, where other business leaders might cower in disappointment or defeat, these men and women come through the fires with strengthened character, clarified values, and a heightened sense of meaning and purpose. Experience is the best teacher, and the rougher the experience, the deeper the learning. I have seen that core truth played out in company after company, and I can see it as I look back across the tumultuous history of Constellation Brands. And that brings me now to the heart of it, to where our story truly begins:

With our Grandpa Mack.

Now Rob and I could probably write an entire book about Grandpa Mack; our family lore is full of stories about the man and his cranky, indomitable spirit. That said, we can't give you a first-hand account of what Mack was like back in 1936 when he started the Car-Cal Winery; Rob and I only knew him many years later. But this much we know to be true: young or old and every age in between, Mack was a classic. A true original. A man about whom everyone would say, "Ah, Mack. With him they broke the mold!"

Mack was not an easy man to understand. He was short in stature, no more than five-foot six or seven, and on the surface he was rough, gruff, irascible, and never without a cigar. Morning to night he smoked his cigars, and his every move was accompanied by huffing and puffing and noxious billows of smoke. As kids, we recoiled from the smell that permeated his clothes, his skin, and every corner of his office and car. The worst part, though, was his temper. Rob and I and most everyone else tiptoed around Mack, for fear we might incur his wrath and unleash his legendary tongue. Still, beneath his prickly, volatile exterior, Grandpa Mack could be as warm and comforting as oatmeal on a winter morning. He wasn't that way often – just often enough to surprise you and make you think.

Mack's personality had many layers and contradictions. He was one part savvy, hard-driving entrepreneur, one part tight-fisted, domineering boss, and one part reckless riverboat gambler. Okay, two parts reckless riverboat gambler. What glued those layers together was ambition. Mack had come to America as an immigrant, and he had a burning desire to prove himself, to succeed, to move up the economic and social ladder. The wine business was his chosen vehicle, and he was not about to let anything – or anybody – slow his ascent. Mack did have many good traits and the best of them was loyalty. If they had earned his respect, Mack was fiercely loyal to his friends, his business associates, and members of his family, even though they too, sooner or later, would feel the sting of his tongue. There was only one person on the planet who enjoyed special dispensation from Mack's volatile temper: his son and only child, Marvin. Dad knew how to handle Mack. And Mack had infinite respect for his son and his abilities. Theirs was a fascinating relationship and, as you will see, it helped shape the early years of Constellation Brands.

And I'll tell you this: Grandpa Mack was one tough cookie. Whatever he lacked in stature and brawn Mack made up for in gumption and bravado. Later in life, after decades of incessant cigar smoking, Mack suffered cancer of the larynx and the doctors had to remove it, leaving Mack with a hole in his throat and a voice that was reduced to a gravelly rasp. But that barely slowed him down. At the Car-Cal Winery and when he came up to Canandaigua to work with Dad and his team, if something piqued his anger, Mack could still let loose with terrible invective, and his raspy voice would echo through the fermenting tanks and rattle the glass on the bottling lines. Yes, Mack was quite a character, and he loved nothing more than to sit down with friends, smoke a few cigars, enjoy a nip or two, and swap a few tall tales about what the wine business was like back in the good old days, back before wine in America became respectable and genteel.

Mack's personal history is quite revealing. Nothing in his early life was easy or safe; as a kid he had to scrap and live by his wits almost every step of the way. He was born on June 19th, 1898, and his given name was Mordechai. He was born into a Jewish family in Russia; our family roots trace back to the town of Kremenchuk, in the Ukraine. Our family name was Sandomirsky. Mack's father Elias was an imposing figure: strong and intelligent, with an authoritative bearing. There are conflicting accounts of what Elias did in Russia but he was clearly a man of substantial means. He and his wife Dora had nine children. Beyond that, we know little about the family's circumstances. But this much we know: this was a terrible period for Jewish families in Russia. Jews lived as outcasts from Russian life and society, whether it was in Moscow or St. Petersburg or in the towns and villages across the countryside. Official discrimination was severe: Jews were barred from many areas of Russian commerce, and schools maintained rigid quotas limiting the number of Jewish children who were allowed to attend. The worst were the pogroms. These were periodic, orchestrated, and often violent anti-Jewish campaigns, where Jewish homes were summarily burned to the ground and men, women, and even children were often brutally murdered. These pogroms touched off a mass exodus. From 1880 to 1920, about two million Jews fled their homeland. One of the worst pogroms extended from 1903 to 1906. Thousands of people were murdered and thousands more chose to uproot their families and flee, in the hope of escaping the violence and making a better life somewhere else. The Sandomirsky family was among them.

The family sailed for America in 1907 and records show that they traveled first class. Their port of entry was Ellis Island. Young Mordechai, then only nine years old, arrived

Elias Sandomirsky, above, brought the family from Russia to America in 1903. At Ellis Island, immigration officials changed our family name to "Sands."

Never great in school, Young Mack's real education came from the streets of Brooklyn.

with his parents, Elias and Dora; his six brothers Harry, Nathan, Benjamin, Fred, David, and George; and one sister, Vera. Another sister, Eva, had earlier died in Russia of whooping cough. As was so often true in the land of the great melting pot, the family's Americanization began right on the spot: immigration officials at Ellis Island changed their name from Sandomirsky to Sands. At the stroke of a pen, the Sandomirskys had a new name, a new land, and a new beginning to their lives. Dora soon renamed herself "Dorothy" and Mordechai soon became known as "Mack."

We don't know much about Mack's early boyhood in Russia; like so many immigrants he drew a curtain down on that part of his life and rarely, if ever, chose to look back. I imagine, though, that his early years in Russia were harrowing, for throughout his life our Grandpa Mack was haunted by a terrible fear: that somehow he had entered the United States illegally, and that sooner or later the authorities would track him down – and ship him back to Russia. Because of that fear, Mack never applied for a passport, and once here he never again set foot outside the United States. For the same reason, he never allowed his name to appear on any official documents. When he created the Car-Cal Winery, for instance, and whenever he bought stocks, he put everything in the name of his wife.

Mack's family settled in Brooklyn. I'm sure life wasn't easy for him – he had to learn a new language, adapt to a new culture, make new friends, and start anew in a wholly different school and neighborhood. Still, he was free. And he loved his new surroundings. Brooklyn at the time was home to thousands of Jewish immigrant families and businesses, and many of his pals were newcomers just like him. Mack never had any fondness for school and he dropped out early. Still, he was naturally intelligent and sharp with numbers, and Mack was known for his "street smarts" – a reputation that would follow him throughout his later life in the world of business.

Even as a youth Mack was a restless spirit: by his late teens he was eager to leave Brooklyn and make his mark in the world. His older brother David had already moved to Cleveland, Ohio, and was doing pretty well. David invited Mack to join him and he promised to help his younger brother get started. Still, Mack had one tiny problem: he had no money to make the trip west. Would that slow him down?

No way. As Marvin enjoyed recounting to Rob and me, Mack went to his father and asked him for a small loan, just enough to make the trip to Cleveland and get settled. Now Mack's father was by no means penniless. Soon he would have the means to purchase a small apartment building in Brooklyn. But Elias Sands was no fool either. He knew that simply loaning his headstrong son the money would not make a deep enough impression on him – and Mack might never bother to pay him back. So Elias came up with an astute alternative. Elias had a pocket watch that he absolutely cherished. Whatever its value in dollars paled next to the sentimental value it held for Elias. Nonetheless, Elias gave the watch to Mack and told him to hock it at the local pawnshop and use that money for his trip. In this way, Elias impressed on his son the true value of the loan. As our own father was always happy to report to Rob and me, in time Mack dutifully paid off the loan and made sure that his father got back his beloved watch. And don't imagine for an instant that Rob and I failed to get the underlying message.

With that money, Mack moved to Cleveland and promptly started to make his way. Early on, he met a tantalizing, high-spirited young woman named Sally Kipnis. They had much in common. Her family, too, had emigrated from Russia, and she was energetic, ambitious, and even more social and outgoing than Mack. Before long, they were married and running their own business, an ice cream parlor, and it quickly became successful. On January 28th, 1924, Mack and Sally had their first and only child, a son they named Marvin Lewis. Our dad. For awhile, everything went along swimmingly. Mack had plenty of cash in his pocket and he was perceived as a smart businessman, a rising star in the local business community. Before long, some tantalizing real estate deals were ushered his way. In my mind's eye, I can see Mack puffing out his chest and, like many young people who taste early success, imagining that he was invulnerable, that he could do no wrong.

Then he started to gamble.

Mack loved to play cards. Gin rummy, poker, bridge, hearts – Mack loved them all. Nobody knows for sure how it happened, but Mack started to gamble – and not just for nickels and dimes. Mack also liked to drink and party. This was, after all, the Roaring Twenties, the era of Prohibition, a time of bootleggers and speakeasies, of clandestine gin mills and gambling dens. While Temperance Leagues and religious leaders railed against the evils of gambling and "demon rum," the Jazz Age was in full swing, thumbing its nose at Puritan America and tugging at the straps of the prevailing social and sexual strictures. In 1925, F. Scott Fitzgerald published The Great Gatsby, featuring a fabulously wealthy bootlegger named Jay Gatsby and heralding a more liberated period in American social history. In line with the times, Fitzgerald and his high-stepping wife Zelda would go on celebrated benders, often ending up in the fountain in front of New York's fabled Plaza Hotel. I'm sure that plenty of plain, down-home Americans back in Cleveland shunned this sort of revelry, in favor of abstinence and proper decorum, but in those ranks you would not find our Grandpa Mack.

Inevitably, I suppose, it all came crashing down.

How comforting it would be to blame Mack's downfall on a failure of his ice cream shop or on some sudden economic downturn in Cleveland. But no, Mack had no one to blame but himself. Even though he had a wife and baby at home, Mack continued to gamble – and lose. Then his real estate deals went south. Whatever profits they were making from their ice cream parlor were not enough to stave off disaster: soon Mack and Sally found themselves without a dime. With few other options, they packed up little Marvin and their belongings and headed back to Brooklyn. According to our mom, one humiliation then led to another: back home, Mack had to turn to his father for help. I doubt Elias was happy about it, but he gave them lodging in the basement apartment in the building he now owned in Brooklyn. For Mack, it was quite a fall. One day he was a young star on the rise, the next he was a loser on the slide.

Mack's recklessness and resultant fall put a terrible strain on his marriage – and his volatile temper only made matters worse. According to Mom, Mack and Sally had some terrible fights. During this period, Sally became very nervous about what was going to happen to her and little Marvin. Mack, after all, had dropped out of school, he had no training

F. Scott Fitzgerald, above, captured the spirit of the "Roaring Twenties" in his American classic, "The Great Gatsby."

The Great Depression was a period of trauma and challenge for the nation and for our family. Photographer Dorothea Lange captured the human toll in a single image, "Migrant Mother."

and few marketable skills, and the one business he had started had ended in failure. That was hardly a track record that would propel him to success – or provide Sally and Marvin with any comfort or security. Yes, by any measure, for the young Sands family these were desperate times indeed.

Then came Black Tuesday and the Great Depression.

I refer, of course, to Tuesday, October 29th, 1929, the infamous day when the stock market crashed, sending the U.S. economy into a devastating tailspin. In a matter of hours, huge stock portfolios became totally worthless; major brokerage houses on Wall Street and across the country were plunged into ruin. In New York, Chicago and far beyond, more than a few brokers and businessmen hurled themselves from top-story windows. No sector of the American economy was spared. Heavy industry, mining, logging, and construction were crippled, as demand for their products plunged and their workers had to be laid off. In rural areas, farmers watched prices for their crops fall by as much as 40 to 60 percent; thousands of family-run farms failed to survive. The crisis quickly spread around the world; international trade slumped. The Great Depression persisted deep into the 1930s, and there was heavy political fallout as well. In 1932, on a tide of voter anger, Franklin D. Roosevelt was elected President and immediately launched his "New Deal," a sweeping series of programs that promised to bring relief, recovery, and reform to American businesses and workers.

And where did all this upheaval leave Mack Sands? Not exactly dancing in the streets of Brooklyn. Times remained rough for him and Sally. Still, in this period of crisis, Mack brought to the fore a better side of his nature: he was a fighter and he was determined to set things right. I'm sure he knocked on every door and tapped every friend he had, looking for a job – or at least a lead. Somewhere along the line, Mack caught a break: by 1932 he had hooked on with a Brooklyn outfit called J. Rabinowitz Brothers. They manufactured and sold bottles to a variety of businesses, including many wine producers. Mack started out driving a truck, then moved up the ladder and became a salesman. Mack worked hard and did well. Sally, I'm sure, was relieved. Their marriage still had some festering sores, but Mack could now claim some measure of redemption; he was pulling his family out of the crisis.

During this period, Mack's larger ambitions remained undimmed. Once he had saved up a little money, he set up a side business: in Rockaway, Queens, he opened a small shop that sold malt and hops to people eager to do a little home brewing, a popular hobby during the long years of Prohibition. Also, in making his sales calls for Rabinowitz Brothers, Mack began building ties with influential people in the wine business. One of them was a local kingpin named Little Joe Applebaum. Little Joe owned Geffen Industries, a firm in Long Island City that made sacramental and kosher wines. (Though Prohibition was still in effect, there was a loophole in the law that allowed for the production and sale of wine for sacramental purposes. More on that in a moment.) Little Joe was a clever operator and he ran a very successful business. Geffen's wines were strong, flavorful, affordable, and, above all, legal. So demand for them was consistently high, and while Prohibition put hundreds of other wineries out of business, Little Joe managed to thrive.

Mack and Little Joe hit it off. Their common bond was the wine business but their relationship went beyond that. Mack looked up to Little Joe, he admired his success, and soon Mack was like a member of Little Joe's extended family. Little Joe ran his business like a benevolent patriarch. He employed several members of his own family, including a cousin who was also named Joe. To avoid confusion, Joe the boss was known as "Little Joe" and his cousin was known as "Big Joe." Big Joe's brother, Max Applebaum, was the chief winemaker at Geffen, and Max's daughter, Bea Applebaum Block, worked in management along with her husband Seymour Block. Mack fit right into the mix. Little Joe became his mentor and his godfather in the world of wine. Little Joe gave Mack guidance and showed him the tricks of making a sale and getting ahead. Their friendship would last for decades and it would have a profound impact on the history of our family.

Mack became a very able salesman and he loved to wheel and deal. In the mold of Little Joe, he was always playing the angles, looking for new ways to make a buck. And of course Mack dreamed of hitting it big. His real estate ventures back in Cleveland were in line with his wheeler-dealer ambitions and so, in a more muted way, was the malt and hops shop he opened in Rockaway. In 1933, when Congress finally lifted Prohibition, Mack immediately sensed this could be it: his big opportunity. So he went to Little Joe and proposed that he quit selling bottles for Rabinowitz and come to work for Geffen. I can just imagine his pitch: "Listen, Joe, I can sell. I've proved that. And with the lifting of Prohibition, demand for wine is going to skyrocket, all across the country. I can hit the road and double, even triple your sales. I can do it. Just give me a shot!"

Little Joe agreed, and it turned out to be a shrewd move for both of them. Demand for wine did soar, and Mack traveled up and down the East Coast selling bulk wine to the scores of new bottlers that were rushing into the wine business. Back then, the wine business was a relatively simple proposition. Each city had two or three bottlers, and they bought wine in bulk – most of it dessert wines – from outfits like Geffen. Most of the source wine came from New York and California and, in some areas, from local growers. The bottlers then put on their own names and labels and sold the wine to retailers mainly as generic port, sherry, and muscatel. At that time, wine sales were almost entirely local or regional; there were next to no national brands. Mack worked hard and built for Geffen Industries a solid network of customers up and down the East Coast. In fact, he did so well that Little Joe made him director of sales. As both an incentive and a reward, he also gave Mack a 10 percent stake in the company. At last, Mack and Sally were back on a firm financial footing. They could breathe again; they had survived the hottest of fires. Still, Mack was never one to sit still. Even as he sold wine for Little Joe, Mack already had his eye out for the next opportunity, his next step up the economic and social ladder.

Now you might be wondering why I've recounted Mack's formative years at such length and in such detail. I did so for several reasons. First, I wanted to show the difficult path that our family followed in its first steps into the wine business, and show how those steps were shaped by the hardships of the Depression and by the lifting of Prohibition. But I also wanted to reveal a few things about Grandpa Mack's character and values. That's key. For these were not only formative years for Mack Sands; in many ways they were also formative

"Listen, Joe, I can sell. I've proved that. I can double, even triple your sales. I can do it, just give me a shot!"

MACK SANDS

The arguing, the money woes, his mother's gnawing insecurity about the future, his father's volatile temper and the whip of his tongue — I'm sure all of these made a deep impression on our father.

years for his young son Marvin. As a boy, Marvin was highly intelligent, perceptive, and sensitive. Throughout his life, he displayed what today we call "emotional intelligence." I'm sure Marvin saw and absorbed much of what was going on in his parent's lives, usually right in front of his nose. The arguing, the money woes, his mother's gnawing insecurity about the future, his father's volatile temper and the whip of his tongue — I'm sure all of these made a deep impression on our father. Mom has told us that, and Rob and I and our older sister Laurie could see it for ourselves.

And what we all saw was this: in many fundamental ways Dad was the mirror opposite of his father. Where Mack was volatile and quick to anger, Marvin was controlled and rarely lost his temper. Where Mack was extroverted and emotionally transparent, Marvin was inward and guarded about revealing his inner thoughts and feelings. Where Mack was indulgent with alcohol and gambling, Marvin never was. Where Mack was haphazard about planning for the security of his wife and child, Dad was exemplary in this regard. In fact, I've never seen anyone so conscientious about making sure that every possible financial and legal safeguard was in place for his wife and children.

When it came to running a business, too, Mack and Marvin had very different styles and approaches. Mack was an old-fashioned, dictatorial patriarch — his way or the highway; Marvin was a gentle persuader. Mack was a bellower; Marvin was a listener. Mack was an igniter; Dad was a defuser. Mack often trampled blindly on even his closest aides and staff; Dad never did. Dad had wonderful people skills, and he knew how to empower his people and motivate them through praise and respect. Mack and Marvin also had very different attitudes toward risk. In considering new business ventures, Mack had that taste for gambling; he was eager to hit the jackpot and saw risk simply as part of the game. Marvin was not risk-averse, but he was always more cautious, keenly aware of how quickly risk can turn into ruin.

Still, Mack and Marvin did share many admirable qualities. Both men prized loyalty and trust. Both men preached and practiced rigorous financial discipline, especially in holding down costs. In deals involving tens of thousands of gallons of wine, they both understood that a quarter of a penny could translate into tens of thousands of dollars in profit or loss. Both men understood, too, that the wine business was mercurial and constantly in flux. So you had to be vigilant and nimble. A bad storm out in California could drive the cost of wine through the ceiling, or some new beverage fad could tilt the wine market for years to come. So you had to keep your ear to the ground and stay close to your suppliers, your sales people, and your customers. And you had to be ready and able to turn on a dime.

There was one other admirable trait that Mack and Marvin shared, one that shaped both their lives and proved to be a determinant factor in the development of our family business: in times of adversity, both men were exceptionally tough and resilient. Mack proved that during the Depression and later in his bout with cancer. Marvin would prove it too — first in his service in the war and then in his own struggles in the wine business.

CHAPTER 2

The Launch

By 1936, Mack Sands was getting restless.

Life, by and large, was good. As head of sales for Geffen Industries, Mack was traveling up and down the East Coast, schmoozing, selling wine, making friends with grape growers, winemakers, and bottlers, and making good money in the process. While the country at large was still in the throes of the Depression, Mack and Sally were living well, and this time Mack was being careful about his money; he was even managing to put some away.

Still, Mack wanted more. With his usual drive and ambition, Mack was eager to run his own business, be the boss, show what he could do. And why not? He was smart, energetic, a good salesman, and through Geffen he had built a vast network of contacts in the wine business, running from Boston to Atlanta. Mack also knew where to find good, drinkable, inexpensive bulk wine – from Geffen for starters. So a new idea now began percolating in Mack's mind: why not set up a bottling business of his own? Why should he be a salesman and pour all those profits into Little Joe's coffers, when he could be a kingpin himself? Sure, it wouldn't be easy. He'd need a good place to start: not too expensive, agreeable for living, and with easy access to good grapes. Brooklyn of course would never do; they would have to pack up Marvin and start somewhere new. And he would need a little capital to get started. But he had that. The real challenge would be to convince Sally that the potential jackpot justified the risk of leaving a secure job, leaving their home in Brooklyn, and jumping into the complete unknown. I can just hear Mack making his pitch:

"Yes, Sally, of course there will be risk. But there's always risk in business. And think of the potential payoff! More money, a better future for us all! We'll run our own show! And we can move from a city apartment into a proper house. Marvin will have much more space to grow and spread his wings…"

There was one other factor that I'm sure spurred Mack and his dreams: the timing. By 1936 the American wine industry was in a frenzy of expansion and change. Three years after Prohibition had been lifted, wine was a hot commodity and insiders like Mack could smell it, they could feel it: this was the wine industry's moment, its own version of California's fabled Gold Rush of 1849. The industry was in a fever, and there were vast fortunes to be made – if you had the guts, and if you got in early. Knowing Mack, there was nothing that could hold him back.

Mack's instincts, as it turned out, were right on the money. Leon D. Adams, a distinguished wine historian and connoisseur, describes those feverish days in his authoritative history, The Wines of America. As Adams notes, the thirteen dry years of Prohibition had put many American wineries out of business, and it had depleted the vineyards and cellars of almost all the others. Fine wines were the hardest hit, but many of the bulk producers – Geffen being a notable exception – were hurting too. As soon as Prohibition was lifted, demand for wine – all wines – immediately soared, but supplies of grapes and wine remained painfully scarce. "Almost the only fine, aged wines available," Adams writes, "were held by the few altar-wine producers for the Catholic clergy, who have always demanded quality in the wines they use to celebrate the Mass."

The upshot was a rush for gold, this time liquid gold. "Speculators, expecting quick profits, reopened many old cellars, some with casks moldy from disuse," Adams reports.

Vast fortunes were there to be made – if you had the guts, and if you got in early.

Prohibition devastated the American wine industry, as authorities such as these in Detroit enforced a national ban on the sale of wine, beer, and spirits.

"Wines hastily made in October and already half-spoiled flooded the country during that frenzied December. Their contents still fermenting, bottles blew up on thousands of store shelves and in windows, creating an odorous reputation for all products of the grape. In California, several million gallons of wine were condemned by the State Department of Public Health as unfit to drink."

By 1936, not much had changed in the supply and demand equation: wine remained scarce and demand was still soaring – a business opportunity that Mack simply could not resist. I can just see the wheels turning inside his head: "The heck with the risks, the heck with Little Joe, the heck with staying in Brooklyn; I'm ready to go out on my own! It's now or never! Full steam ahead!"

By this time, Mack knew all the major wine hubs up and down the East Coast, and in considering where to launch his own business, he had plenty of promising locales to choose from. I'm sure Mack brought out his maps and carefully examined several options. Now nobody alive today knows exactly why, but Mack finally settled on Greensboro, North Carolina. From our vantage point today, that might seem an unlikely spot to start a wine business. But North Carolina had a rich history in wine and growing good quality grapes, and Greensboro had its own special charms. Back then it was a sleepy town of 40,000 people, with a lovely climate and several good colleges and universities close by. With its central location, midway between Washington D.C. and Atlanta, Georgia, Greensboro was also a busy railway hub – a valuable asset for shipping wine. "And Sally," I can hear Mack saying, "just wait 'til you see some of the homes! You're going to love it!"

So it was that Mack and Sally packed their belongings, corralled young Marvin, and said good-bye to their friends and family in Brooklyn. Once in Greensboro, they found a nice little house near the center of town and began what was truly a brand new life. While Sally got the family settled in, Mack began building the Car-Cal Winery and establishing his own foothold in American wine. "Car-Cal" was short for Carolina-California, Mack's two most important sources for grape juice. At the outset Mack was only bottling wine, but I'm sure he used the name "winery" in anticipation of future growth and diversification. The word "winery" also had a certain cachet, making it a good fit for Mack's long-term business and social ambitions. His days as a contract salesman were over; Mack was ready to be a king of the hill.

This was a defining moment for Mack and for the history of our family. Our grandfather was leaving a comfortable job, uprooting his family, and setting out on his own, in a new place, and with absolutely no guarantee of success. Sure the risks were high, but the gambler in Mack would have it no other way. Still, I believe there was also another impulse that was propelling Mack. Like so many other immigrants before him, Mack was not just launching a business. He was laying claim to his share of the American Dream.

Where was the American wine industry at that precise point in time? What forces and business models shaped Mack's approach to launching his company? And how did Mack's experience help lay the groundwork for what Dad accomplished and for what Rob and I did later with Constellation Brands?

To properly answer those questions, I first need to step back and paint for you a capsule history of wine, in the United States and far beyond. Our wine traditions here are very different from those in Europe, Australia, New Zealand, and South America, and I'm sure that many of our readers abroad have little idea of how the American wine industry was born and how it was eventually transformed into what it is today. Besides, the story of East Coast wine is fascinating in and of itself, filled as it is with turmoil and an array of colorful characters and pioneers.

The history of wine, of course, traces back thousands of years. No one knows for sure how or where wine first made its appearance; its precise roots remain shrouded in mystery and mythology. There is an ancient Persian tale, for instance, that tells of a princess who, in a fit of sadness, drinks the juice of spoiled grapes and – miracle of miracles – becomes giddy and light-hearted, and then falls into a long, restorative sleep. When she awakes, she finds her mood has improved and her worries have eased. She returns to this surprising elixir, and again it improves her mood and spirit. Elated, she shares her secret with the king of her realm, and he too marvels at this mysterious drink. The king then celebrates wine and its miraculous powers and spreads the word far and wide. Now I don't give much credence to this tale, but it does contain a kernel of truth: most scholars today agree that wine was discovered by accident. No Einstein or Pasteur of ancient times went into his lab and came out with the nectar that would later be celebrated in the Bible and in the figures of Dionysus in Greek mythology and Bacchus in the Roman.

The noble roots of wine trace back thousands of years, to Greek and Roman mythology and far beyond. Here the Italian master Caravaggio pays homage to Bacchus, the Roman god of wine and grape cultivation.

We do know for certain, though, that there was grape cultivation and winemaking around the Caspian Sea and in Mesopotamia as far back as 4000 B.C., perhaps even as far back as 6000 B.C. Texts found in Egyptian tombs reveal that priests and royal families were enjoying wine as far back as 2700 B.C. The Egyptians also developed the first arbors, the first scientific methods for pruning vines, and perhaps the first wine "cellars" – to avoid spoilage from the heat, the Egyptians stored their wine in sunken jars, as revealed by several archaeological excavations. To my knowledge, no archaeologists have turned up any tell-tale remains of chewed cigar butts, but I can still imagine some distant ancestors of Grandpa Mack running a rudimentary winery or two back in Egypt, on behalf of some broad-minded king who had taken a shine to a wandering and very clever Sandomirsky.

The ancient Greeks too revered wine and its unusual powers. In both the Odyssey and the Iliad, the Greek poet Homer wrote extensively about wine. Though many scholars disagree on when Homer published his works, most of them put the time somewhere between the 8th and 6th Centuries B.C., and by then grapes and wine were already a mainstay of Greek agriculture, trade, and culture. Even at that early stage, the Greeks believed that wine held an array of healthful benefits. Centuries before anyone spoke about "The French Paradox" – the beneficial effects of drinking wine in moderation – Greek doctors, including the highly respected Hippocrates, were prescribing wine as a healthy tonic for the body, mind, and spirit.

The Romans went even further, methodically developing wine science and working to

This elegant Persian wine pitcher in the form of a water bird dates back to 800-600 BCE.

spread grape cultivation, winemaking, and wine knowledge throughout Western Europe. By 1000 B.C., the Etruscans, predecessors of the Romans, were growing grapes and classifying grape varieties according to soil preferences, taste, color, and ripening characteristics. From there, the Romans made many advances in pruning, irrigating, fertilization, and maximizing crop yields. The Romans are also credited with inventing wooden cooperage to facilitate the maturing, storage, and shipping of wines. The Romans may even have been the first to use glass for bottling wine. In Germany, archaeologists unearthed two stone sarcophaguses containing glass wine bottles, which carbon-dating traced back to about 325 A.D. No labels were found on those bottles, so I can't substantiate the oft-heard claim – in our family at least – that this was the first vintage of "Old Maudius," the forerunner to Grandpa Mack's storied Old Maude.

By the first century A.D., the Romans were exporting wine from Italy to Spain, Germany, England, and Gaul, what is now France. Soon each of these countries was making their own wines, with native-grown grapes, and developing their own wine industries. The French showed a particular flair for growing grapes and making wine, and they soon became the dominant force on the international wine market. French monks played a decisive role. They planted vineyards in Burgundy, Champagne, and the Rhone Valley to make sacramental wines for Mass – foreshadowing the way our California wine industry was later developed. By the Renaissance, drinking wine had become a cornerstone of daily life throughout Europe, and by the 1500s and 1600s the Europeans were exporting wine to South Africa, Mexico, Argentina, and beyond.

The history of grapes in America traces back a thousand years. In The Wines of America, Leon Adams reports that when the Norse explorer Leif Erikson landed in North America around 1000 A.D., he found so many grapes growing wild that he referred to the continent as "Vineland." It is unclear whether the berries he found were grapes or some other form of berry, but North America's climates and soils were clearly hospitable to the growing of wild grapes and berries. According to Adams, Frenchmen were probably the first to make wine here. French Huguenots first arrived between 1562 and 1564, in a territory that is now Florida, and using grapes they found growing wild, the Huguenots made their own wine. Scientists later determined that the Huguenots had used the same native-growing varietal that Grandpa Mack would often use some 300 years later: Scuppernong.

That was the beginning. By 1609, the Jamestown colonists in Virginia were fermenting native grapes and making home-made wine. In 1621 the Mayflower Pilgrims at Plymouth made their own wine to help celebrate the first Thanksgiving. Because these early wines were barely drinkable, the early settlers began importing Vitis vinifera cuttings, the species of vine that yielded the best wines in Europe. Their hope was to make Vitis vinifera grow in the different soils and climates of the East Coast and then use them to make better wine.

Many prominent settlers tried their hand with Vitis vinifera. In 1619, Lord Delaware brought over vinifera vines, along with French specialists to turn the grapes into wine. In 1643, Queen Christina of Sweden promoted the planting of Vitis vinifera in New Sweden, a tiny Swedish settlement on the Delaware River. In 1662, Lord Baltimore planted Vitis vinifera in Maryland, and there were similar experiments in Florida, Georgia, South Carolina, Rhode Island, and New York. None succeeded. A century later, Thomas Jefferson tried his hand with the persnickety Vitis vinifera at Monticello, his estate in Virginia. But his effort failed too. As Leon Adams explains, the European vines would take root and sometimes produce small quantities of wine. But they soon lost their leaves and died – along with the dreams of their growers.

The upshot of these failures was clear: if Americans on the East Coast were ever going to develop a wine industry, they would have to start with native grapes. There was another upshot as well: with no good wine being made in abundance, the New World colonists and their descendants drank hard apple cider and later strong applejack and rum. Ultimately, the colonists made whiskey their alcoholic beverage of choice. There is a poignant irony here: if those early attempts to make good wine of moderate alcohol content had succeeded, whiskey might never gained such popularity, and the wine and beverage industries might never have suffered the imposition of Prohibition and all of its dire consequences.

The Charles Krug Winery, above, created in the Napa Valley in 1861, was one of the first wineries in California.

Throughout the 1600s and most of the 1700s, despite numerous efforts, no one succeeded in making good wine in commercial quantities. So when and where did the American wine industry truly begin? That distinction belongs to an outfit called the Pennsylvania Vine Company, located on the Susquehanna River northwest of Philadelphia. The company, founded in 1793, made wine in underground vaults, using grapes that they grew in an adjoining vineyard. The varietal they used was a hearty native red called Alexander. From that modest beginning, the American wine industry began to grow.

Over the next 50 years, the industry grew at a very brisk pace. Nurserymen and grape breeders worked hard to develop varietals that were better than the Alexander. In 1823, Catawba grapes made their debut. In 1854, Concord grapes, still so popular today, made their appearance in Massachusetts. By 1880, there were active wine-producing ventures all along the East Coast, from Massachusetts, New York and New Jersey in the north to Virginia, West Virginia, Tennessee, North and South Carolina, and Georgia in the south. The industry had also spread westward, producing some surprises. In the 1850s, for instance, Ohio was the leading wine-producing state in the Union, until it was eclipsed a decade later by Missouri. Ohio? Missouri? Looking at America's wine map today, who would have imagined that?

Father Junipero Serra, above, led the creation of 21 Franciscan missions in California and encouraged them to grow high-quality Vitis Vinifera grapes, the roots of today's California wine industry.

Now we come to California, where the history of wine has different roots and a very different set of flavors. According to Charles L. Sullivan, an expert on the history of California wine, the first true visionary in California wine was an innovative Franciscan friar named Junipero Serra. Padre Serra is celebrated in California history today as the man who led the construction of the 21 fabled missions that dotted the state and anchored its early development. In 1769, Serra brought a load of Vitis vinifera cuttings from Mexico and made their cultivation a central activity at several of the missions. Though it suffered on the East Coast, Vitis vinifera prospered in the California climate and soil, and for the next 60 years the Franciscan friars used Vitis vinifera to make their wines. They did not make wine for commercial purposes, only for Mass and their own use at the communal

In California the soil was rich, the climate ideal, and in the late 1880s immigrants from Italy, Germany, and across Europe came to the Golden State to grow grapes and make wine.

table or for medicine, just as the Greeks had done thousands of years before.

In the 1840s, though, a tough, adventurous trapper named George Calvert Yount went to the Franciscan mission in Vallejo, just northeast of San Francisco, and purchased from the friars a substantial quantity of their vinifera vines. He then took them home and planted them on his ranch, in the fertile, mineral-rich soil that is found in the center of the Napa Valley. According to Sullivan, Yount's was the very first vineyard planted in the Napa Valley. The vinifera grapes thrived there, and I think we can say that was the true birth of the California wine industry. That same locale, by the way, is now a thriving wine and gourmet hamlet named, aptly enough, Yountville. And just to the north of there is a lovely winery called Franciscan, which is now a prominent part of our portfolio at Constellation Brands.

George Yount soon had a lot of company. In the second half of the 1800s, many other settlers from Europe came to the Napa Valley and began their own plantings and winemaking. With its rich soil, its hot days and its cool breezes at night, the Napa Valley proved to be an ideal terrain for growing high-quality grapes. And California's fertile Central Valley, running inland from Sacramento down to Fresno, proved to be ideal for growing good grapes in very large quantities. With those twin assets, the California wine industry soon began to develop and prosper. To promote this young industry, the California legislature offered landowners tax incentives to plant vineyards, and by the mid-1880s the result was abundantly clear: scores of vineyards dotted the hills and valleys up and down the Golden State, many of them producing very good wine.

In the Napa Valley, several of the new settlers began making and aging some excellent, European-style fine wines, using Vitis vinifera vines. Charles Krug was one, Joseph Beringer was another, and their names are still revered in California wine today. The fine wine industry that was taking root in California drew a great deal of interest in Europe, especially in France. As Leon Adams tells us, in 1862 the French journal Revue Viticole ran a laudatory piece about this new frontier in wine. California, it said, was one American region "capable of entering competition with the wines of Europe." But not right away. As the French revue noted in a sniffy conclusion, that would be sometime "in the distant future." Well, they were right. It was not until 1976, more than a century later, that a handful of Napa Valley wines beat the very best wines of France, red and white, in a blind-tasting in Paris carried out by a blue-ribbon panel of French judges. Still, that 1862 article seems to me an important benchmark in the history of American wine: it signaled to the barons of European wine that these upstart vintners in California would, sooner or later, emerge as a colossal power – and competitor – in the world of wine.

Now, let me add a few more dashes of fact and color, to set the stage for Grandpa Mack and how he launched his business. As you might imagine, the rise of California's wine industry created tensions with the wine powers back East. In the 1860s and 1870s, there were East/West arguments over market turf, wine quality, and the origin of what was in the bottle. Specifically, the East Coast vintners accused California shippers of selling their wine under counterfeit French and German labels and of putting their own California labels on East Coast wine. To fight back, some unscrupulous merchants in New York and Boston put California labels on rotgut they had imported from Europe. Nasty business. In counter-attack, the Californians railed against what was – then as now – a standard practice on the East Coast: adding sugar to the wine in order to "ameliorate" its quality.

We'll talk more about the process of amelioration as our story unfolds. But the crux of the matter is this: California's short, hot growing season gives its grapes naturally high sugar content and low acidity. The growing seasons in the East and Midwest are, by contrast, cooler and often rainy. That, plus using different varietals, produces wines that are often tart to the tongue, being low in natural sugar and high in acidity. To remedy that, East Coast producers routinely ameliorate their wines with a solution of sugar and water. The sugar enables the wine to ferment to stable alcohol levels, while the water reduces the acidity and softens the taste.

Even in the 1800s, "amelioration" was an accepted fact of life in East Coast wine-making. But the Californians used it to try to gain advantage both politically and in the marketplace. In Washington, they pressed the U.S. Congress to enact national legislation against "adulterated" wines. East Coast vintners bitterly opposed the measure, claiming it would destroy their business. Finally, in 1894 Congress settled the dispute by enacting a law that permitted wine producers to use only a limited amount of sugar in making their wines.

Despite such disputes, by 1900 the American wine industry had made tremendous progress in a very short time. Grape growers and winemakers across the country, despite their different origins, climates and varietals, had laid the foundation for a thriving and highly competitive industry. About 90 percent of all the wines produced and consumed in America at that time were dessert wines. They were strong, very drinkable, and their high alcohol content helped them prevent spoilage. That said, the small handful of wineries that were making fine wines were having excellent results. At the Paris Exposition of 1900, American wines were matched against the best wines of France and the rest of Europe – and came away with three dozen medals. The Americans were also making inroads on the international wine market. California wines were routinely exported in barrels to Canada, Mexico, and Central America, as well as to England, Germany, Australia, and the Far East.

Then two nasty plagues descended.

The first was natural. This was phylloxera, a voracious louse that attacks and destroys the roots of grapevines. It can shrivel an entire vineyard in just a few years. The almost microscopic insect is native to the Mississippi River Valley and is known to have destroyed the grape plantings of early American settlers in Virginia in the 17th Century. Later, in the 1850s, the nasty louse made its way to France, possibly on American vines imported for research. Over the next 20 years, phylloxera ran wild through the vineyards of France and destroyed almost every vine in the country, from the most humble to the most noble. It was one of the worst plant disease epidemics of all time.

The savior, ironically enough, was of American origin. Some of our native American rootstocks, like St. George, turned out to be genetically resistant to phylloxera. These were imported by the French and grafted onto the few remaining European vines not affected, making them resistant too. It took time, but the French wine industry did come back. The next victim, though, was California. The pest moved slower there than in Europe, giving vintners time to replant their vineyards, but that replanting cost millions of dollars and was

By 1900 the American wine industry had made tremendous progress in a very short time. Then two nasty plagues descended...

The imposition of Prohibition in 1919 nearly killed wine-making on America's East Coast. But three loopholes in the law enabled a few intrepid souls, including our Grandpa Mack, to stay in the wine business.

a heavy blow to the California wine industry.

The second plague that hit American wine was man-made – and the damage it did was far worse: Prohibition. Most of us tend to think of Prohibition as a self-contained period starting in 1920 and lasting until 1933. But the truth is more complex. As early as the 1830s, many preachers and anti-alcohol groups were railing against the evils of alcohol, using such fiery slogans as "demon rum" and "devil's poison." By the 1840s, scores of towns and counties from New York to Iowa had declared themselves "dry" and had banned the sale of alcohol. Then whole states went dry: Kansas in 1880, Iowa in 1882, then Georgia, Oklahoma, Mississippi, North Carolina, Tennessee, West Virginia, and Virginia. As Leon Adams points out, some of these states permitted their wineries to make wine for sale elsewhere, but this provided only short-term relief. Barred from selling their wines locally, and unable to compete with wines from California, countless wineries closed their doors and disappeared.

Emboldened by their progress, the temperance leagues and other anti-alcohol forces stepped up their campaign, demanding that any and all mention of wine be expunged from school and college textbooks, including classical Greek and Roman texts. Anti-alcohol campaigners wrote scholarly papers trying to explain away the Bible's positive references to wine, and they saw to it that all favorable references to wine and alcohol were removed from medical textbooks and the U.S. Pharmacopeia, the official listing that governs the sale and marketing of all prescription and over-the-counter medicines, tonics, and supplements. In this climate, the imposition of national Prohibition in 1920, via the Volstead Act, was not an abrupt legislative action; it was the culmination of a long, vigorous, well-orchestrated political campaign.

Prohibition badly damaged the American wine industry, but it did not wipe it out. For several reasons. For one, wine was not the No. 1 target of the anti-alcohol forces. Back then, a gallon of wine sold for about four times the price of a gallon of whiskey, making it a luxury item that could not be easily tossed into the furor over "demon rum" and "the devil's poison." Also, in the august precincts of Washington D.C., wine enjoyed a positive reputation, starting in the White House. As Treville Lawrence reveals in his book *Jefferson and Wine*, the first five presidents of the United States – Washington, Adams, Jefferson, Madison, and Monroe – were all close friends who enjoyed drinking wine together on many occasions. Moreover, many of them wrote about the positive effects of wine, which they viewed as a respectable beverage of health and moderation.

Thomas Jefferson, our first true wine connoisseur, was a champion of the virtues of cultivating grapes and drinking wine in moderation. Born and raised on a farm in Virginia, Jefferson went on to serve as Minister to France, an opportunity he used to pursue his passion and knowledge of wine. He traveled throughout Burgundy, Bordeaux, and beyond, tasting and selecting the very best wines for his cellar back in Virginia. When he returned to Washington D.C., Jefferson became the White House's unofficial sommelier, recommending and procuring fine wines for George Washington and several later presidents. Jefferson never drank spirits and he shunned strong wines. But he cherished fine wines and he used the genius of his pen – to which our Republic owes so much – to celebrate the virtues of wine as both a beverage of civility and temperance. Like the Greeks, he saw it as a "natural medicine for health." In these ways, Thomas Jefferson was centuries ahead of his time and was the true godfather of fine wine in America today.

Perhaps the continuing influence of Jefferson and the other Founding Fathers helps explain why the Volstead Act, while banning all other alcoholic beverages, contained three important exceptions when it came to wine: 1) sacramental wines, 2) medicinal wines, and 3) various wine tonics that purportedly improved everything from digestion to blood circulation. The first exception enabled religious leaders to secure federal permits to procure enough sacramental wine to serve the needs of their congregations. They were not allowed to sell their wines, but they could give each member of their flock up to five gallons for use in the home. The second and third exceptions allowed doctors to secure a federal permit to provide medicinal wines and tonics to their ailing patients. I imagine that churches and synagogues across the country witnessed a dramatic rise in the number of people seeking such aid and comfort, and so, I'm sure, did countless family physicians.

Another loophole in the Volstead Act allowed families to purchase a limited amount of grapes per year so that they could make wine at home for their private family use. This was especially appreciated by immigrant families from Italy and other parts of Europe, for whom table wine was an integral part of their daily lives and family traditions. In one case, a group of Italian workers in the iron ore mines of northern Minnesota deputized a trustworthy colleague named Cesare Mondavi to go to California, select good grapes, and ship them back to Minnesota, so they could make their own wine at home. Cesare Mondavi did that. But out in California he saw an exciting opportunity: to set up a business buying grapes and shipping them back to other Italian enclaves across the Midwest and East. Cesare grabbed it. Soon he moved his entire family out to Lodi, California, in the rich Central Valley, thus sowing the seeds for his pioneering son Robert Mondavi to go into the wine business in 1936, the very same year as our Grandpa Mack.

Now we can bring up the lights for Grandpa Mack. During the 13 dark years of Prohibition, those three loopholes kept the flame of the American wine industry alive – and they kept Mack and his family financially solvent, with help from Rabinowitz Brothers in Brooklyn and Little Joe Applebaum at Geffen Industries. When Prohibition was lifted, Mack was ready to make his move. And Old Maude was waiting for him just around the corner.

The enduring influence of one man may have ultimately saved the American wine industry: Thomas Jefferson.

It is now time that I bring into our story Captain Paul Garrett, by no means a household name but definitely a legend in East Coast wine and another man who played a role in our family history. Paul Garrett was born on a farm in North Carolina; the year was 1863, the third year of the Civil War. By trade his father was a doctor, but by passion he was a winemaker. In 1865, at the end of the war, Garrett's father and his wealthy uncle purchased the Medoc Vineyard, a 30-year-old venture that enjoyed the distinction of being North Carolina's first commercial winery.

As with so many Southerners of the time, young Paul's family was pushing him toward

The American wine industry and our family owe a tremendous debt of gratitude to Captain Paul Garrett, above, a North Carolina pioneer whose Virginia Dare wines blazed an exciting path for us to follow.

a military career. He attended a military prep school as a teenager, but then he caught the wine bug. At the age of 14, Paul dropped out of military school and joined his uncle, who was running the winery. Paul plunged right in. He worked the vineyards, bought grapes from growers in neighboring counties, made the wine, and then loaded the barrels on wagons bound for the bottling plant. At 21, when his uncle died, Paul took over sales for what was now the Garrett Winery. He traveled through Arkansas, Tennessee, and Texas with a magic sales tool in his pocket: a vial of pure Scuppernong wine.

Garrett told anyone who would listen that this native East Coast grape made "the finest wine in the world." On his sales route, he would call on local saloon keepers, offer them a taste of Scuppernong, and dare them to compare it with whiskey. The ploy worked, sales soared, and Paul Garrett was on his way. At the age of 37, he left the Garrett Winery and set up his own wine-making operation, Garrett & Company. There, he earned from his staff the honorific title "Captain." He had the bearing for it. Captain Garrett was tall, portly, and charismatic, a quality enhanced by his deep voice and soft Southern twang. Over the next 19 years – right up to the imposition of Prohibition – Garrett built a nationwide empire, and he did so on the strength of two brilliant innovations.

The first was his decision to blend his beloved Scuppernong with additional wine from both New York and California, being careful to keep the Scuppernong flavor predominant. This allowed Garrett to make larger quantities of wine than he ever could have using pure Scuppernong alone. California's Vitis vinifera grapes married well with Scuppernong and so did wine from New York. Garrett's blend not only tasted good; it built a welcome bridge over that East/West wine divide.

His second innovation related to how he named this new blended wine. Garrett had no desire to emulate the Europeans and name his wine after the family chateau or its region of origin, the way the French do. Garrett wanted a name that sounded uniquely American, a name that conveyed spirit, character, and personality. That led him to a new idea: name his wine after a person or historical figure. What could be more unique, what better way to convey character and personality than through a person's name? So he began searching for just the right one. For awhile he toyed with calling his white wine "Minnehana" and his red wine "Pocahontas" – you can't get more distinctively American than that. Still, those were not names that would roll easily off the tongue or stand happily in the consciousness of the American consumer. Then Garrett nailed it. He chose to name his new wine after the very first child born of English parents in America: "Virginia Dare."

Well, with those two inspired bits of innovation, Captain Paul Garrett wrote himself large into the early history of American wine. In short order, Virginia Dare became a household name and a national sensation. Soon Garrett had five wineries churning out Virginia Dare in North Carolina. Then, as the temperance leagues gained strength in his home state, Garrett built a larger plant in neighboring Virginia. Soon, though, both those states went "dry." Garrett moved north to New York State and created vineyards and wineries in Hammondsport and Canandaigua, the home of our company. True to his vision of building a business that would bridge East and West, Garrett built a sister operation in California: the Mission Vineyard and Winery, located in Cucamonga, due east of Los Angeles. Captain

Garrett's national strategy paid off handsomely: in the two decades leading to Prohibition, Virginia Dare reigned as the biggest-selling wine in all of America. By wit and brass, Garrett survived Prohibition, and when Prohibition was lifted he was the only one ready with a strong national network of production, sales, marketing, and distribution. In American wine at the time, Captain Paul Garrett was definitely The Man.

Grandpa Mack, I'm sure, gazed upon Captain Garrett's achievements with a mixture of admiration and envy. Moreover, when he started his own business in 1936, Mack borrowed a page or two from Captain Garrett's playbook. First, Mack's business plan was East/West in nature and was based on the same Carolina/California axis as Garrett's: he would buy wine from producers in California and North Carolina and bottle it as his own. The name "Car-Cal" embodied that strategy. Also like Garrett, Mack planned to feature Scuppernong grapes, among others, in his line of wines. And there was something more. At first, Mack bottled a line of generic dessert wines and labeled them "Sands Port," "Sands Sherry" and the like. Soon, though, he saw that he needed a more colorful and memorable name, and again it was to Captain Garrett that he turned for guidance and inspiration. Mack's wines were for the masses, not the classes, so he wanted a name that was warm and friendly and by no means high-falutin', a name that had a touch of good old American marketing magic.

Old Maude.

Now no one knows for sure how Mack came up with that name. There is a bit of lore that says that Mack named Old Maude after the waitress who regularly served him breakfast at his favorite eatery in downtown Greensboro. I wouldn't swear to that in a court of law, but it certainly sounds like Grandpa Mack. What we do know to be true is this: Old Maude was a fortified dessert wine – a full 20 percent alcohol – and to celebrate its kick, someone on Mack's team designed for its label a sassy kicking mule. It was an arresting image, but it didn't last long. According to an article from the Greensboro Record, several rival vintners complained about the label, noting that federal rules barred wine companies from promoting a wine's strength either through its name or its label. The authorities responsible for overseeing the wine industry agreed and "ordered the mule to the barn," as the Record deftly put it.

Mack changed the label, but Old Maude still kicked its way into the hearts of legions of consumers. Former employees of Grandpa Mack estimate that in its early years Car-Cal sold some 20 million bottles of Old Maude wine. Old Maude put Car-Cal on the map, and soon Mack was eagerly launching new brands of the same ilk and spirit. I have a letter that Mack wrote to my father in 1945, and the letterhead tells the story: it reads "Car-Cal Winery, Originators of Old Maude Brand Wine." In smaller letters, it then lists eight other brands that Mack had created: Maude, Old Duke, Old Tradition, Sun-Ray, Old Mr. Mack, Captain Jack, Seven Star, and Nectar.

Those names alone tell us volumes about the spirit of the American wine industry in those tumultuous years after Prohibition. And I think they tell us a thing or two about the spirit of our Grandpa Mack. Unlike so many winemakers today, Mack didn't go into the wine business with soaring dreams of crafting a gold medal Cabernet or Chardonnay, or of

Our family's first successful brand was Old Maude, a fortified wine with character and kick.

having his name on a prestigious label for generations to come. Nor did Mack or any of his cohorts have visions of rubbing shoulders with the aristocratic families of Europe, men and women whose families had been in the wine business for several hundred years or more. No, Mack went into the wine business to bottle good wine, sell it as fast as he could, and make good money in the process. It was a tough, volatile business, with fierce competition, and to survive you had to have guts, guile, energy, stamina, and the daring of a riverboat gambler. Captain Garrett had all those traits. And, bless him, so did our Grandpa Mack.

THE TOOLS

An antique corkscrew

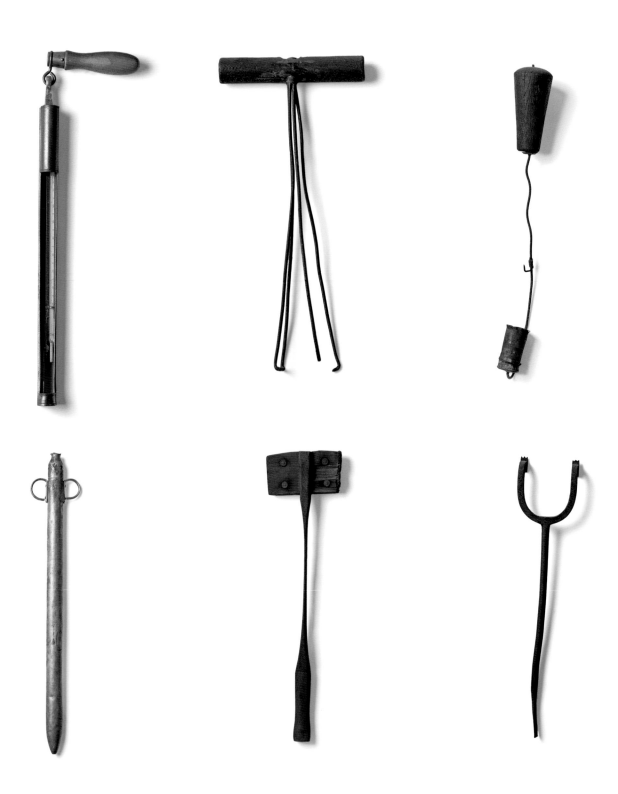

Above, Antique wine-making tools.

Opposite, Storage tanks at the Robert Mondavi Winery, Oakville, Ca.

Following spread, A stainless steel auger, to move grapes into the crusher/de-stemmer at the Robert Mondavi Winery.

Above, An antique hand-operated press for crimping foils on champagne bottles.
Opposite, Arbor Mist Peach being bottled at Canandaigua Winery.

Above, A "bung," the top hole on an oak barrel.
Opposite, The wine lab at Franciscan Estates, Rutherford, Ca.

Above, A hand-operated wine pump made in 1888.

Opposite, A bottling line for J. Roget Champagne at Canandaigua Winery.

Following spread, Stainless steel fermenting tanks at Opus One Winery, Oakville, Ca.

Above, An antique, hand-cranked basket press.
Opposite, A stainless steel tank valve.

Above, A hose connection station to move wine throughout the Canandaigua winery
Opposite, Stainless steel fittings, valves and gaskets used for wine filtration.

Above, Stainless steel hose manifold.

Opposite, Test bottles of wine for tasting.

Following spread, Oak barrel storage at Franciscan Estates.

CHAPTER 3

Young Marvin

As I sit here now and write about Grandpa Mack and the early days of our business, one thought keeps surfacing in my mind: How far we've come. How far my family has come – and how far the American wine industry has come.

Think about it: 70 years ago when Mack moved to Greensboro, the only fine wines you could buy in America, with only a few exceptions, were crafted in Europe, and much of the table wine being made here was mediocre at best. No longer. Today we are crafting some of the finest wines made anywhere in the world, wines that are every bit as good as – and often better – than those being made in France, Italy, Spain, Germany, or anywhere else. Yes, the American wine industry has been totally transformed, and our family business has been transformed as well. We still produce inexpensive dessert wines of the sort that Grandpa Mack made, but in our portfolio we also have many fine wines of towering international reputation, wines that Mack, no doubt, would deem too fancy to drink.

So how did we and the American wine industry come so far in 70 years? How did we, in a few decades, attain levels of quality, character, and finesse that it took the French, the Italians, the Spanish, and the Germans several centuries to achieve? And how did the Sands family business grow from a tiny start-up in North Carolina into a global power and the largest wine company in the world? The answers will become clear in the pages ahead, and in the case of our family business, most of the answers will emerge from a single source:

Marvin Sands.

Our father, by any measure, was an exceptional man. He was a gifted businessman, a respected community leader, a dedicated philanthropist, a decorated war veteran, a caring husband, a trusted friend and, as Rob and I can assure you, he was a remarkable father and grandfather. As you will see, Dad was a man blessed with many natural gifts. But his life and character were also shaped by a series of extraordinary challenges and setbacks. How he overcame them, what he learned in the process, and the lessons and wisdom that he then passed along to his children form the backbone of the story of Constellation Brands.

Marvin's formative years were divided between two very different places and cultures: Brooklyn, New York, and Greensboro, North Carolina. We know very little about Marvin's early years in Brooklyn. We know that he was a sensitive youngster, and we know that as an only child Marvin received plenty of love and attention from both his parents, despite the frequent turmoil between Mack and Sally. In his early years, Marvin was, by all accounts, an outgoing kid, with handsome dark eyes, an even temper, and a playful sense of humor. He loved playing outdoors with his pals, and I can easily imagine him playing stickball in the streets of Brooklyn and then going over to the corner drugstore for a cream soda, a milk shake, or a root beer float. At school, Marvin showed himself to be a good student and a good athlete. Watching Mack and Sally bicker must have been painful, but in almost every other way Dad had a happy childhood and, while by no means devout, Dad felt very much at home in Brooklyn, with its large Jewish community and its rich ethnic feel.

Marvin, like his father, was a whiz at math. His facility with numbers was downright amazing. Like anyone who's good in math, Dad could add, multiply, and divide big numbers in his head; to him that was child's play. And like anyone who is very good in math, Dad had little trouble solving complex fractions and algebraic equations in his head, and

Sally and Mack Sands, in the 1950s.

It was one thing to be a smart Jewish boy in Brooklyn in the 1930s, but it was quite another to be a smart Jewish boy in the South of that time.

whatever he couldn't do in his head he could easily do with pencil and paper. That was no big deal. But Marvin's talents went way beyond those. He and our Grandpa Mack used to have contests to see who could add up huge columns of numbers the fastest. Their only point of competition was speed; it was a given that both men would get the answer right.

Where Dad's math talent really shined, though, was in business. He was an absolute marvel when it came to the math needed for the wine business, both in terms of production and finance. Let me make up a very basic example. If a grape grower in New York had a field of ten acres of land planted with, say, Concord grapes, Dad could quickly tell you the number of tons of grapes the grower would expect to bring in at harvest time and how many gallons of wine that would yield. That was basic stuff. But he would also know how much sugar and water he would have to add to the grape juice to ameliorate it and how much distilled spirits he would need to fortify it. He would also know the different costs of transporting the grapes back to his winery in Canandaigua, crushing them, fermenting the juice, and bottling the wine. He would know down to the penny the profit he could expect to make on every case he sold. I could go on, but you get my point: Dad was gifted with numbers, especially the complicated algebra that is central to the wine business.

Dad often said that if he hadn't gone into the wine business, he would have been happy going into teaching. I can see why: he was a born teacher, whether at the office or at home with Laurie, Rob, and me. I still have vivid memories of driving to Sunday school with him. It was a good hour's trip, and as he drove he would make up math problems for me to solve. We would start with simple problems with one unknown. For instance, Joe started with X number of oranges. If he sold two and had eight left, how many oranges did he start with? In other words, what was X? When I could do that kind of problem, he would add another unknown to the equation, and when I could solve that kind, he would make it two variables in two equations. I, too, was naturally good in math, but working with Dad just made me that much better. Whenever I'd mastered something, Dad pushed me to another level – and he did the same thing later when he was teaching me the specifics of the wine business. As a teacher and mentor, Dad was patient and stimulating, and he had an uncanny way of making things clear and simple to understand.

Dad was happy growing up in Brooklyn, but Greensboro was a somewhat different story. When Mack and Sally moved south, Marvin was 12 years old. Few kids at that age like to be uprooted from their friends and their neighborhood, but for Marvin the move was especially unsettling. Greensboro at that time was typical of the South of the 1930s: it was a small town, predominantly white, and staunchly Christian. In both culture and geography, Greensboro and North Carolina were part of that wide swath of the South that in the 1920s the influential writer and pundit H.L. Mencken labeled the "Bible belt." Before they left Brooklyn, Mack and Sally sat Marvin down and warned him that life in Greensboro was going to be "different." Everything he said or did was going to be carefully scrutinized, they said, so Marvin had to be extremely careful to always maintain "proper" behavior. Their underlying message was clear: it was one thing to be a smart Jewish boy in Brooklyn in the 1930s, but it was quite another to be a smart Jewish boy in the South of that time.

How did Marvin adjust to his new life in Greensboro? In front of me now is a stack of

Dad's report cards from his junior and senior high schools. They are quite intriguing. The first is from Dad's first semester in the 9th grade at his new school, Central Junior High. For the first grading period that semester, Marvin got an A- in English, an A- in science, a B in history, a C in spelling and, for some reason, only a C+ in math. Worse, he got a D in "Guidance," which was akin to "comportment." There is a portion of the report card where the teacher can alert the parents to any problems in the student's attitude, comportment, or work habits. Marvin's homeroom teacher, Carrie S. Bigham, makes no comment there whatsoever. Marvin did pull his math up to a straight B by the end of that semester, but throughout his next three years, in senior high, he was never more than a B student in math, and he was a B student in most of his other subjects as well.

Now don't get me wrong: there is nothing wrong with a B. But given Dad's evident gift for math, I do find his math grades a bit perplexing. My first inclination is to think that Dad simply didn't like school. After all, his greater gift, as he showed later in life, was for inspiring and managing people. Mom, though, has a different point of view. Marvin loved living in Brooklyn, she says. He felt comfortable there and he shined at school. Beyond that, he felt very much at home in Brooklyn's Jewish neighborhoods and its enveloping culture. "In Brooklyn," Mom explains, "everyone was the same. Everyone was Jewish. I think Marvin was very happy up until he was twelve and moved to Greensboro. That was the time in his life when he became very reticent and very conscious of things and very aware of the differences."

This context puts Marvin's report cards in a clearer light. In his first weeks at Central Junior High, I imagine that he felt uncomfortable, on edge, an outsider in every way. Maybe that D in Guidance stemmed from acting out a little, or getting teased, or being hassled in the hallways, as kids everywhere often do to newcomers. It was in this same period that Dad got that C+ in math. Sure, maybe he was being taught math by a different method. Or maybe he was just responding half-heartedly to an uninspiring math teacher. Or maybe he was discovering girls. But I still can't help but wonder if Dad wasn't simply holding himself back a little, keeping his natural talents under wraps. He did pretty well in all his subjects – well enough to get B's – and he never received any sort of official reprimand. So what I see coming into view is the Marvin Sands that Rob and I knew growing up: a highly intelligent and sensitive man who was extremely guarded about revealing his thoughts and feelings, a business leader of enormous natural gifts but who was always a little shy, a little reticent about unfurling those gifts in public. As Mom will tell you, for instance, for many years Dad was absolutely terrified of speaking in public.

Still and all, Marvin and his parents prospered in Greensboro. With Old Maude leading the way, Mack's business at the Car-Cal Winery was booming, and soon Mack and Sally moved into a larger, more elegant home at 3300 Starmount Drive, in an area of stately homes on the northwest rim of the city. Theirs was a big white house on a corner lot, with a wonderful garden out back and a patio that, with its brightly colored umbrella and chairs, was perfect for cocktail parties and backyard barbecues. Mack and Sally joined a small reform congregation, and when he was 13 Marvin was confirmed there, in line with the reform Jewish tradition.

Greensboro Public Schools
HIGH SCHOOL REPORT

Central Junior High — School

Report of _Marvin Sands_

Semester Beginning _9-7_, 193_6_   Semester Ending _____, 193_7_

Session Room _S I C_   Advisor CARRIE S. BIGHAM

Principal H. A. HELMS

Parents or Guardians:

This report presents a summary of your child's school activities for each period of six weeks during each semester. An evaluation of his scholarship, attitudes, and habits, and a record of his attendance is furnished for your information. The effectiveness of this report will be determined by the response of parents and pupils to the evaluation presented of pupil's school life. The report is presented in two parts.

Part I deals with the progress made by your child in the regular school subjects. A mark of A shows that the pupil is among the group whose progress is evaluated as above the average of the class. The mark B indicates that his work ranks with the group of average progress. A mark of C shows that he is grouped with those whose progress is below the class average. The mark D indicates that his work has fallen below the accepted standard and is considered as incomplete or unsatisfactory.

Part II lists a number of traits as habits and attitudes which we consider as essential to satisfactory progress in his school activities. A check √ is recorded so that you may know our estimate of your child's outstanding qualities, those in which he is improving and those in which both school and home should co-operate in order to secure greater improvement.

The school and home should work in harmony; therefore your earnest co-operation in our efforts to raise the standards of the school and to extend its usefulness, is earnestly solicited.

The school authorities feel that your co-operation is essential to the best interests of your child's school life.

B. L. SMITH, Superintendent.

Young Marvin was an absolute whiz at math. At school, though, his grades in math were never outstanding, and our family has an intriguing idea as to why…

Once Mack's Car-Cal Winery began to prosper, Mack, Sally, and their son Marvin moved to the Starmount section of Greensboro, where Marvin enjoyed playing golf at the Starmount Country Club, above.

In this house, Sally – always gregarious and social – blossomed into a prominent hostess and party-giver. According to Mom, the Sands' house became a favorite weekend gathering place for young girls from the nearby Women's College of the University of North Carolina, and for young men from the colleges and military bases in and around Greensboro. If they were in the area to entertain the troops, a few Hollywood celebrities might even stop by. The actor, singer, and dancer Donald O'Connor was a frequent visitor, and so were Red Buttons and Ray Middleton, a popular singer of the time. If the mood was right, they would play the family piano and sing the popular songs of the late 1930s and early 1940s. I'm sure all of this festivity thrilled Grandpa Mack. The harsh memories of his failure in Cleveland and the miseries of the Depression were now far behind him, and Mack had become a respected man in and around Greensboro. As a little icing on his cake, Mack was now tooling around town in a shiny new Buick convertible.

By the age of 16, young Marvin Sands was also emerging as a dashing man about town, albeit in his quieter way. Marvin was very handsome now, with intense dark eyes and a shock of wavy dark hair. He was also well-built and athletic, and – according to Mom – he had a shy, understated charm. In the spring of 1940, Marvin graduated from the local high school and that fall he entered the University of North Carolina at Chapel Hill, 50 miles to the east. That was exactly a year after Hitler and the Nazis had marched into Poland and begun their sweep into the rest of Europe. As Marvin entered college, President Roosevelt was already putting the U.S. economy and the entire country onto a wartime footing. Marvin was getting ready too.

At 19 and as a junior at Chapel Hill, Marvin was enrolled in the V-12 program, which prepared young men to go into the U.S. Navy. That he would soon go off to war was a foregone conclusion; the only real question was when. In the meantime, Marvin often came home on weekends. There he could take a breather from his studies and his naval training and meet the winsome young ladies whom Sally regularly invited out to the house. According to Mom, there was nothing veiled about Sally's match-making; she wanted her one and only child to have his choice of the finest young women in Greensboro and far beyond. I'm sure Dad enjoyed playing his mother's game, but I'm also sure that he found every excuse to go off and play tennis or golf, or borrow his father's Buick convertible. Donald O'Connor, who was a year younger than Dad, became a friend of Dad's, and they would often slip away together to play a round of golf.

It was on just such a weekend at home that Marvin was introduced to Marilyn Alpert, a very bright, very attractive young student from the Women's College of UNC. Everyone called her Mickey. At 17, Mickey was two years younger than Marvin – in fact they were born on the very same day – and both of them were dating other people at the time. But no matter, Mickey was immediately smitten. "I liked him. A lot," Mickey laughs now. "He was a lot of fun, fun to be with, and he had a nice car and a nice uniform, and he was very nice to me. I loved his mother and dad, and I loved going out to his house. You know, when you live in a dormitory, it's so nice to have a lovely house to go to." Before long, her beau of the time was ancient history. And from that point on, Mickey Alpert only had eyes for Marvin Sands.

Marvin was smitten as well, though he was more guarded about showing his feelings. Still, young Mickey Alpert was quite a catch. Her family had roots in Connecticut and she had been born and raised in Manhattan, on the Upper East Side. Her father was a haberdasher who owned and managed three shops featuring men's shirts, ties, jackets, and accessories. One was on 86th Street in Manhattan, the second was in New Haven, Connecticut, and the third was on Fordham Avenue in the Bronx. In sum, the Alperts were a proper, upstanding Jewish family in Manhattan, with two happy, attractive, well-educated, very intelligent children. Mickey's older brother Norman studied physiology and later became chairman of the physiology department at the University of Vermont Medical School. Mickey was bright and blonde, blessed with common sense, and she was very wise and mature for her years. Naturally, she had no shortage of potential beaus: "I was very popular," Mom recalls, "and I was very nice. I enjoyed school, I enjoyed my life."

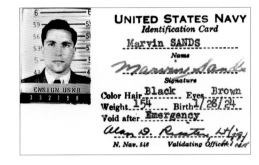

Marvin went off to war when he was just 19, leaving Mickey at home to eagerly await his return.

Smitten though they both were, the ensuing romance of Mickey and Marvin was anything but smooth; in fact, it was frequently punctuated by upheaval and tears. I guess that was inevitable. For one thing, Mom and Dad were very young when they met, and both of their lives were in a great deal of flux. During her very first month away at college, Mickey's father died, the victim of a weak heart. Her mother, a very strong woman, had no business experience but she stepped right in, along with her two brothers-in-law, and took charge of the Alpert family's three stores. Overnight, Mickey's life and the internal chemistry of her family were abruptly and permanently changed. From this vantage point, it is easy to understand why Mom so enjoyed bicycling over from her dorm to Mack and Sally's house in Starmount and why she so enjoyed the socializing and the many family comforts she found there.

Marvin's life was in flux as well. In early 1944, when he started dating Mickey, the war was raging both in Europe and the Pacific. Even though Dad was by nature a meticulous planner, I doubt he could even begin to consider making any life plans, not with imminent deployment staring him in the face. Also, as his later letters to Mom make clear, Marvin was up in the air about a career. At that stage, he had little interest in either his father's Car-Cal Winery or in the wine business in general. In fact, he had no idea at all of what future path he wanted to follow.

Fate and the U.S. Navy were not kind to their courtship. Soon after he started dating Mickey, Marvin got the call. The Navy wanted him to report for duty – now. As a first stop, Marvin was sent to Midshipman's School at Northwestern University in Evanston, Illinois, just north of Chicago. Then in March of 1944 Dad was sent to New Orleans for his first duty at sea. There he was assigned to an LST, specifically the USS LST 657, as a full ensign, an officer of the deck. A month or so later, Marvin was sent to Norfolk, Virginia, and then on to New York City to await the orders that would send him to the European front. It was in New York that he and Mickey began seriously courting. But their time together was brief. Soon Marvin got his orders. He gave Mickey a final hug and shipped out for Europe, as a gunnery officer aboard the USS LST 995. It had been built in the Boston Navy Yard and commissioned on May 20th, 1944, under the command of Lieutenant (Junior Grade) G.W. Chamberlain.

Marvin crossed the Atlantic aboard LST 995, a transport ship like those pictured here. After a stop in North Africa, he and his shipmates saw plenty of action in the European theater.

The LSTs – shorthand for Tank Landing Ships – were the rugged workhorses of the U.S. Navy. As their name suggests, LSTs were used to land troops, tanks, and support materiel onto enemy shores, usually as part of an Allied offensive. The LSTs were built in different sizes, but they all had bow doors and ramps that cranked down to facilitate rapid unloading, often under enemy fire. Inside, they had different decks, with lifts and turntables to facilitate the loading and unloading of the heavy tanks and other materiel. Over the course of the war, the Navy's fleet of LSTs played a vital role in the landings in Italy and the south of France. A few weeks after Marvin shipped out, LSTs landed troops on the beaches of Normandy, as General Dwight D. Eisenhower launched the climactic D-Day assault against Hitler and his forces.

Fortunately for all of us, Dad was a letter-writer. I have a sheaf of letters that he wrote during his years in the Navy, starting with his trip across the Atlantic and his arrival in North Africa, en route to the European front. These letters reveal Dad's intelligence and his sharp eye for observation. They also reveal a lively wit and a great deal of grace under pressure. Listen to this passage, written to his parents in July of 1944, just after his LST had docked at an unnamed port on the coast of Tunisia. On his first day off, Dad hitched a ride aboard an Army truck and headed for Tunis, the capital city:

"The countryside in general appearance might look like any of the western states approaching the Rockies. The land is mostly flat, but every few miles a range of large hills and sometimes mountains breaks the monotony of the straight roads… Olive groves and sugar cane fields were scattered throughout the countryside. Homes, or should I say the farmers' dwellings, were small huts constructed of mud-like brick. Here and there it was amusing for the first time to see Arab men riding their mules next to the road with their women trailing close behind. Arabs are Mohammedans, very religious and with a great many sacred customs. For one thing, I don't think they approve of career women. You will never find a female out in public with her face exposed, and never will you find one walking alongside her man… I arrived in Tunis with 5,000 francs in my pocket and raring to go. With the sound of so much jack I thought I was a millionaire… The population of Tunis is 200,000 and it looked like a large town. I bumped into a little Italian boy who spoke five languages and I adopted him as my guide. He has two brothers in Brooklyn who like America very much. He's anxious to get there too."

From there, Dad recounts visiting the local casbah, or market, joining up with an Army sergeant, meeting two French girls, testing out the two or three ragged words of French he knew, and generally having a fascinating day playing tourist. "I had a swell time," he wrote his parents in closing, "but had to start back at 2300. So ended an interesting day. In about a week we shove off, and on to a new place. Your loving son, Marvin."

Those were the good times. Dad didn't write much about the bad times, and Navy censors would have squelched it if he had. But from his letters and from Navy records we know that in August and September of 1944, the USS LST 995 and its crew saw plenty of action – and plenty of bloodshed. In that period, U.S. Naval forces pushed up through the Mediterranean Sea, then landed tanks and personnel onto the shores of France and Italy. The ships involved came under heavy enemy fire during those landings, and naval forces suffered many wounded and killed. Dad never told us much about what he went through; silence was a part of the code of what Tom Brokaw later called "The Greatest Generation." But we can glean a lot from the many medals he earned: the American Campaign Medal; the African-European Campaign 1 Medal, with star; and a World War II Victory Medal. His ship was awarded one star for its valorous service in some of the climactic naval operations in the European theater of World War II.

For Dad, the Navy was an education unto itself. As I now read and re-read his wartime letters, I find many passages that reveal the kind of business leader he was going to be – and the kind of tightly run organization he was going to build. In his stateside training and early postings, Dad was clearly unimpressed by the Navy's bureaucracy and lack of organizational discipline. There was starch in the uniforms, sure, but no starch when it came to precision execution or cost-conscious financial management. Dad's attitude toward the Navy changed, though, once he and his boat had shipped out and were making their way to the front. Now he saw that every man knew his job, knew the responsibilities it entailed, and knew that executing his job with skill and professionalism was essential – not just to his shipmates but also to the fleet and to the entire war effort. Heading to the front, Dad saw come into play all the fundamentals of effective management: Vision. Strategy. Planning. Recruitment. Communication. Teamwork. And chain of command. He saw, too, that what made each of those fundamentals work in harmony, and what made each seaman proud to serve and be the best he could be, was inspiring Leadership, with a capital L.

For any operation to succeed, whether in the military or in business, Dad saw that you need leaders with self-confidence, self-control, and a deep understanding of how to motivate people and ensure their trust, loyalty, and performance under fire. In his eyes, everything flowed from inspiring leadership, from General Eisenhower on down. During that Atlantic crossing, Dad saw that despite its many faults, the Navy had created some magnificent leaders; it had taken ordinary men and precision-trained them to do extraordinary things. Seeing that made a deep impression on Dad, and as he and his shipmates headed into the fighting, his view of the Navy began to lift, and his own spirits lifted in kind:

"I like the Navy much better now that I'm really in it," he wrote to Mack and Sally from aboard ship. "Around here one doesn't feel a certain contempt for what appears to be over-organization, waste, and criminal inefficiency in the armed forces back home – at least I don't. A new and more thrilling perspective creeps across one's horizon. The seed planted in the U.S. is magnificently in bloom here. We have a real army and navy here, and I'm sure it won't be long before everyone is home again."

As I type those words and feel their power, I can see how those words – and the values they define – later shaped the way Dad ran his operation in Canandaigua. Dad detested anything that smacked of useless bureaucracy. He made sure that his own organizational structure was light and nimble. Waste annoyed him; he managed every deal and every corner of his operation as if each penny was gold instead of copper. And just as he had seen aboard his ship, he knew that every single person was crucial to the performance of the larger enterprise, and every single person had to know his or her job perfectly and be proud to do it in the hottest of fires. Reading his words now, it is no wonder to me that

In the Navy, Dad saw that you need leaders with self-confidence, self-control, and a deep understanding of how to motivate people and ensure their trust, loyalty, and performance under fire.

After his tour in Europe, Marvin was sent to San Francisco to await orders to ship out to the Pacific. As his tour in the Navy unfolded, Marvin learned valuable lessons about leadership, organization, and building a first-rate team.

when he was interviewing job candidates, Dad always asked them if they had served in the armed forces. If the answer was "yes," Dad would be much more inclined to hire them. It wasn't just because they had served; it was because Dad knew that the Army, the Navy, or the Marines had already shaped their character and values – and put them to the test.

In the Navy, though, Dad also witnessed management and leadership at their worst, starting with one of his own assignments. Though he was a trained navigator, for some reason Dad was assigned to the LST 995 as a gunnery officer. "This makes no sense to me," he complained to Mickey. "I don't know a damned thing about guns!" Nor was the captain of his ship a paragon of grace under fire. According to Mom, at one point, in a fit of pique, the captain ordered most of his officers confined to quarters – and he had almost nobody left to run the ship! Through those kind of experiences, Dad saw only too clearly the limitations of the Navy's "command and control" leadership model, and he later evolved for himself a leadership style that put a premium on humility, patient listening, and treating all of his employees as if they were family – not just numbers and pay-grades.

Irony of ironies, too, it was a bit of bureaucratic inefficiency – the kind that Dad deplored – that derailed his deployment to the brutal fighting on the Pacific front. After his service in the European theater, Dad was shipped back to the U.S. and assigned to San Francisco, to await his orders to the Pacific. Dad arrived in San Francisco in April of 1945, and while awaiting his orders to ship out, he was assigned to a unit of the U.S. Naval Hydrographic Office, which provided vital maps, charts, and sea conditions to the U.S. fleet in the Pacific. Week after week Dad waited for his orders to ship out but they never came. Somehow, the Navy had lost his records. So from April to December of 1945, Dad served the war effort from behind a desk.

While Marvin was serving in San Francisco, two people back on the East Coast were eagerly anticipating and planning for his return: Mickey Alpert and Grandpa Mack. On Mickey's mind was love and marriage; on Mack's was business and wine. From the time Marvin first shipped out in 1944 and all through 1945, Mickey wrote to Marvin almost every day. While he was stationed in San Francisco, Marvin used some of his furloughs to come back to New York to be with Mickey, and by the spring of 1945 their love was in full bloom. On April 29th, 1945, Mom wrote: "Dearest Marvin, Fourth letter in four days. Golly, but I'm an awfully good gal. However, I do have lots of time and I enjoy writing to you. Wonder why? Maybe it's because I love you..."

In December of 1945, Dad was formally discharged from the Navy, after two and half years of service and just shy of his 22nd birthday. He had come through the war alive and intact, and the entire nation was celebrating the end of hostilities. Marvin was intent on returning to Greensboro for the holiday season – but not before he first stopped in New York City to formally ask Mom for her hand in marriage. For some unknown reason, though, he begged her not to tell a soul. Of course Mickey rushed to share the news with her mother, who promptly told everyone in her family. Then came the stunner: a week later, Marvin abruptly changed his mind and called off the engagement.

According to Mom, Marvin never clearly spelled out his reasons. Maybe he was upset that Mom had leaked the news. Maybe he just got cold feet. Or, as Mom suggests, when

Marvin got back to Greensboro, maybe Mack or Sally said, "What's the rush, son? You just got home!" Either way, Mickey was irate and humiliated and her mother was none too pleased either. I wasn't there, of course, and I am not well-placed to guess what prompted Dad's decision. But there is another side to this story, another "marriage" on the horizon, and I can't help but wonder if it wasn't that which gave our father pause.

CHAPTER 4

Mack's Grand Plan

The Seneca Indians referred to New York State's Finger Lakes area as the "chosen spot."

Grandpa Mack, I'm sure, had the best of intentions.

In mid-1945, when Marvin was still in the Navy, Mack decided he should set his son up in business, to give him a leg up when the war finally came to an end. His own father had done little to help him get started; Mack wanted to do better for his own son. With that in mind, Mack decided to pay a call on Little Joe Applebaum, the head of Geffen Industries and his godfather in the world of wine. Maybe Little Joe would have an idea or two about how best to help out Marvin.

Little Joe was doing well. Just as he had managed to thrive during Prohibition, Little Joe was thriving during World War II. At the height of the war, in 1943 and 1944, when wine was in terribly short supply, Little Joe was selling all the wine he could produce – and he had plans to sell even more. To that end, Little Joe had a valuable ace up his sleeve: sugar. At that time, supplies of sugar and many other staples were controlled under wartime rationing. But Little Joe, clever as always, had secured for himself a generous quota of sugar, more than enough to boost his production of bulk wine – provided he could secure more grapes and find another facility to make the wine.

To that end, in early 1944 Little Joe sent his cousin Big Joe on a high-priority mission: go up to the Finger Lakes region of western New York State, just outside Rochester, and find an existing winery or other facility where Little Joe could set up shop – as cheaply as possible – and start churning out wine. Joe didn't care much about quality; he needed quantity and he needed it fast; no one knew how long the current demand would last. That was Little Joe: see an opportunity and grab it.

The Finger Lakes region has a long and rich history, though I doubt Big Joe paid it any mind. The area's topography is dominated by five picturesque lakes shaped like fingers and aligned like a hand. According to historians, the Seneca Indians, who resided in the region for hundreds of years, considered this to be sacred land, a "chosen spot." Specifically, they believed that those five lakes were actually formed by the hand of the Great Spirit, pressing down into the Earth. The Seneca named the western-most lake "Kanandarque," which in their language means "the chosen spot." When white settlers moved in, they started referring to the region as the "Finger Lakes" and the name of that western-most lake evolved into "Canandaigua." The lake itself is 16 miles long, 262 feet deep at its deepest point, and it is surrounded by magnificent hills and lush green forests. With so much natural beauty, it is little wonder that Canandaigua and its surroundings attracted throngs of summer tourists and many small industries, including wineries. As a result, Big Joe had plenty of potential sites to consider for Little Joe's new operation. Soon, though, he found an unusual solution, and it came with a startling history:

Sauerkraut.

That's right. In the town of Canandaigua, Big Joe found an old, abandoned sauerkraut plant that had been formerly owned by a packing company called Snyder of Berlin. Now not many people would have seen the potential of the Snyder plant, but Big Joe did. Though it had long been idle, the plant was still equipped with huge wooden tanks that had been used for making sauerkraut. And as Big Joe quickly learned, the process for making sauerkraut was not too distant from the process for making wine. Here's the gist of it: at harvest time, Snyder purchased large quantities of fresh cabbage. Then their team finely sliced the cabbage and put the cuttings into those wooden tanks. There, using lactic acid bacteria, the cabbage was fermented and turned into sauerkraut. The Germans had been making sauerkraut that way for centuries; it went perfectly with the vast array of sausages and boiled meats that the Germans love to consume. If Snyder could use those tanks to ferment cabbage, Big Joe figured, surely we can use them to ferment grapes and make wine!

That is exactly what they did. In May of 1944, Little Joe purchased the old Snyder facility. Then Big Joe and Lou Goldberg, another Geffen employee, cleaned out those wooden tanks, purchased used hoses and filters, and added a makeshift refrigeration system – with 50-pound blocks of ice – to hold down temperatures during fermentation. They did everything on the cheap, and they got the job done quickly. With that, Little Joe had a second facility that could churn out decent bulk wine in industrial quantities. Little Joe arranged for Lou Goldberg to stay in Canandaigua to run the operation, and he tapped his cousin Max Applebaum – Big Joe's brother – to oversee the winemaking and give guidance to Joe Noble, who was to be the resident winemaker. It was a good plan. Max was Little Joe's most talented winemaker, and Joe knew that Max would make sure the new venture turned out a very drinkable product. To round out this family team, Little Joe sent Max's daughter Bea and her husband, Seymour Block, to help manage the operation. That way Max could still help oversee the winemaking at Geffen's facility on Long Island and he could stay with Bea and Seymour when he was in Canandaigua. With that team in place, Little Joe put a respectable name on the door – the San Gabriel Wine Company – and he was off and running.

Now let's be clear: Little Joe's wines would never win any prizes. Likewise, in speaking of the great innovators and pioneers of American wine, you would never even mention Little Joe's name, much less compare him to North Carolina's Captain Garrett or California's Junipero Serra. But when it came to making money, Little Joe knew his stuff. He knew every aspect of the wine business; it was both his passion and his life. He had no wife or children. And Little Joe liked to live well; he kept a suite at the Waldorf and loved to go to Florida to play the ponies. The success of Geffen made all that possible, and in the final years of World War II, Little Joe's operation in Canandaigua churned out substantial quantities of both wine and profit. Before long, Little Joe decided that the San Gabriel Wine Company needed a name that better reflected its growing muscle in the market: Canandaigua Industries. And when Little Joe considered the profits it was generating, I'm sure he thought that he had found his own "chosen spot."

Which makes what happened next all the more surprising.

It was the following year, in the late summer of 1945, that Grandpa Mack paid his call on Little Joe. Even though Mack had left Geffen and was now out on his own, he and Little Joe maintained a tight relationship. So when Mack needed advice and counsel, or maybe a favor, it was only natural that he turn to Little Joe, just as he did now. As Mack explained to him, Marvin was now 21, he was out in San Francisco doing admirable duty in the U.S. Navy, he had been in combat and had won lots of medals, and Mack wanted to set him up in business, get him a good start in life. "So tell me, Joe. What do you think? Do you have

Now let's be clear: Little Joe's wines would never win any prizes.

With the war coming to an end, Mack saw an exciting opportunity in wine – and he wanted to grab it.

any ideas?"

Now I wasn't there, of course, and no one today knows exactly how it played out. But in my mind's eye, I can see the scene unfolding: Little Joe is sitting at his desk, listening patiently to Mack, and maybe even thinking back to when he knew Marvin as a young boy playing on the streets of Brooklyn. Then, as Mack is talking, I can see a tiny light bulb going off in Little Joe's brain.

Like many a shrewd businessman, Little Joe watched trends and carefully followed the fluctuations in the wine market. This was the summer of 1945 and Little Joe knew the war was coming to an end; Hitler's forces had already been defeated and the Germans had officially surrendered on May 7th, 1945. The Japanese defeat would not be far behind. With the end of the war, Little Joe knew that big changes would hit the wine industry: the rationing of sugar would be lifted and distilleries that had been converted to wartime use would quickly return to producing spirits. The wine industry could very well be slammed, meaning that the market value of Little Joe's Canandaigua operation could very well plummet – almost overnight.

Beyond that, Little Joe was thinking of quitting the wine business altogether. According to Mom, he was eager to cash out and retire to Florida. He was dreaming of warm weather, playing the ponies every afternoon, and leaving the daily stresses of the wine business far behind. At that time, there were also rumors in the industry that Little Joe had antagonized some rival clans in New York wine, so maybe he had some other reasons to head to Florida. I don't know. Still, I can well imagine that when Mack asked him about ways to help out Marvin, Little Joe might have seen this as a godsend; this could be an ideal way for him to start selling his assets.

I can picture the scene: Little Joe's mind is racing, but as cool as ice he would lean back in his chair and offer Mack a fresh cigar. "You know, Mack, we go back a long way," I can hear him saying. "And that's awfully good of you to want to give your son a hand. An excellent gesture. Very noble. Just what a good father should do. And you know what, my friend? I do have an idea that you might find interesting..."

Little Joe then suggested that – for the right price, of course – he might be persuaded to sell his sweet little money-maker, Canandaigua Industries. Geffen Industries, after all, was the primary engine of his empire and his main source of income. Canandaigua, by contrast, was only a sideline, and it would be an ideal spot for Marvin to get a good start in the wine business. Besides, Canandaigua was a beautiful spot, not expensive to live, and it would be a fine place for a young man to settle down and raise a family. "You know, Mack, this might be a perfect opportunity for you and Marvin..."

Mack's first inclination, I'm sure, was to jump out of his chair and shout "Yes!" Little Joe's idea was extremely enticing: Canandaigua would indeed be a fine spot for Marvin – and it would be a very fine fit for Mack's own business ambitions as well. Mack was buying bulk wine from Geffen and other suppliers for Car-Cal; now he could buy the source wine he needed from his own son – to the benefit of both businesses. This would be vertical integration at its best: Marvin's team would buy the grapes and make the wines; Car-Cal would become one of its biggest customers. Marvin could sell to other bottlers as well.

Working in tandem, they could grow both businesses, while holding down costs and gaining leverage with growers, shippers, and distributors. Did Mack see any downsides? Well, he may have foreseen, like Little Joe, that the end of the war could bring upheavals to the wine market. But Mack never worried too much about risks or downsides; he kept his eyes set on the potential jackpot. And what a handsome jackpot it would be. For Mack, purchasing Canandaigua Industries would be a big step up the economic and social ladder and it would be a chance to join with his beloved son Marvin in a fabulous business marriage. Who could ask for more?

Still, Mack would be careful not to tip his hand. Seeing himself as a shrewd negotiator, Mack would probably make an elaborate show of downplaying his interest. After all, down the road he and Little Joe would have to do some hard bargaining on a final purchase price for Canandaigua Industries. "Gee, Joe," I can hear Mack saying, "that's a generous and very intriguing idea, but I just don't know. What with the war still on and all… And no one knows for sure what the Navy's going to do with Marvin. Heck, by tomorrow morning the poor guy could be on his way to the Pacific…"

Still, Mack and Little Joe agreed to meet again soon to discuss the deal. And knowing Mack, he probably danced his way home, bursting to tell Sally all about the brilliant coup that he had set into motion. "Honey, Canandaigua's a sweet little operation, very profitable and with plenty of future potential. It's a perfect fit for Car-Cal! And we can go up there in the summers and spend time with Marvin. Maybe we can rent a little place right on the lake. This is going to be great, you'll see. And think about it: Marvin will be set for life – and so will we!"

Still, Grandpa Mack was a long way from closing the deal – and he had some daunting hurdles to cross first. He had to negotiate a good purchase price. He had to find a way to keep Max Applebaum on as winemaker, since Marvin knew absolutely nothing about making wine. And, too, he would have to find a legitimate way to get Marvin out of the Navy, quickly but honorably of course. And, of course, there was one other tiny hurdle that Mack had to surmount: somehow he had to convince his son to set aside all of his other future plans – be they marriage or whatever – and join Mack in his grand plan for the future of the Sands family.

Now how in the world was Mack going to accomplish that?

"Marvin will be set for life – and so will we!"

MACK SANDS

CHAPTER 5

The Good Son

When the war was finally over, Marvin was eager to marry Mickey – but Mack's grand plan got in the way.

On October 9th, 1945, in his office in Greensboro, North Carolina, Mack pulled from his desk several sheets of quality bond, each imprinted with the letterhead of the Car-Cal Winery. Then, in a rough, scrawling hand, he penned to his son Marvin a three-page letter laying out an enticing, almost irresistible plan. To set just the right tone, Mack opened the letter by announcing a very sweet fatherly gesture:

"Dear Marvin,

"You will find enclosed a list of the family holdings. Last Saturday when Pepsi dipped after that 3½ point rise, I placed an order for 100 shares. There were 30,000 shares traded that day and only 2,000 at 34. You had what I call beginner's luck and got yours at the bottom price. From now on you must say Pepsi; no more Coke."

The list of family holdings that Mack refers to is attached at the end of the letter. Marvin's individual holdings are featured at the very top of the list, above those of Sally, Mack, and Mack's older brother Dave. It shows Marvin owning 100 shares of a now-defunct company called American Ice, plus 300 shares of Burlington Mills, and the newly purchased 100 shares of Pepsi. Sally's holdings are listed as 400 shares of Burlington Mills. Mack has 200 shares of Burlington, 100 shares of an outfit called Atlas Corp, and 400 shares of Pepsi. The only shares listed for Dave are 100 shares of American Ice.

With the stage thus set, Mack then takes up the real purpose of the letter: convincing Marvin that together they ought to accept Little Joe's generous offer and buy Canandaigua Industries. Mack had already spoken to Marvin about the basics of the deal. But now Mack really lays on the honey: he tells his son this is more than a sweet business deal; played right, it could mean for Marvin an instant ticket out of the Navy: "Joe and I are of the opinion that if you take the matter up with the proper authorities you may get out now. Your parents are ready to buy you a business where you are essential... and will give employment to a good number of people."

Let me explain. During the war, many men were exempted from service or given early discharges if they could show they were running a vital industry or employing a large number of people. Mack clearly had such an exemption in mind, and he wanted Marvin to pursue this option – right away. To speed the process, Mack even offered to intervene personally with Marvin's commanding officer: "Is it possible for you to get 30 days leave in November so that you can go to New York to be investigated by N.Y. liquor authorities to get your permit? If you want, I will be glad to write to your skipper asking him advice on this matter." (We can only imagine how Dad's skipper would have reacted to that!)

In the letter, Mack then brings Marvin up to date on Car-Cal's activities and he asks Marvin if he would please contact a California grower about supplying Car-Cal with another 300,000 gallons of wine. The underlying message here could not be clearer: "You see, son, we're already a team, working hand in glove. Together we can do great things…" With similar subtlety, Mack signs off as the perfect, generous father: "With the best regards from all, Dad. P.S. Do you need cash? Let me know…"

Now Mack's letter might not merit a featured display at the Smithsonian, but in terms of our family history and the history of Constellation Brands, I believe it should be framed and given its due. The letter clearly sets forth the dimensions of what I think of now as

"Marvin's Choice." On the one hand, the letter shows Mack's very honorable intention of helping his son. On the other, it also shows how much conniving he'd do to persuade his son to accept Little Joe's offer. Stripped down to its essence, in this letter Mack was pressing – perhaps "manipulating" is a better word – his son into a life-defining decision. Marvin was still only 21 years old, he was still serving in the Navy, he was still uncertain about what career path to pursue, and yet here he was confronted with a decision that could shape his life and his financial health – and those of his parents – for many long years to come.

Which way would he turn?

I wish Dad were here now to tell us how he felt when he received that letter back in October of 1945. I'd also like to hear, in his own words, why he called off his marriage to Mom. I have other questions too: how did Dad really feel about the wine business, before he became a part of it? What reservations, if any, did he have about Mack's grand plan for his future? I'd love to ask him, too, about how serving in the wartime Navy had shaped his attitude toward words like honor, duty, family, and country – words that influenced many of Dad's later decisions in business and in life.

Without Dad here to provide the answers, I can only piece together what happened next from conversations with Mom, from letters that she and Dad wrote to each other, and from an array of other sources that shed light on what happened with Dad in the closing months of 1945. And what a tumultuous year that was. On April 12th, 1945, President Roosevelt died in office of a massive cerebral hemorrhage. Right away he was replaced by his Vice President, Harry S. Truman. On April 30th, Hitler committed suicide, purportedly by gunshot and cyanide poisoning. On May 7th, Germany officially surrendered, though the Japanese went on fighting. On August 6th, President Truman ordered three B-29 bombers to Hiroshima, a city on the southern tip of Japan. Once over the target, one of the planes, the Enola Gay, dropped the first nuclear bomb ever used in combat. On August 9th, a second nuclear bomb was dropped on the city of Nagasaki. The next day the Japanese surrendered. World War II was thankfully over. But Dad's duty in the Navy was far from finished.

Throughout the war, the port of San Francisco served as a critical hub for naval operations in the Pacific. The Navy's headquarters at the Presidio, a sprawling compound of barracks, offices, and command centers built right beside the bay, teemed with activity. Day and night ships came and went under the Golden Gate Bridge, shuttling men and materiel to the worst fighting in the Pacific, in now-legendary places like Guadalcanal, Midway, Bataan, Corregidor, Okinawa, and Iwo Jima. At the U.S. Naval Hydrographic Office where Dad worked every day, I'm sure that everyone cheered when the Japanese surrendered, but I'm equally sure that tension and a sense of duty remained high for many months to come, as the Navy's many carrier groups, destroyers, submarines, and LSTs either made their way home or were redeployed to other areas across the Pacific.

When Mack's letter reached him that October, Dad had been in the Navy for a little over two years and was by no means due for a discharge. And I doubt he was very pleased about Mack's plan to buy him an early ticket out. According to Mom, Dad felt torn between his sense of duty to the Navy and his country and his sense of duty to his father. One voice

At the age of only 21, Marvin was confronted with a decision that could shape his life – and those of his parents – for many years to come.

"Listen, boy, your father's absolutely right: this is a great opportunity; you'd be a damned fool to pass it up!"

inside him was saying, "Take your time, go back and finish college, and find your true passion and calling in life." But another voice was saying to him, "Listen, boy, your father's absolutely right: this is a great opportunity; you'd be a damned fool to pass it up!" So there it is. By any measure, Mack's grand plan had placed Dad onto the horns of a very painful dilemma.

There was another element here too. As he told Mom at the time, Dad was reluctant to accept the offer laid before him by Mack and Little Joe because he felt as though he had done nothing at all to earn it. Accepting their offer would be too easy. Too cushy. Dad was a man who wanted to prove his merit and earn his stripes. He wanted to have the lasting fulfillment of making it on his own, by his own mettle and wit. How could he do that if his entire future was handed to him on a silver platter?

Today, Rob and I can sense how much this aspect of the decision must have weighed on our father: with us and our sister Laurie, Dad never tried to influence our career paths or decisions. He always told us to chart our own course, to follow our hearts and passions and find our own sources of personal fulfillment. Dad never openly expressed to us any regret about how he resolved "Marvin's Choice," but I do see in his advice to us kids the residue of his own ambivalence and torment.

Dad also had reservations about doing business with Little Joe Applebaum. In a letter that he wrote much later to Little Joe's niece, Bea Applebaum Block, Dad recounts the early history of his dealings with her family. As always, he was gracious and diplomatic in the letter, but he also truthfully described the deal that was being placed in his lap, including the price and final terms of the purchase: "By December 1945, the second world war was over, sugar was no longer rationed, and Little Joe recognized (he was always very shrewd, as we knew) that the picnic was over and that the wine business would become more competitive and tougher in the years ahead. With that in mind, he developed an idea. Joe was very bright and always a great schemer…. He made an offer which *on the surface* [the italics are mine] seemed most attractive. He would sell me the winery for $70,000 cash and take notes for one-half million gallons of wine with a market value at that time of approximately $1.00 per gallon." In sum, the deal called for Dad to pay Little Joe $70,000 up front and give him notes for $500,000 more, to be paid off over time. That number had been worked out by Mack and Little Joe based on the fact that Dad was purchasing all of Little Joe's inventory of 500,000 gallons wine. The agreement fixed this part of the sale price at the current market price of $1 per gallon.

That letter is very revealing. It underscores that right from the outset Dad recognized that Little Joe was a schemer. It also underscores Dad's belief that even before the deal was signed, Little Joe knew that "the picnic was over" and that the wine industry could be in for a fall. Still, as Dad says, "on the surface" the deal that Little Joe was offering "seemed most attractive." And to young Marvin's eye, those notes for $500,000 did appear to be manageable. At that time, demand for wine was strong, and Dad had every reason to imagine that as he turned that inventory into sales, he could comfortably pay down that note – and in short order too. Then he would own Canandaigua Industries outright and be set for a long time to come. Not a bad position to be in for a young man of 21.

Other aspects of the deal also seemed attractive, at least "on the surface." Dad lays them out in that same letter: "During the discussions it was suggested that it might be a good idea to have Max Applebaum as a 20 percent partner, as he was a good practical wine maker and very energetic. It was not contemplated that he move to Canandaigua because there was a wine maker that we would inherit, Joe Noble. One problem was that Max didn't have any money. We made Max a 20 percent partner anyhow and arranged for him to pay out his $20,000 investment out of earnings, with no time specified. The $20,000 was arrived at because of other borrowed money put into the company and also because my uncle, Louis Kipnis, (Sally's brother) became a 10 percent partner for a $10,000 investment... My father had no financial interest, being very happy to operate his most successful wine bottling company in Greensboro."

Yes, to Dad all of these terms must have seemed enticing indeed. If all went according to plan, he would leave the Navy right away, honorably, and become the owner of his own thriving wine business in "the chosen spot" of New York State. Max Applebaum would stay on to ensure the quality of the wine and teach him the inside secrets of wine production. His Uncle Lou would come in as a minority partner and business guide. As an added incentive to Marvin, Mack had agreed to loan him the lion's share of the up-front payment of $70,000 to Little Joe. So at a single stroke Marvin would own his own business with little of the up-front money coming out of his pocket. On top of all that, Mack was not going to take a piece of the action. He wanted his son to be the sole captain of his ship, the sole master of his fate. Yes, "on the surface," everything looked perfectly grand, just as Mack had promised. How could Marvin turn down such a deal? Indeed, how could any good son rebuff such a generous offer from his father and his father's friend?

Ah, how looks can deceive…

In my view, a seasoned business executive would have examined this deal in much greater depth and from several different angles. For instance, let's look at it from Little Joe's perspective. He gets $70,000 up front and an iron-clad note for another $500,000. In today's dollars, that note would be worth about $5,425,000 – not chump change. Joe also secures a lovely part-time job and a piece of the action for his cousin Max, even though he puts in no up-front money at all. Little Joe also secures continued employment for his niece Bea and her husband Seymour. That's a sweet deal for Little Joe. If he does cash out of the wine business, he can now do so with plenty of cash and lots of pride, knowing he has taken good care of his own.

And Mack? With this deal, Mack secures for his Car-Cal Winery a strong sister operation in New York and a reliable source of quality bulk wine. Through vertical integration, Mack moves into the enviable position of becoming his own supplier. At the same time, he secures a piece of the action for Louis Kipnis, his brother-in-law, pal, and longtime bridge partner. Also, with a sister operation in New York, Mack climbs a few steps higher in the world of wine and, no doubt, in the business and social whirl of Greensboro. Financially, too, this is a good deal for Mack. Working in tandem with Marvin's operation will help him cut costs and increase his profits at Car-Cal. Are there risks for Mack? Some, sure. But Marvin, of course, will pay back the initial loan to buy the business, probably with interest. And while

Yes, "on the surface," everything looked perfectly grand, just as Mack had promised.

Mack's decision not to accept a piece of the action might look a generous gesture, it also had a silver lining for Mack: it meant that the burden of paying off that $500,000 to Little Joe was not Mack's direct responsibility. No, that responsibility would fall primarily on the shoulders of his beloved son Marvin, a young man of 21 with absolutely no hands-on experience either in business or in the world of wine. How sweet – for Mack.

Marvin, of course, could see none of this. He was not a seasoned business executive, and he had neither the time nor the experience to undertake a careful process of due diligence. I'm sure he assumed that his father, as a business veteran, had done all the necessary homework and had dutifully considered the risks and all the many things that could go wrong. Moreover, Dad was stationed across the country in San Francisco, he was working in a high-pressure unit of the Navy, and he never had the opportunity to sit down with Little Joe, look him in the eye, and go through the deal line by line. Nor did Dad have the time to seek outside advice. Instead, despite any reservations he might have had, Marvin chose to trust his father and his father's judgment. In the end, I think he simply could not imagine that his own father might steer him wrong.

And so it was that in December of 1945 Dad finally resolved the agonizing issue of "Marvin's Choice" – he agreed to the business marriage that his father had taken such pains to arrange. In those same weeks, Dad secured his early discharge from the Navy and rushed back East for the holidays. He first stopped in New York City to be with Mickey and ask for her hand in marriage. Then he rushed home to Greensboro to see Mack and Sally and get ready to take command of Canandaigua Industries. It was all happening so fast: in the blink of an eye, his entire life was being totally transformed.

Once back in Greensboro, when he finally had a chance to catch his breath and grasp all of the new responsibilities that he had agreed to take on, Dad abruptly called off his engagement to Mickey. Now I think we can understand why. Having agreed to a new business marriage, marrying Mickey at the same time was just too much to handle. Dad's instincts turned out to be right. Within weeks of taking the helm of Canandaigua Industries, Dad discovered that his new business marriage was riddled with problems and deceit. Mack – with all of his grand ambitions and plans – had been blind to the many risks and pitfalls embedded in Little Joe's deal. Instead of being properly set up in life, Dad would now find himself in another struggle to survive. Still and all, Marvin honored the vow "for richer, for poorer." He never openly complained about the terms of Little Joe's deal, and he never said an angry word to his father. In his world, in his system of values, good sons never do.

PART II

Learning the Hard Way

When Marvin took over Canandaigua Industries, he was 22, he had no idea how wine was made, no idea how to source grapes, and no clue how to run a business. His education was about to begin.

CHAPTER 6

Shock Upon Shock

In many people's minds today, the word "winery" conjures up images of rolling hillsides, immaculate vineyards, beautiful surrounding gardens, and polished production facilities where the wine is fermented, barreled, and then patiently aged.

Canandaigua Industries was never that kind of facility. When Marvin first arrived in the town of Canandaigua, in January of 1946, the facility was located, as it still is today, on Buffalo Street, in a quiet neighborhood several blocks away from Main Street, with all the shops and commercial activity to be found there. The facility itself had changed little since the days when it was owned by Snyder's of Berlin. In look and feel, it was drab and functional, with a railroad spur running conveniently alongside. Day and night, though, it smelled richly of fermenting grapes, instead of cabbage. There were no vineyards anywhere near the plant; the company bought grapes and juice concentrate from providers in New York State, California, and other locales. Then they made the wine in those same huge fermenting tanks that had once been used for sauerkraut.

Within weeks of his arrival in Canandaigua, Marvin was hit with a series of crises…

Dad arrived in the dead of winter, and if he had stood outside Canandaigua Industries at the end of the day, he would not have seen a change of shifts; the company at that time counted only eight employees, with Dad and his winemaker Max Applebaum chief among them. Dad's office was located in a small wood-frame building in front of the facility; the production area was located a short walk to the rear. It, too, was modest and functional. The old wooden fermenting tanks were shop-worn and musty, and at that stage the facility didn't even have a bottling line. This was, in truth, a small, no-frills operation, and I'm sure that in his first days there Dad had plenty of reservations about calling it "home."

Indeed, when he first arrived, Dad had neither the time nor the inclination to properly install himself in an apartment or house. Instead, he chose to live at the Canandaigua Inn, an historic gathering place in the heart of Main Street. The inn burned down long ago. At that stage, Dad's sole preoccupation was work, digging in and learning everything that he needed to know about running a business and everything he needed to know about producing, bottling, selling, distributing, and marketing wine. Starting from scratch the way he did, the challenge was enormous – and so was the stress. In those winter weeks, Dad spent all of his days and most of his evenings there on Buffalo Street, making decisions as best as he could and trying to learn as fast as he could.

Then the feds came knocking. For some time, Dad now discovered, federal regulators had been investigating the way that Little Joe Applebaum was making wine both in Canandaigua and at his Geffen Industries operation out on Long Island. Specifically, agents of the Alcohol Tax Unit, or ATU – the precursor to today's TTB – suspected that Little Joe's winemakers were "adulterating" their wines, meaning they were using outside ingredients to boost production in excess of the wine actually derived from fresh grapes. That was a very serious charge.

For Marvin, this was not just one shock; it was three. First of all, it seems that Mack's dear friend Little Joe had never bothered to mention the ATU probe during his negotiations with Mack; Dad was totally blind-sided. Second, as a novice in the wine business, Dad had no idea how extensive and detailed the federal regulations were – or how heavy the penalties were for breaking them. Third, Dad knew nothing at all about the chemistry

Unsure of his future in the wine business, Dad took temporary quarters at the Canandaigua Inn, above, a town landmark that later perished in a fire.

of making wine. Dad simply took it for granted that with Max Applebaum overseeing the Canandaigua operation, it would be run in full compliance with all federal and state regulations and guidelines. Indeed, that was one of the many reasons they had wanted to retain Max and even gave him a piece of the action, to avoid just this sort of problem.

The ATU probe was a rude awakening, and it was also Dad's first hands-on lesson in how to manage a crisis. In response, he moved forcefully on three fronts. First, Dad began a crash course in wine-making and government regulations; from then on, he wanted to be an expert in every aspect of how wine is produced and shipped, from grapes in the vineyard to the finished product's point of sale. He also wanted to be an expert in every guiding state or federal law pertaining to wine and alcohol. Second, Dad tightened his command over every aspect of his company's operations. Never again would he leave compliance issues to his winemakers alone, nor would he leave any other critical decisions solely in the hands of others. He had been blind-sided once; that would not happen again. From that point forward, Dad would monitor every aspect of the company and hold his staff directly accountable for whatever they did. Third, acting on some good legal advice, Dad made a crucial strategic decision: he wanted to make the ATU probe go away as quickly as possible. In his eyes, the ATU probe was more than a legal problem; it threatened his personal reputation and the credibility of his company. He simply couldn't move forward with that cloud hanging over his head. Dad also wanted to make clear to the feds and the wine industry as a whole that Marvin Sands would not be doing business like Little Joe Applebaum.

To halt the ATU probe, Dad turned to a trusted legal procedure: "offer in compromise." It took some negotiating, but Dad and his advisers were able to come to terms with the ATU. Without admitting any culpability, he agreed to pay a fine and the ATU agreed not to bring any formal charges. This was a suitable solution for all concerned. And it reinforced in Marvin a set of values that he already held dear. First, never break the law in the first place, either in letter or in spirit. It's not worth it – ever. Second, be careful never to do anything that even appears to break the law; even a false or unproved allegation can taint your reputation and credibility for a lifetime. Third, if you make a mistake, own up to it right away – then do whatever it takes to fix the problem. Lying or denying the mistake inevitably makes the problem worse. These were lessons that Marvin adhered to throughout his life and then deeply impressed upon Rob and me. As he always emphasized to us, a strong and accurate moral compass is your most important business tool.

Then came two more shocks: Dad next discovered that he had inadequate working capital and an inadequate supply of grapes coming in. Here again, Dad was blinded-sided. When he took over Canandaigua, his near-term plan was simple: sell his existing inventory to the different bottlers that Canandaigua was already servicing, including Mack's Car-Cal Winery. With profits from those sales, he would start paying down his $500,000 note to Little Joe. In the first six months of 1946, Dad was able to follow that plan. By harvest-time, though, he faced the same hurdle that almost every wine producer, no matter where in the world, faces every year: securing the quality and quantity of grapes he needs to meet his targets and serve his customers. And here Marvin slammed into a wall. With the end of the war, demand for wine was soaring, and grape and wine production could barely keep pace.

At the same time, Canandaigua Industries was in only its third year of operation, and it had yet to develop a strong, reliable base of suppliers. And it had no clout in the marketplace. So when Marvin made cold calls to volume growers, looking to buy additional grapes, their first reaction inevitably was: "Marvin who?"

The situation put Dad in a terrible bind. To replenish his inventory, Dad was forced to buy grapes from grape brokers – and pay them a hefty premium. That was a very expensive fix, but Dad had no other choice. But that put him in a cash crunch and made it extremely difficult for him to pay down that big note to Little Joe. What to do? Here Marvin was in a terrible quandary. Should he go to the bank for a loan and get himself deeper into debt? Or should he lay off people, cut salaries and costs, and try to squeeze by? Or should he simply raise the white flag and chuck the whole thing? Get out. Sell the company. Go back to college, finish his degree, get a job, and start fresh doing something completely new?

His mother, for some reason, was pushing him to come back to the University of North Carolina, to finish his degree. I'm not sure why. Maybe Sally wanted her son to follow a different path from her husband Mack's. Or maybe, being a good Jewish mother, she wanted her only son to be a doctor, lawyer, or college professor. Either way, her pushing only made Dad's quandary all the more intense. And so Marvin did the one thing that he was always so reluctant to do: he put aside his usual stoicism and revealed the full depth of his inner torment, and he did so to the only person he knew would understand:

Mickey Alpert.

Dad's decision in December to call off their engagement had put a chill into their relationship, of course, and during the first few months of 1946 he and Mickey had next to no communication. Besides, Marvin was focused on his problems inside Canandaigua Industries and Mickey was focused on her studies at Hunter College in Manhattan, to where she had transferred from her college in Greensboro. Still, by the spring of 1946 Dad was aching to see her again. I'm sure he felt lonely in the small town social life of Canandaigua, but I'm also sure that he knew Mickey was a true jewel and that his feelings for her ran extremely deep. In any case, in the spring of 1946 Dad went to New York City to see Mickey and try to repair their rift. Somehow he succeeded, and soon they were actively courting again. On weekends they would meet in the Catskills to play golf, relax, and enjoy each other's company. In between their weekend visits, they resumed their letter writing, and during this period Dad reaffirmed his intention of marrying Mickey.

Now, here at my desk, I have a sheaf of letters that Mickey wrote to Marvin throughout 1946. They read like a map of the ups and downs of their courtship and, in my eyes at least, each letter is a testament to the steadfastness of Mickey's love, even after the pain and humiliation she felt when Dad had so abruptly called off their engagement. In some of her early letters, Mickey is guarded with her feelings, unsure of Marvin's feelings and true intentions. In some of them, she signs off "Love ya," as if to dial down her own feelings and protect herself against future hurt. But in a letter dated May 31st, 1946, when their marriage plans are back on track, she once again opens the letter with "My darling Marv" and signs it "All my love, Mickey."

Still, the letter that is the most poignant is the one that Mom wrote to Dad one Thursday

Marvin was in a terrible quandary. Should he take out a loan? Cut salaries and costs? Or just raise a white flag and chuck the whole thing?

"I'm not saying that I'd stop loving you, but you can't marry for love alone."

MICKEY SANDS

in the fall of 1946. She was responding to a letter that Dad had written to her about his many problems at Canandaigua and his torment over what to do next. I don't have Dad's original letter, but clearly he had laid everything out to her, right down to his desire to chuck the wine business and go back to school. Mom's response makes clear that this was a moment of truth, not just for Dad and his business but also for their relationship. It is rare that any son or daughter gets such a deep and intimate look into a parent's relationship, and it is with a great deal of hesitancy – and with my mother's full permission – that I share her words with you now. They reveal the depth of her understanding of my father and also the wisdom and maturity that she displayed at the tender age of 20. What a remarkable young woman she was:

> *My dear Marvin,*
>
> *I would have written sooner but I really wanted to give myself a chance to think things out clearly. I've thought about this whole business an awful lot, and every time I've come to the following conclusions.*
>
> *If you're being completely honest with me, you have two problems. The first is getting married and the second is Business. School, dear, is nothing more than a plain and simple escape from both problems.*
>
> *If you go back to school you are avoiding the major issue by pushing the problems of marriage and business into the future. However, when that time is over nothing will have been settled. In fact, before school starts, or if you want to put it off another few months, we can become engaged in September and married in January. Thus giving you a chance to finish school and still fulfill one of the promises you made.*
>
> *It is also foolish of you to consider going into another business or working for someone else. The only way to prove that you have any ability and that you can make something more of yourself is to stay where you are now and learn the business as quickly and as thoroughly as possible, even if it takes you five years or more. If you quit now, honey, you'll only be doing a cowardly thing by not giving yourself a chance. And I'm sure that everything will be twice as hard because the same mess will confront you in even greater proportions after having put it off for a few months. If you were interested in a profession, or if your degree meant everything to you, then I could understand the sudden desire to go back to school. But Marvin, if such had been the case, you would certainly have had your B.A. by now. But by giving into Sally you are just taking the easy way out, even though you might fool yourself into thinking you're being strong... [Leaving Canandaigua now] will just be something else uncompleted to add to the list. It will show that you hadn't the nerve or the gumption to try yourself out.*

Those are stiff words – and very good advice. And from there, Mom gives Marvin an ultimatum: in terms of marriage it is "now or never." And she won't stand for another engagement followed by another postponement:

> *The same applies to marriage. The longer you put it off, the harder it's going to be. That's*

one of the reasons why it has to be now or never with us. The other is that I could never marry someone I'd distrust or dislike as much as you, if this happens again. I'm not saying that I'd stop loving you, but you can't marry for love alone. And I feel sure that the feeling of disgust that I'd have for you if this happens again would soon overpower my love for you.

Marvin, I couldn't have been more honest or sincere than I have been in this letter. I have always felt this way but it's hard for me to say these things without becoming emotionally upset. I do hope that I've made myself and my feelings clear to you.

Love, Mickey

Mickey was bright, blond, cheerful, and blessed with insight and wisdom beyond her years. When he was uncertain about staying in the wine business, Marvin turned to Mickey for guidance and support.

Now I knew my father extremely well, but I still can't imagine how he must have felt reading Mickey's letter. Her words were gracious, her feelings were clear and understandable, and yet those three little words – "now or never" – could give any man pause. With so many other problems staring him in the face, I'm sure that a part of Dad responded to her letter with an exasperated "Oh boy," or something close to it. But now consider it more deeply, the way I'm sure my father did. He had opened his heart and revealed his turmoil to Mickey, and she had come back with advice that was calm, supportive, and right on the mark. How many men have a partner they can rely on like that? How many men have a partner in life whose love is so steadfast and yet so clear-eyed at the same time? As Mom had so wisely put it, "You can't marry for love alone."

As you might have gathered from the way he went into the deal with Little Joe Applebaum, Dad was something of a pleaser; he wanted to make everyone happy. In his eyes, to do otherwise would be selfish, it would be being less than a good son. Now again Dad tried to put things right with everyone: with Mickey, with Sally, with Mack, and with his own self-respect regarding Canandaigua Industries. First, despite her ultimatum, Dad somehow convinced Mom to put off their marriage once again, for only a few months more. Then, to please Sally and himself, that fall he returned to the University of North Carolina. He wrapped up his B.A. in business in a single semester, all the while managing Canandaigua from afar. Finally, in a move that must have brought a sigh of relief from Mack, at the start of 1947 Marvin returned to the helm of Canandaigua Industries. And he did so with a much clearer sense of purpose: to learn as much as he could and to put things right inside the troubled company. In sum, he followed Mickey's precise advice in that regard, and I'm sure that her advice and wisdom drew them even closer than before.

Seven months later, on May 29th, 1947, Marvin Sands and Mickey Alpert joined their lives in holy matrimony. The ceremony and wedding dinner were held at the Waldorf-Astoria Hotel in New York City, with a rabbi officiating and 200 guests celebrating their union. Mickey remembers the day as if it were yesterday: "The ceremony was a traditional Jewish ceremony and Marvin's uncle, Emil Rosen, who was a cantor, participated. The wedding was held in the Sert Room of the Waldorf and then we all moved to the Wedgewood Room for champagne and the dinner afterwards. Our families were extremely happy and so were Marvin and I."

As delighted as she was to be married, Mickey was still shocked when she moved to

Their courtship was tumultuous, but in the spring of 1947 Marvin and Mickey finally joined hands in marriage. Their wedding at the Waldorf-Astoria in New York City unfolded in storybook fashion.

Canandaigua. "I cried every day for two years," Mom recalls. "My home was Manhattan, and Canandaigua seemed like the end of the world." Several months after she and Dad had settled in together, Mickey's grandmother came to visit, in the middle of winter. She would never return, not once. "She was afraid that if she died here," Mickey explains, "there would be so much snow on the ground they would never be able to get her to the graveyard!" Still, Mickey and Marvin had a cute little apartment and their life as a married couple began in earnest. Almost immediately Mickey became pregnant, and their first child, our older sister Laurie, was born in early 1948.

But another shock was coming down the road.

In the spring of 1947, just as Mom and Dad were tying the knot, the price of wine began to plummet. And I mean plummet. Week after week the price of wine dropped, and there was no bottom in sight. Within a month or two, the wholesale price of wine dropped from $1.00 a gallon to 50 cents. New York State wines were hit especially hard. At one point, the price of a gallon of New York wine dropped a full 75 percent, down to 25 cents a gallon. The reasons were not mysterious. With the lifting of wartime rationing, the price of sugar had dropped, making bulk wine cheaper to produce. On top of that, with grain and corn once again in ample supply, there was a huge jump in the production of spirits – and the public's demand for them jumped as well. Suddenly, saloons and restaurants were filled with people drinking whiskey, bourbon, vodka, gin – anything but wine. In this period, national consumption of wine dropped to levels not seen since before World War II. For Dad, this was a crippling crisis: he had that huge inventory of wine to sell. But no matter how low he dropped his prices, he couldn't close the deal. George Bresler, a cousin of Dad's and a trusted legal adviser and a longtime member of our board of directors, later told me about the crisis:

"The price of wine so plummeted that it would have been economically more viable to open the hoses and pour it into the sewer," George told me. "The price of wine was less than the federal and state taxes owed on the wine."

Marvin was not alone in his misery: Mack's business down in Greensboro got pummeled too. By October of 1947, Mack's sales had dropped a full 60 percent from the year before. Car-Cal had shipped only 86,000 cases for the entire year, putting Mack's company into serious financial trouble. There was also a rebound effect. Since Dad was providing bulk wine to Car-Cal, Mack's woes kicked right back onto him.

By any measure, the situation was now dire. And I can only imagine how Dad must have felt. Thanks to Mack, Marvin had bought a business that was now heading for insolvency. Dad was up to his neck in debt. Mom was pregnant. The price of wine and the public consumption of wine had both collapsed. On top of that, Dad still had to pay Little Joe nearly $500,000. What could Marvin do? Sell the business? Take pennies on the dollar, just to get out from under? Some sons, burdened by similar problems and a similar history, might see this as an opportune moment to say, politely, "Thanks, Dad, for all you've done. But from now on I have to go it alone. Mickey and I are starting a family and we have to chart our own course. That goes for my business too."

Marvin, of course, would never do that. Instead, he and Mack sat down and worked out a plan. They decided to close down the Car-Cal operation and move the bottling line to Canandaigua. From there, Mack could continue to service his southern customers. Mack and Sally would move north until the crisis either eased or passed. From this consolidated position, the Sands family could draw together, tighten their collective belts, and see where the American wine industry would evolve to next. No matter what the pressures, Marvin was not about to turn his back on his father, nor did he flinch from the stark reality that he now shouldered three huge responsibilities: saving his company from bankruptcy, protecting the health and security of Mickey and the baby to come, and protecting the financial future of Mack and Sally. Even at the age of 23, Dad carried it all; few men are made of such sturdy stuff.

After growing up in Manhattan, Mickey hated the small town life of Canandaigua. "I cried for the first two years," she says, but later she and Marvin came to love the place.

To weather the collapse in wine prices, Marvin knew he had to do two things simultaneously: raise money and further lighten his financial load. Specifically, he had to do something about the $500,000 note that he owed to Little Joe Applebaum. The value of that note had been set by the market value of bulk wine at the time of the sale: $1 a gallon. But with the fall in the price of wine, the value of his inventory on hand was now worth half of what it had been, making that note twice as hard to pay off. To stay in business, Dad still had to honor his commitments to his bulk wine customers and to Car-Cal's customers in the South. But as he depleted his inventory, at 50 cents a gallon and worse, his ability to pay back Little Joe depleted as well. So that note was now threatening to sink Dad's entire ship.

By nature, Dad was an optimist; he treated people well and, generally, he assumed they would treat him well in return. In this instance, he figured that he could pay a call on Little Joe, explain how dire the situation was, and make Little Joe understand that the very existence of Canandaigua Industries – and his family's future – were hanging in the balance. He would then ask Little Joe to renegotiate the terms of the loan. Surely Little Joe would agree, right? After all, he and Mack were best of friends; they went way back all the way to the Depression. Beyond that, Marvin was employing three members of Little Joe's family; their future was hanging in the balance too. And there was one thing more: that ATU probe. In concluding the sale to Marvin, Little Joe had not disclosed that federal authorities were investigating the way Little Joe's operation was making its wines – and Marvin had never issued a single complaint. Given all this, Little Joe would surely cut him some slack, right?

With his hopes high, Dad paid that call on Little Joe. Calm and controlled as always, Dad explained that the value of his inventory had depreciated by 50 percent. Wouldn't it be fair, therefore, if Little Joe cut the loan down by an equal 50 percent? As Dad later told us, Little Joe considered Marvin's plea for a few moments and then he posed a simple question in return: "Tell me, Marvin, if the price of wine had gone up by 50 percent, would you be here now to offer me 50 percent more?" Of course, Dad knew the answer was no. So he was stuck: he was honor-bound to pay that $500,000 in full, no matter what the current price of wine happened to be.

Looking back now, you can understand why I refer to this period as "Learning The Hard Way." Inexperienced and naive about business, Dad had signed onto the deal with Little Joe without doing a proper investigation first. Instead he had relied on the judgment of his father – and boy, was he paying the price. On the brighter side, Dad was learning from his

Dad made us understand that in our business, wine is money. He had learned that the hard way.

RICHARD SANDS

mistakes. In an effort never to get caught short of grapes again, he vowed that the company would forge solid and enduring alliances with key grape growers around the country. He wanted to build a reliable network of loyal providers who would stick with him through thick and thin. To that end, many years later he hired someone specifically to nurture those relationships, a position that only a few other wine companies were prescient enough to create.

Dad learned other crucial lessons as well. In evaluating deals and negotiating contracts, Dad learned to look at potential risks from every conceivable angle. He learned that in the wine market, supply and demand are always mercurial and you have to be prepared for that. He also learned that no deal is ever as good as it looks on the surface; you have to build a first-class team that can pore through every corner of a company's finances and operations and then accurately project future performance and profits. Not doing that is an invitation to disaster. As you will see in later chapters, Rob and I and our management team built Constellation Brands into the largest wine company in the world through a series of vigorous – and judicious – mergers and acquisitions, and it was Dad who showed us the way. The painful lessons that he learned in this period he later passed on to us, and those lessons are now burned deeply into the DNA of Constellation Brands. To our benefit, believe me.

When Little Joe refused to renegotiate, Dad had little choice but to go deeper in debt. He went to the Lincoln First Bank of Rochester and obtained a loan. As Mom recalls, Dad took out a loan for twice the amount that he actually needed, so that he could make his payments during this period of crisis, and then be in a position to pay off the loan quickly once the crisis had passed. "By paying them back faster," Mickey explains, "he could borrow more later." The loan was a good first step. Then Marvin set out to become an expert in every aspect of financial management. His primary goal was to understand money, how to make it, manage it, and leverage its power. Here his innate gift for math came into play, and Marvin soon became a master at managing money. And this was absolutely key to everything he did at Canandaigua Industries – and that Rob and I later did at Constellation Brands.

In our business, Dad made us understand, wine is money. He had learned that the hard way in his deal with Little Joe: what an inventory of wine is worth one week could be worth only half as much the following week. This is an essential fact of the wine business. So when you are negotiating in April to buy grapes from a California producer who will harvest in September, you have to be extremely careful about fixing the financial terms of the deal. Likewise, when you are evaluating the potential benefits of acquiring another company, or when you are projecting future profits to Wall Street analysts, you have to look long and hard at the potential shifts in both the wine market and your resultant costs and profit margins. Moreover, the financial particulars of wine production in California are very different from those of wine production in New York State – and you had better master those differences. Mastering the money, Dad taught us, was also the key to expanding opportunity and mitigating risk. Some business people, like Grandpa Mack, manage by instinct and are quick to see the proverbial pot of gold at the end of the rainbow. With them, success can be a hit-or-miss proposition. But when you first master the money, you can make far more intelligent choices, and success is not something you stumble upon, it is something you plan, carefully manage, and build.

Through his first crises at Canandaigua, Dad was learning how to master money and build success. In working with Lincoln First, for instance, Dad learned first-hand the value of building a close, trusted relationship with a strong financial institution. As collateral for his loan, Lincoln First wanted firmer guarantees than the assets of Canandaigua Industries; they demanded, additionally, personal guarantees from Marvin and Mickey and also from Mack and Sally. So I am not exaggerating when I say that in the crisis of 1947 the financial future of our entire family was at stake. In giving him the loan, Lincoln First put their trust in Marvin Sands – and Marvin did not let them down. Over the next five years, through hard work, raw smarts, and rigorous financial management, Marvin put things right, and in the process he built a strong working relationship with Lincoln First. Lincoln was later acquired by Chase Bank and then Chase became JP Morgan, but here's the essential point: these same bankers remain partners of ours to this very day. Over the years they have helped us with debt financing and with many of the acquisitions that have helped us become the largest wine company in the world. They have benefited and so have we. It has been "relationship banking" at its very best.

Mickey had a degree in biochemistry, but once in the lab she made a firm decision: leave the wine-making to the professionals.

The crisis of 1947 taught Dad something else: in an industry as volatile and unpredictable as wine – with so many factors beyond your control – you had better not keep all of your eggs in a single basket. In 1946 he had focused on selling wine in bulk to bottlers, who then put their own names and labels on the bottles. That strategy had led to profits on the year of $50,000 – not a bad showing at the time. Marvin planned to stay in the bulk wine business, but he also foresaw, correctly, that there would be advantages to setting up a parallel operation: producing and bottling his own line of wines and selling them to wholesalers under his own labels. This diversification would provide twin benefits: better profit margins for the branded wines and stronger insulation against future fluctuations in the wine market. Many years later, Rob and I followed this same reasoning when we diversified Constellation Brands into spirits and beer.

Right here I have to stop and bow my head in admiration. Dad's first five years in business were a brutal fight for survival. He endured shock upon shock: a serious legal crisis, a crash in the price of wine, and a desperate need for money. In this period, he did suffer one bout of disillusionment, when he considered dropping the whole thing, but then Mom bucked him up and set him on the right course. From there, on every front, Dad managed to put things right. And, always learning from his mistakes, he got stronger and wiser in the process. Still, it would be wrong to leave you with the impression that Marvin had done all of this on his own. By the end of the 1940s, he had started to build a first-rate team, a group of remarkable men and women who, with passion and skill, would help Marvin turn the 1950s into a decade of excitement and growth. And at one critical juncture, when he needed a little help and guidance, it would again be Mom who provided the magic touch.

Portfolio

NEW YORK

City Hall, Canandaigua, N.Y.

Previous spread, The city pier, Canandaigua Lake.
Above, Grapes going into the conveyer, Canandaigua Winery.
Opposite, Labrusca grapes, native to New York State.

Antique Glassware Collection from Constellation Brands offices, Fairport, N.Y.
Following spread, A 28,000-gallon redwood tank at the Canandaigua Winery, still in use today.

Above, Charmat process tanks for champagne production, Canandaigua Winery.
Oppostite, Labrusca grape vines.

Previous spread, Widmer's Wine Cellars, Naples, N.Y.
Oppostie, Eric's Office Restaurant, Canandaigua, N.Y.
Above, A door on an outside tank, Canandaigua Winery.

Previous spread, Sculpture by Albert Paley, outside Constellation Wines offices.
Opposite, A Canandaigua home.
Above, A parade on Main Street, Canandaigua, N.Y.

CHAPTER 7

Striking Gold

In one of their issues in 1948, Life Magazine included Marvin and Mickey in a feature spread about young couples finding happiness in the American countryside.

I have to laugh.

On my writing desk now I have an article that Life magazine did on Mom and Dad and seven other couples back in 1948. The article is headlined "Escape To The Country," and it portrays these eight handsome couples as part of a cultural vanguard that has chosen to leave behind the stresses of big city life and create new, much happier lives on the farms and in the small towns of the American countryside. To read the introduction, you'd think that Marvin and Mickey and the other couples were donning overalls and going back to the land to grow beans and sprouts:

> *Every day in big cities like New York and Chicago young people jamming their way into elevators, dodging taxis and sweating out office routines wish they were somewhere else, doing almost anything else. Wiping soot from their furniture, they long for some clean, fresh air to breathe and a safer, roomier place for their children to play. But financing is the big problem. Still, each year, particularly since the war, an increasing number of Americans are managing one way or another to leave crowds, noise and rush behind for a simpler existence on a farm or in a small town. On these pages Life shows eight couples who found a way to make the break and make a living too.*

The Life report was more of a photo spread than an in-depth look at an emerging social trend, but in one sense the story was truly prescient: young married couples would soon be leaving our big cities in droves. But they wouldn't be creating new lives on farms or in small towns; they'd be moving just outside the big cities and creating the modern American suburb. Life got the surface of the trend right, but nothing beyond that.

What really makes me laugh, though, is the way Life's editors put Mom and Dad into this supposed cultural vanguard, into this hunger for quieter lives on a farm or in a small town. The truth, of course, was starkly different. Mom had been born and bred in Manhattan, and in 1948 she was not at all happy with the small town life of Canandaigua. Later she would grow to love it and would sink contented roots into Canandaigua's social and cultural life. At that moment, though, she felt as though she had been sent into exile. Napoleon had Elba; Mom had Canandaigua. Nor did Dad fit the template. He had never, in Life's imagery, sweated out office routines or wiped soot from his furniture. Nor was he now leading "a simpler existence." To the contrary, he was working in a cramped winery office, dodging a showdown with federal agents, and sweating out a crippling cash crunch and a complete collapse in the price of wine. That was his bucolic "escape to the country." Yes, I have to laugh.

Nonetheless, I can see why Mom and Dad were happy to be a part of that feature story. At that time, Life was a clarion voice in America and a weekly feature in nearly every American home. No other publication, with the possible exception of the Saturday Evening Post, even came close. Also, being photographed for the pages of Life, in front of a wall of wine cases ready to be shipped – each case brightly lettered "Canandaigua Industries" – certainly wouldn't hurt Dad's business. In fact, this was marvelous publicity. The truth was that in those dark days of 1948, Mom and Dad were dancing on the edge of bankruptcy, so why let the truth get in the way of a positive and very uplifting story?

In one way, though, the editors at Life had it right: this was a young couple that was indeed bound for success. Not because of where they chose to live, but because they had the right stuff. The Life story highlighted Marvin's years in the Navy and Mom's training in chemistry, and one photo shows Mom in the wine lab. Mom says she rarely worked there, but Life's larger point was valid nonetheless: here were two able, well-educated, strong-willed people who were determined to create a new life on their own terms, doing it their own way. In that sense, I have to say that Life was right on the money. They were just a few years premature in portraying the shining success of Marvin and Mickey Sands.

By the early 1950s, Dad had dug out of his deep financial hole and was really starting to build the business. And he had some wonderful brains working at his side. One of them was Bob Meenan. Bob had learned sales while working for a liquor company in Boston; Mack had met him back in the days when he was selling bulk wine for Geffen. Dad had brought Bob to Canandaigua in 1946, and it proved to be one of the best staff moves that Dad ever made. Bob had a perfect pedigree for the wine business. He was Boston Irish, with a natural charm and an easy, gregarious manner. He made friends quickly and had a joke for every occasion. In the lore of our business, it is often said that Robert Mondavi could sell refrigerators to Eskimos; the same could be said of Bob Meenan. Bob knew the wine and liquor businesses inside out and had good friends in each of them – a key asset for any salesman.

Bob Meenan, above, was Marvin's right hand when it came to sales, marketing, and building a brand.

There was something else: Bob was creative. He had flair. He knew what a strong brand could do, and he loved the challenge of creating brands and testing them in the market. In many ways, Bob was also the perfect complement to Marvin Sands. Where Dad was new to the wine business, Bob was a seasoned pro. Where Dad was quiet and introspective, Bob was outgoing and lively. On top of that, the two men liked each other, respected each other, and relied on each other. Moreover, it was Bob Meenan who urged Dad to diversify his business and develop his own blends and brands, and it was Bob who anchored the sales department and built an extensive network of loyal customers for the company, a network that radiated out to Connecticut and Massachusetts and west to Ohio and Michigan.

Bob also led Dad and the company into the art of branding. Dad was very supportive of the move; he knew that one strong brand could make a business soar. He had seen what Old Maude had done for Mack, and he had seen what Virginia Dare had done for Paul Garrett. Still, when it came to the art of branding Dad had an even bigger success that he dreamed of emulating: Frigidaire. As Dad often told us, Frigidaire was more than a magical brand; it had actually become synonymous with a proprietary product, the modern refrigerator. Now that was impact. That was power. Kleenex was the same. When sneezing, nobody grabbed a generic "tissue" – they grabbed a Kleenex. Once he had put things right inside his company, Dad began dreaming of creating a brand of comparable power, something that consumers would instantly equate with a unique and satisfying glass of wine.

Still, creating a brand with that kind of power was no easy feat, as Dad and Bob learned the hard way. Starting in 1949, they produced and bottled Sands Port and Sands Sherry, and while those were solid, serviceable brands, they carried no touch of magic. That same year they tried to be a little hip with a wine called "Be Bop." That proved to be a flop and

Compare Tissues... Compare Boxes —

There is only
ONE
KLEENEX*

LITTLE LULU SAYS:

No other tissue gives
you all the advantages
of KLEENEX!

America's
Favorite Tissue

ONLY KLEENEX
HAS THE
SERV-A-TISSUE
BOX

Marvin had a guiding dream: he wanted to create a wine brand that would be as powerful and as easily recognizable as Kleenex or Frigidaire.

a costly one at that. So was a later creation of Bob and Marvin's, a brand called "Parade." Then they created "King Solomon" for the kosher wine market and introduced "Hog's Head" for Mack's customers in the South. None of those became big hits either. By the end of the 1940s, Dad and Bob had yet to strike marketing gold. There was no brand like Old Maude in the house or even on the horizon. Still, they were learning as they went, and Dad was hoping that all their effort with branding would soon pay off.

Bob Meenan brought something else to our little family business. He instilled an important ethos in Marvin and in our company's DNA: Innovate. Create. Pioneer. Some things will work, some won't, but that's just the nature of any business. So never stand still. Never be content with the status quo. And never be afraid to experiment. Bob also helped put into our DNA a quality of joy and spirit: this is the wine business; make it fun. Make it playful. Make it energizing and creative. Now I'm not claiming that Bob Meenan was the Steven Jobs of his time, but he had a similar gift. And when you combined Bob's creativity with Dad's leadership skills and his rigorous financial management, the result was a winning combination.

The numbers proved it. In 1951, Canandaigua Industries registered $1 million in sales, split evenly between bulk wines sold to other bottlers and the branded case wines that Bob was selling to their various distributors. To give you an idea of what pricing was like in those days, Dad was selling bulk wine at about 75 cents a gallon, while the branded case wines went for only about 10 to 15 cents more per gallon – a reflection of the fact that branding was still an underdeveloped art form both at Canandaigua and in most of the American wine industry. Still, those sales figures showed that our little family business was improving its profits and gaining strength.

One clear sign of the improving picture came from Grandpa Mack. Now that the price of wine had stabilized, along with the financial footing of the Sands family, Mack decided it was time to leave Canandaigua and return to the South, the better to manage his network of customers in Virginia and the Carolinas. He and Marvin were also eager to cut down one of their heaviest operating costs: shipping glass and wine from New York State to Mack's customers in the South. Instead of returning to Greensboro, though, Mack found a suitable plant down in Petersburg, Virginia, a charming little town 23 miles south of Richmond, the state capital. Mack outfitted the plant with used crushing equipment, used tanks, and a serviceable bottling line, and very quickly he was back in harness, running his own operation. And right here is where a new element came into play:

Me.

I was born on March 3rd, 1951, and I want to affirm right here that, despite some reports to the contrary, Mom and Dad did not ask the U.S. Congress to declare that date a national holiday. But they did the next best thing: they talked it over with Mack and together they decided to name the new Petersburg operation "Richard's Wine Cellars." Canandaigua's history books do not record whether or not I greeted this decision with an approving gurgle, but I'm sure Mom and Dad were pleased. In fact, this was the beginning of a family tradition. Rob was born on June 10th, 1958, and the following year, to hold down his shipping costs and create a new revenue engine, Dad launched "Robert's Trading Company." At one time, we also had a holding company named Laurie Ann, after our older sister. Growing up, Rob and Laurie and I felt very lucky indeed; how many kids get to see their name on wineries, trucks, and company letterheads?

While these were welcome developments, Dad's business was still missing a key element of success: a hot product, a winning brand, something that could really start driving sales and growing the business. Dad and Bob were definitely on the hunt. This was a time of great upheaval in American wine, on both the East and West Coasts, and Dad and Bob were looking down several avenues to see which way to go: fortified dessert wines, sparkling wines, or even fruit-flavored wines. To put their search into proper context, I need to relate some of the history of New York State wines and show where our side of the American wine industry was headed.

The history of wine in New York State begins in an improbable place: on the island of Manhattan. Yes, it may be hard to imagine it today, but in the mid-1600s, there were thriving vineyards in Manhattan, and early colonists from Europe were using grapes from those vineyards to make homemade wine. For these immigrants, wine was a natural and healthy part of their daily lives and their family table – and the political leaders of the day supported this Old World tradition. Peter Stuyvesant, who was governor of what was then called 'New Netherland," carefully regulated the sale of hard liquor, but he actively endorsed the consumption of wine in moderation. In fact, according to Leon Adams in Wines of America, Stuyvesant, following the British Navy's example of providing rum to its sailors, set forth an ordinance requiring that sailors on the high seas be provided with a daily ration of wine.

Over the next two hundred years, grape growing and winemaking spread far and wide across what is now New York State. Settlers used either Vitis Vinifera vines imported from Europe or native-growing Vitis Labrusca vines, especially the abundant varietals Isabella and Catawba. Concord grapes, though plentiful in the Northeast, proved wonderful as table grapes and for making jams and jellies, but they produced wines that were very harsh in taste. As New York's winemakers became more skilled, though, they were able to blend Concords with softer varietals and make some lovely New York ports and Kosher wines. Still, not everyone in New York State viewed wine as a healthy beverage. The nation's first temperance movement was formed in 1808, in Chautauqua County in the far western part of New York facing Lake Erie. From that tiny root, the anti-alcohol campaign grew into national Prohibition 112 years later.

In our neck of the woods, the Finger Lakes region, wine-making has a rich and distinguished history. It began in earnest in 1860 with an event of lasting import for New York wines: the creation of the Pleasant Valley Wine Company. The winery, which is still in existence today, is located in the town of Hammondsport, 40 miles south of where we are in Canandaigua. Pleasant Valley was started by a man named Charles Davenport Champlin along with a few of his neighbors, all of them farmers who were growing grapes. They started the winery with $10,000, and their varietals of choice were Isabella and Catawba. To craft their wines, Champlin turned to Joseph Masson, a winemaker who had trained in France and had earlier worked for a winery in Cincinnati, Ohio. As I noted before, back

An early map of our magnificent Finger Lakes region, which has long been a pillar of the New York State wine industry.

The Urbana Wine Company, with its award-winning Gold Seal Champagne, helped establish New York State as a major power in American wine. So did Taylor, Widmer, Great Western, and the Pleasant Valley Wine Company.

then Ohio was one of the leading wine-producing states in America – until it was hit by two devastating plant diseases: black rot and a powdery mildew named "oïdium." When those wiped out the grape crops in Cincinnati and other parts of Ohio, Masson came to Hammondsport. He was later joined by his brother Jules, who was also an experienced winemaker.

In 1865, as the Civil War was drawing to a close, Champlin and the Massons unveiled something new for New York State: a delightful sparkling wine made from Catawba grapes. Joseph Masson had developed a sparkling Catawba back in Cincinnati but this one was much better. It was crisp, fruity, and festive – just what a good sparkling wine should be. And over the next few years they made it even better. In 1870, the Massons unveiled their latest vintage at a meeting of the Pleasant Valley Grape Growers. As Leon Adams reports, presiding at the meeting was a respected horticulturist and wine connoisseur named Colonel Marshall Wilder. Upon tasting the Massons' sparkling Catawba, Colonel Wilder smacked his lips and exclaimed, "Truly, this will be the great champagne of the West!" By West, he was referring to the continent of America, and he meant that this was the New World's answer to French Champagne. Impressed by Wilder's verdict – and eager to exploit it – Champlin and the Massons named their sparking wine "Great Western Champagne" and a New York legend was born.

Champlin then entered Great Western in competitions in Europe, and it won several prizes, even in France. Emboldened, Champlin set up a post office station inside the Pleasant Valley Winery and got the necessary authorities to name it "Rheims, New York," in reference to the champagne capital of France. The sparkling Catawba, its name, and the supporting marketing campaign all clicked with the American public. For the next 50 years Great Western was the leading sparkling wine made here in America. And that, in turn, helped make the Finger Lakes region one of the preeminent wine regions of New York State.

Champlin blazed an inviting path. In 1865, the Urbana Wine Company began operations in nearby Hammondsport, and it soon recruited wine-makers from the top champagne houses in France: Louis Roederer, Moët et Chandon, and Veuve Cliquot Ponsard. Urbana's sparkling and still wines soon gained prominence under the label "Gold Seal." Then in 1888 a Swiss emigré named John Jacob Widmer and his wife Lisette started a vineyard and wine business in nearby Naples, New York, and it soon became known for its high-quality table wines. Widmer's Wine Cellars grew into a prominent producer and a pillar of the Finger Lakes region.

In 1880, all of this pioneering activity in our little corner of the world caught the eye of a young cooper named Walter Taylor. Seeing an exploding market for his skills as a barrel maker, Taylor and his wife Addie came to Hammondsport and set up shop. As Taylor had hoped, his business quickly boomed. Two years later he bought a 70-acre farm on a picturesque hill north of town. Broadening out from cooperage, Taylor planted half of his farm with Ives and Delaware, two grapes then being used for making red and white wines. These were the humble roots of the Taylor Wine Company, and it would soon become a powerhouse brand in New York State and across the nation. I will have more to say about both Taylor and Widmer as our story unfolds; both of them are now in our portfolio. In fact, Constellation Brands today owns all of them: Taylor, Widmer, Great Western, and Gold Seal.

Now let me bring this brief history of New York State wine home to Dad and Canandaigua Industries. Walter and Addie Taylor had three sons and two daughters, and all five of them went into the family business. For the next several decades they produced a wide array of sparkling and still wines. When Prohibition came along and put most of the other wineries in the Finger Lakes out of business, the Taylors shifted quickly out of wine and into making high volumes of non-alcoholic grape juice. They were smart. They were nimble. They survived. All because they maintained a pragmatic, non-elitist, business-first attitude toward the production and sale of wine. Fred Taylor, one of Walter's sons, summed up their approach perfectly: "we make uncomplicated wines." To that end, they produced port, sherry, sauterne, rhine wine, burgundy, claret, rosé, champagne, sparkling burgundy, and vermouth. If they saw a niche, the folks at Taylor worked hard to fill it. This strategy paid off handsomely: by almost any measure, Taylor was a resounding success. Dad and Bob Meenan, as you can imagine, regarded Taylor with great admiration.

Now we come to the marrow of it. Back in the 1940s and 1950s, the American wine industry was dominated by one thing: dessert wines. In fact, dessert wines – most of them fortified to 20 percent alcohol – represented a full 75 percent of all the wines being consumed in America at the time. A successful brand of dessert wines brought companies profit and power. The evidence was abundant: for Taylor, its dessert wines helped make it the largest winery in New York State. In California, Ernest and Julio Gallo built their entire empire on a foundation of white port, sherry, and muscatel. Italian Swiss Colony, also in California, ranked as the third largest wine company in the nation, thanks to its strong portfolio of fortified wines. So for Dad and Bob Meenan, there was no mystery here: if they wanted to grow and prosper, they had to create a winning dessert wine, one with a unique flavor and a proprietary blend, a wine that retailers and consumers alike would flock to as new, different, and exciting. In the early 1950s, they vowed to do just that; they made it their mission.

As a first step, Dad gave Max Applebaum a top-priority assignment: create for us a bold new wine, one with a proprietary blend that no one else could copy. Dad and Bob felt that a Catawba flavor had to be part of the mix. The ongoing success of Great Western's sparkling Catawba influenced their thinking, but down south Mack was also doing well with a pink Catawba dessert wine that he sold under his Richard's Wine Cellars label. However, Catawba grapes were not in bountiful supply, and Dad was worried about their ongoing availability and cost. So he asked Max to come up with a blend that featured Catawba's distinctive fruity flavor and pink color, but included other Labrusca varieties that Dad was sure he could buy in sufficient quantity. This was a tall order, even for a winemaker of Max's skill and experience.

In his lab, Max played with white Labrusca varieties, with red varieties, and he played with various combinations of the two, looking for a brand new flavor. The final result, Max knew, had to be 20 percent alcohol and 6 degrees Brix, a measurement of the percentage of sugar in wine by weight. Those were the standard numbers for fortified dessert wines. Max

Great Western Champagne helped launch the New York State wine industry and became a legend in the process.

Max was a perfectionist. He didn't want to create something that was "good enough." He wanted to create something that would make everyone stand up and cheer.

also knew what the color and flavor should resemble. Within those parameters, though, Max was free to invent, to be creative. In fact, he had to be: Dad and Bob wanted a product that was truly unique, not a knock-off of someone else's success. So Max tinkered and tasted, tried and rejected. I have no doubt that it was a very frustrating process. Like all serious artists and craftsmen, Max was a perfectionist. He didn't want to create something that was "good enough." He wanted to create something that would make everyone stand up and cheer.

I wish I could have been there to see Max at work. By this time, Max was by no means a young man; he was older than our Grandpa Mack. And as a winemaker he was extraordinarily deft – though not in the ways that you might imagine. If you think of the most celebrated winemakers today – the men and women turning out the finest wines in Napa or Sonoma, in France, Chile, Australia, or New Zealand – you are probably thinking of winemakers working in the European fine wine tradition, using grapes grown on their own estates, aging them in the finest oak barrels, and managing quality at every step, from the vineyard to the glass. The wines they craft are very expensive, so they don't have to watch every single penny; they have the luxury of always putting top quality first.

Max had none of those luxuries. He was blending different varieties of grapes and they were coming to him from many different sources. Moreover, whereas a small Napa winery back then might produce 40,000 cases of wine a year or less, Max would consider that a three-week vacation. Just to give you an idea of the difference in scale, that same winery on Buffalo Street today bottles 35,000 cases a day – and often more than one million cases in a single month. To produce a fortified dessert wine on that kind of scale, with consistency of quality and flavor, takes an enormous amount of expertise and a very unusual skill set. Let me say it plainly: in his realm, Max Applebaum was a genius. And for our family business, thank God that he was.

For what Max now created was a true sensation. The old winemaker stepped from his lab with a wine that had an array of dazzling qualities. First of all, it had a wonderful and very distinctive color. It was not a rich purple-red like the ports and Kosher wines that Concord grapes produce. Nor was it a feathery pink like a typical Catawba or a classic rosé. Instead, its color was a very bright light red, dazzling to the eye and begging to be consumed. There was no other dessert wine on the market that looked anything like it. The taste was just as unique. It had the lovely fruit-forward quality typical of a good Labrusca, but it also tasted exceptionally light, fresh, and cheerful. Even at 20 percent alcohol, the wine was not overpowering; it was just right. In sum, what Max created looked new, it tasted new, and it totally broke the mold of traditional dessert wines. Canandaigua's Be Bop and Parade now seemed like pale efforts next to this; Max's creation had that certain indefinable quality that I often describe simply as "Wow!"

I wish I had been there to see the reaction of Marvin and Bob Meenan. I was only two at the time, though, and it would be awhile before I was invited in for new product tastings. With his savvy sales and marketing mind, Bob must have been elated; here was a wine that could really ignite sales and generate excitement among his distributors and customers. Dad's reaction, I'm sure, was far more careful. After all, he dreamed of a breakthrough product that could become the Kleenex or the Frigidaire of the world of wine. I'm sure he felt that Max's creation was promising, and it definitely had a unique color and flavor, but were those really enough to create a magical brand?

No. And both Dad and Bob knew it. They would have to surround Max's creation with all the other necessary components of a breakthrough product. First and foremost, they had to find just the right name, a name that would become synonymous with a light, bright, red-colored dessert wine – and a name that no one else could claim. Then they'd need to create a distinctive bottle. And they would need a label that conveyed just the right spirit. As Grandpa Mack often put it, "We make beverage wine for the masses. We make quality wine, but it's not snooty wine." The label needed to convey exactly that.

Could they do all that – and get it right?

Now it was Bob Meenan's turn to set to work. And right away he had a bold idea: let's bottle our magnificent new baby in a square decanter. That would convey class and prestige and instantly set this new wine apart on retailers' shelves. It would also signal to the consumer, right away, that this was not a typical dessert wine. There were a few liqueurs that came in nice decanters, but this would be a first in the realm of wine. Marvin loved the idea of a square decanter, and he immediately set into motion its design and production. The train was moving.

Then they came back to the big question: what do we call it? Today, of course, there are countless ad agencies and marketing firms that specialize in branding and coming up with ingenious names. They use high-tech market research, outside consultants, in-house creative talent, and in the end I'm not sure their process is any better than how Mack purportedly came up with the name Old Maude – by borrowing the name of his favorite waitress. Bob Meenan started his search for a name in the classic way: he looked at the most exceptional qualities of the product itself. And what he saw first was its bright red color. Let's see, bright red color…. Rose! Yes, rose! Not a fancy French rosé, just down-home American rose. Now, shall we call it Sands Rose? No. We already have a Sands Sherry and a Sands Port; we need something better, something that has a little flair to it, a little music. Music! Yes! Now let's see: rose… What popular songs do I know that feature a rose?

Bob, remember, was Boston Irish, and I can imagine that he soon had a tune right on his lips: My Wild Irish Rose, a ballad that was close to every Irishman's heart. The song and its lyrics were written by a New Yorker of Irish descent: Chauncey Olcott. Olcott had been born in Buffalo, New York, in 1899, and he had become a celebrated singer, actor, and songwriter. He had also produced several shows about Ireland for the New York stage. But Chauncey Olcott's most lasting contribution to American and Irish popular culture was another song that came from his pen: When Irish Eyes Are Smiling, a piece of pure poetry that can reduce even the hardiest Irishman to schoolboy tears. Now I'm only guessing here, but I imagine that when the name My Wild Irish Rose popped into his head, Bob may even have known the refrain by heart:

When you combined Bob's creativity with Dad's leadership skills and his rigorous financial management, the result was a winning combination.

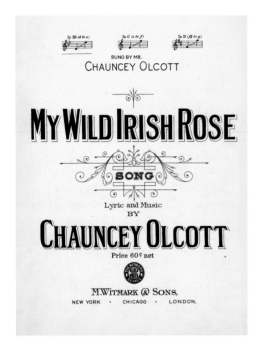

Marvin turned his dream into a reality with the creation of his first big breakthrough brand, Richard's Wild Irish Rose.

My wild Irish Rose,
The sweetest flow'r that grows,
You may search ev'rywhere,
But none can compare
With my wild Irish Rose.
My wild Irish Rose,
The dearest flow'r that grows,
And some day for my sake,
She may let me take,
The bloom from my wild Irish Rose.

Now, how perfect is that? "You may search ev'rywhere/But none can compare/With my wild Irish Rose." If you're looking for a proprietary name to brand a unique product, and maybe advertise it with a jingle on the radio, as Captain Garrett had done with Virginia Dare, you can't do much better than "Wild Irish Rose" and a few lines like that. For Bob it all just clicked. The word "Wild" was perfect for a fortified wine with a lusty kick. The word "Rose" was short and sweet, perfect for a label featuring a bright red rose. Bob then checked and found that the copyright on the song had lapsed; there would be no problem using the name. So Bob was excited. And I'm sure it gave him a special thrill to bring a touch of the Irish into the house of Sands.

That, however, is not the end of the story. From this point forward, there are differing accounts of what happened next. Bob and Dad, alas, are both gone, and no one left from those early years has a clear recollection. Still, many of the old-timers agree on this: when Bob first presented the name to Marvin and everyone else, there was instant applause. The name "Wild Irish Rose" seemed truly inspired and it also seemed perfect for Max's creation. Well, almost perfect. A few people felt it needed one more touch, something to give it a more personalized feel, like so many of those fabled names from the past: Virginia Dare, Old Maude, and Captain Jack. According to some accounts, Bob Meenan had an answer for that. Back in the 1920s, there was a hit Broadway show called "Abie's Irish Rose," and some people say Bob took that title and proposed calling the new wine "Max's Wild Irish Rose" – a charming and very fitting salute to its creator, dear Max Applebaum.

That version may be true, I just don't know. But I have sifted through all the varying accounts, and I am going to go with the one I like best. It goes like this: as soon as he found it, Bob Meenan knew, deep in his veins, that the name "Wild Irish Rose" was a winner. Sure, maybe it needed to be tweaked or personalized a bit, but he knew the core concept was right on the money. Dad, though, wanted to consider other opinions. For he, too, was a perfectionist; he wanted to be certain that every detail clicked into place. And right here is where Mom comes in, with her wonderful instincts and clear-eyed wisdom.

The way Mom recalls it now, Dad came home one night and shared with her the proposed name "Wild Irish Rose." I was two at the time, a bouncy little guy, and of course I was the apple of my mother's eye. What two-year-old isn't? Anyway, Mom felt that the name "Wild Irish Rose" needed an added touch, something to give it more character and personality. So she said the first thing that popped into her head:

"Marv, dear, why not make it Richard's Wild Irish Rose?"

Bingo! That was it – and everyone knew it. With Mom's tiny tweak, a magic brand was now in the making. Dad and Bob Meenan could feel it in their bones: this could be the breakthrough product they had long been striving for, the bolt of energy that could lift their sales and boost their profits. Yes, on the wings of Richard's Wild Irish Rose, Dad and Bob allowed their dreams to soar. But again I have to laugh. Because even they, smart as they were, had not the slightest inkling of what would happen next.

CHAPTER 8

Creating Brand Magic

The success of Richard's Wild Irish Rose turned our little family company into the beginnings of a wine industry powerhouse.

Now came the hard part.

Thanks to the talents of Max Applebaum, Marvin now had an exciting new wine to launch. And thanks to the talents of Bob Meenan – with a little help from Mom – their new product had a winning name and a striking new bottle. The next challenge, though, was by far the toughest: how to build the brand and get Richard's Wild Irish Rose to market without risking a lot of money that Dad simply didn't have.

For guidance, Marvin carefully studied how Pepsi-Cola had become a top-selling soft drink across the United States, using a network of franchise bottlers. That was typical Dad: always eager for knowledge, always looking inside and outside the wine industry for fresh ideas and effective solutions. In studying the Pepsi model, Dad was looking for ways to better handle the wine industry's cumbersome three-tier system of distribution and sales. In the case of all three categories of alcoholic beverages – wine, spirits, and beer – the process was essentially the same. First, you had to convince a local or regional distributor to buy your product and give it a substantial share of his resources and attention. Second, you and the distributor had to persuade retailers in the coverage area to stock your wine, display it prominently, and give it a substantial share of their sales attention. Third, the retailer, building on whatever marketing assets you and the distributor had already provided, had to convince his customers to look past all the other products and buy yours, or at least give it a try. For Dad, mastering that system had long been an exercise in frustration.

Many other products are brought to market in comparable fashion, but in the wine business there was an added headache for producers like Dad: not all the distributors were neutral middlemen, simply taking their cut. Many were also bottlers of wine and spirits – outfits apt to push their own products ahead of yours. Another group of distributors had their own wines and labels that they purchased from local bottlers – and they, too, would be inclined to push their own products well ahead of yours. There were still other distributors who had little interest in small producers like Dad; they were pouring most of their energy and resources into selling established – or emerging – regional or national brands, and many of them distributed beer and spirits as well. So good luck getting them to promote your product line. For Dad, it was a chicken-and-egg problem. He had to make Wild Irish Rose successful in order to pique the interest of distributors. But he needed interested distributors to help him make the product successful in the first place. Without solving this conundrum, even a product as promising as Richard's Wild Irish Rose could sputter and crash, just as Be Bop and Parade had done before.

Mindful of those disappointments, Dad and Bob Meenan decided to launch Richard's in a cautious, step-by-step way. Grandpa Mack, with his go-for-broke instincts, might have rolled Richard's out with a lavish multi-city campaign and all trumpets blaring. Not Dad. Instead, as a first step he chose to test market Wild Irish Rose with a modest launch in Buffalo, New York. Now, the romantic in me would like to think that Dad chose Buffalo as a way of tipping his hat to Chauncey Olcott, the Buffalo native who had penned My Wild Irish Rose. But Dad's decision was dictated purely by business considerations. Bob Meenan had solid relationships with a loyal distributor in Buffalo and several important retailers. More important, Buffalo was an easy 80 miles west from Canandaigua, and Bob could spend time there overseeing the launch and making sure that the distributor was giving sufficient attention to Wild Irish Rose. If not, Bob could work directly with retailers himself. It was a good plan, one that did not involve a gaudy, very expensive marketing campaign.

Was my namesake an instant success in Buffalo? Yes indeed! I'm not saying that all the traffic in the streets screeched to a halt, but Richard's debut was definitely a hit. Next, following the same formula, Dad and Bob went another 100 miles west to Cleveland, a strong market for wine, and there, too, Richard's proved to be a strong success. These markets were a good test: they were manageable in size and the risk was equivalent to their size. As always, Dad had the risk of failure in the back of his mind; he did not want any single failure to sink his entire ship. For this same reason, he waited over 15 years to attack the monstrous New York City market; the risks there were simply too high.

The next test was Mack's. He started distributing Richard's in Virginia and the Carolinas. There, too, Richard's quickly caught fire. To keep pace with sales, Dad stepped up production and the following year, 1954, sales of Wild Irish Rose climbed to $500,000, generating a 30 percent jump in combined sales for Canandaigua Industries and Mack's operation, Richard's Wine Cellars. By this time, everyone could feel it: a real phenomenon was now in the making.

This is where the Pepsi model comes into play. Marvin knew that one of the keys to their success in Buffalo, Cleveland, and the South was that their distributors in those markets were highly motivated to push the product. They had the right incentives. So Dad asked himself a few basic questions: how can I replicate that initial success? What kind of incentives can I offer to other distributors to push the sales of Richard's? In a larger sense, how can I best leverage all the potential of Richard's Wild Irish Rose – but without taking on the risk of a multi-million-dollar investment in more bottling lines, an expanded sales force, and all the attendant costs of recruiting and managing a whole new group of distributors?

With the Pepsi model as his template, Dad went to his five most important bulk wine bottler/distributors with an innovative plan: let's join forces and build our own franchise bottling system. Together we can build a national brand. I will sell you the proprietary blend – Richard's – and then you bottle and distribute it for your local market. Under Dad's plan, his own company and his five partners would gain added profit and competitive edge. For Dad, franchising the bottling as Pepsi did would spare him the costs and the task of building up his own bottling capacity and sales staff. For the bottlers, Dad's plan would provide two streams of profit: one on the bottling side, a second on the distribution side.

As an added incentive, Marvin did a little innovating in his system of pricing. At this stage, Dad had two distinct arms to his business. On the biggest arm, he provided finished case goods to hundreds of distributors across much of the country on an F.O.B. (Free On Board) basis. His second, much smaller arm was delivering bulk wine to a number of bottler/distributors along the East Coast. As an added incentive for both arms of his business, Dad proposed moving to a system called "delivered pricing," a system that enabled him to trim his shipping costs, make a profit, and pass along some of the savings to his distributors. This was a necessary and timely shift. Gallo and Italian Swiss Colony were pushing their dessert wines and both were about to unveil their

In short order, Wild Irish Rose became the locomotive of our business and it became a popular beverage up and down the East Coast and west to the Mississippi River.

By 1963, ten years after its launch, Richard's Wild Irish Rose was generating annual sales of $10 million.

own new systems of transportation and distribution.

Dad's franchise bottling plan proved to be very enticing to his five strongest bottler/distributors. They especially liked its package of incentives. When you strip away all the wrapping, Dad's pitch to them was this: Richard's Wild Irish Rose is a hot new product and I'm offering you a bigger piece of the pie. Right away all five of them signed on with long-term contracts: Ben R. Goltsman in Alabama; Ambrose in Kansas City, Missouri; Consolidated Distilled Products in Chicago; Glazer's in Texas, and the Fairview Wine Company in Gardiner, Maine. Dad was thrilled: he now had a solid alliance of partners and the beginnings of a strong, flexible bottling and distribution system that could help him turn Richard's Wild Irish Rose into a powerful locomotive of expansion, innovation, and brand development.

And that is exactly what happened next.

With their new partner distributors, Dad and Bob Meenan were able to expand distribution and sales across the East Coast and west all the way to the Mississippi River. Mack expanded further across the South. Richard's was a hit in market after market, and with regional bottling and delivered pricing, his partner distributors were able to offer it at a very competitive price. Dad's franchise plan worked brilliantly and it would continue in high gear for the next three decades, adding a very important component to our entire business.

How successful did Richard's Wild Irish Rose become? Well, by 1955 Marvin's and Mack's operations registered combined sales for Richard's of $2 million. By 1957 sales had jumped to $3 million. By 1959, even with stiff competition in fortified wines from Gallo and Italian Swiss Colony, sales had leaped to $4 million. Over the next two years, sales doubled to $8 million. By 1963, ten years after its launch, Richard's Wild Irish Rose was generating annual sales of $10 million. Canandaigua Industries was still producing several other wines, but Richard's was the undisputed champ, consistently generating 80 or 85 percent of total sales. And there was more to come.

In 1959, Dad came forward with another innovation: the creation of Robert's Trading Company. This affiliated transportation arm solved one of Dad's thorniest problems. At that time, trucking was still a tightly regulated industry in the United States. There were high rates – all of them fixed – for shipping every conceivable finished product or raw material, including finished cases of wine. This put a crimp into Dad's profit margins and his ability to grow into new markets. For instance, Cleveland, Ohio, was only 250 miles from Canandaigua. But because of those high trucking rates, it could cost Dad as much to truck wine there as it cost Gallo to deliver wine there by railroad car – a 2,000-mile haul!

Robert's Trading Company solved that problem. As a "trading" company, as opposed to a trucking company, Robert's was not subject to regulated rates. Then, by slowly building his own fleet of trucks, Dad was able to wean the company away from using third-party trucking companies – saving millions of dollars in the process. Also, once the drivers had emptied their trucks, they could stop at our glass suppliers, fill their trucks, and haul bottles back to Canandaigua, generating even more savings. The glass suppliers were happy too because they didn't have to pay for third-party shipping either. Also, with the money he saved, Marvin was able to more rapidly grow his business – and boost his orders for glass, at a lower per-bottle price. Everybody won. And that set the stage for more rapid growth throughout the 1960s.

Wink Lanier watched this amazing story unfold. Wink was Mack's right-hand man, his pilot, and his friend. He was there back in 1951 when Mack built Richard's Wine Cellars down in Petersburg, Virginia, and he was there almost every step after that, working side by side with Mack and with Marvin too. If you want to get a feeling for the way Mack and Marvin worked and the way our little family business spread its wings and learned to fly, the best thing you can do is track down Wink, warm him up a bit, and then listen as he spins stories from those early days and years. I wish I could re-create Wink's warm, distinctive Virginia drawl right here on the page, but I think you'll get a sense of the man from the stories he tells and the way he tells them. Just sit back and have a listen:

"I was born in Petersburg, I'm a native," Wink starts in. "When the war came along, everybody joined the service, and I said I'm not going to be a draft dodger; I'm going to enlist. So I joined the regular Navy and spent three and a half, nearly four years there. When we won the war, I got out. I went to a year of engineering school in Milwaukee, Wisconsin. Then I came back to Virginia and went to William & Mary in Williamsburg."

Wink much preferred to live in his native Petersburg and so did Marie, his brand new bride. So Wink moved to the Richmond Professional Institute, a branch of William & Mary in Richmond, which was much closer to Petersburg. When he finished his degree, Wink returned home and hired on with an engineering firm that was building the Petersburg General Hospital. Once that job was done, the firm wanted to send him to West Virginia, but his wife put her foot down: "Marie said 'No, we're not going to go to West Virginia. Try to find something around here.' So I talked with a fellow by the name of Ed Phillips, a beer and wine distributor here in Petersburg. He said, 'I don't have anything here for you, Wink, but I know of a man that's building a winery over on Pocahontas Island. I'll introduce you to him.'"

That man was Grandpa Mack. "He was a real nice guy, somewhat similar to George Burns but don't quote me on that," Wink says with a twinkle in his voice. "But that gives you an image of him: a short guy, smoked cigars, loved cigars. At that time Marvin was running Canandaigua Wine, and the reason Mack was building a winery in Petersburg was he didn't like the Yankee weather. He wanted to come back south after having the Car-Cal Winery in Greensboro for a number of years. So he and Sally bought this old peanut factory and Mack was changing it into a winery. A couple of weeks after I first met him, I came back to see him and he said, 'You know, Winky, I don't have a job for you, but you can come to work for me anyhow.'"

Pocahontas Island is located between Petersburg and the town of Colonial Heights, and it sits right in the middle of the Appomattox River. Back then the only activity there was a lumber company and the abandoned peanut factory that Mack was converting. "This was 1951, 1952, that's when we first started," Wink says. "The Korean War had started about that time and Mack wanted to build in Richmond, frankly, but then he couldn't get steel because of the war. Then he found this piece of real estate on Pocahontas Island and that's

Wild Irish Rose also became the locomotive for Grandpa Mack's business across the South. To grow his business, Mack bought himself a plane and put Wink Lanier, above with his wife Marie, at the controls.

"Wink, never shut the door to a salesman when he calls on you. Always say hello to him. And show respect to him."

MACK SANDS

why he located there."

The peanut factory needed a lot of work. There was a main plant with shelling and packing equipment, plus two warehouses out back. As with the Canandaigua facility, a railroad spur ran conveniently alongside. Mack was building a bottling room between the main plant and the warehouses, to turn the complex into one integrated production facility. This was the birth of Richard's Wine Cellars. "I didn't know what kind of a job I was getting into," Wink recalls. "So I ended up by helping the brick layers, helping the roofers, helping put up the tanks. We started from the ground up, finished getting the tanks in, then we brought in the wine, filtered the wine, and by that time the boiler room was working. I think maybe the first month we didn't do more than maybe 9,000 cases of product, most of it dessert wines."

Then along came Richard's Wild Irish Rose.

"That was sort of like the Model T for us – don't quote that – but in a way it hit at the right time. And it seemed we couldn't make enough of it," Wink recalls. Mack had his own winemaker making Richard's Wild Irish Rose, and they made it in two versions: 14 percent alcohol and 20 percent. Both sold like wildfire: "Everything we made we sold. We were producing it at Canandaigua, we were producing it in Petersburg, and we also ended up producing it in South Carolina."

With the stunning success of Richard's Wild Irish Rose, Grandpa Mack was in seventh heaven – or pretty close to it. He loved getting out and about to see the distributors, and to make that easier in 1966 the company purchased a small private plane – a family tradition that Rob and I continue today with our two corporate jets. Mack had his own private pilot too: one Winfield "Wink" Lanier. Wink was an experienced pilot – instrument-rated and commercially licensed – and so on top of his other duties in the business, Wink became Mack's chauffeur in the sky. "I learned how to fly when I was in high school," Wink explains. "But I did not get into the Navy's flight training in World War II. Afterwards I took it up again with Mack and ended up having a real nice airplane, a Navajo that we could fly in all kinds of weather."

The Navajo was a small twin-engine plane with seven seats, and Wink spent hours and hours aloft with Mack, visiting distributors up and down the East Coast and flying regularly up to Canandaigua to see Marvin. According to Wink, Mack understood that to have a successful business it was great to have a winning product like Richard's Wild Irish Rose, but you also needed to build and maintain strong relationships inside your industry, from the biggest distributor down to the most humble salesman. "Mr. Sands one day said to me, 'Wink, never shut the door to a salesman when he calls on you. Always say hello to him. And show respect to him. If you don't have anything for him, go outside and tell him, 'We don't have anything for you right now, but please come back.' People would call on us trying to sell us labels and bottles and caps and things like that. We usually had a good supply of them. But one day a fellow called on us, he had been calling on us for about three years. And he happened to call on the day that we were out of a particular item: the little seals that go around the top of the bottles. And this guy hit pay dirt. He happened to be there when we needed him and he got the business. So Mr. Sands was right: always say hello to the guy. You never know when you're going to need him."

Another day Mack got a visit from a man named Jim Staton. "Jim played football for Wake Forest, then went on to become a tackle for the Washington Redskins and a Super Bowl player," Wink recalls. "Then he stopped playing football and went into the beer business. He was from Greensboro. One day he came up to see us. 'Mr. Sands,' he said, 'you got a piece of property on Walker Avenue in Greensboro. It was the former Car-Cal Winery. I've got beer to sell, but I need a place to set up shop.' So Mr. Sands made it easy for Jim Staton to buy that former building and Jim became one of our biggest distributors in Greensboro."

Wink remembers Mack's wife Sally as a tiger in her own right. Because Mack still refused to have his name on any official papers, in the early days Sally served as president of Richard's Wine Cellars. And she did pretty well too, though she soon withdrew from the daily business fray to pursue other activities in the social life of Petersburg. "Sally, she was a great gal," Wink says. "She would be concentrating and if a bomb were to explode next to her, she wouldn't flinch at all because she was so concentrated on what she was doing. Unfortunately at age 58 she got colon cancer and died. That was in 1956."

Two years later, Mack remarried. His new wife Eileen had one daughter who was married and two others who were teenagers. Without batting an eye, Mack assumed the responsibilities of fatherhood all over again. "He accepted those kids as his own," Wink recalls. "Mack educated them, put them through college, and now they have families of their own. He was a good family man."

Wink also saw up close the relationship between Marvin and Mack, and he saw how Marvin grew more confident with the success of Richard's Wild Irish Rose. "They had a very close relationship," Wink recalls. "At first Marvin was new and young and growing up and running Canandaigua, and back then there were conversations every day between father and son. Of course as time went on, there wasn't as much. But they talked frequently. They were very much alike in a way – in looks, in appearance. I think Marvin was a little bit more – I hate to say it – but tougher. He was a tough negotiator. Mack sort of mellowed out a little as he got older, though I think the people up in Canandaigua maybe had a different opinion."

At Petersburg, Mack had his own counterpart to Max Applebaum: a Swiss-born winemaker named Otto Selig. Wink remembers Otto vividly. "I'll never forget when Otto first came over, with a food case with a rope around it," Wink recalls. "He had been making wine in Algeria, in huge concrete tanks, then shipping it back to France in big tankers. When they had the revolution there, Otto got out and stepped off the boat and some guy he'd been corresponding with said, 'Why don't you go down and see Mr. Sands in Petersburg?' Otto came aboard four or five months after we had opened and, boy, he was a character."

Otto was an expert winemaker, but he had his own special way of doing things. And, poor guy, he was prone to accidents. "I'll tell you something about Otto, to give you a picture of him," Wink says, warming to his subject. "If Otto had been a surgeon, he would go up through your rectum to remove your tonsils. I mean you just never knew what the heck he was driving at. But he was very smart. At first he was just clumsy as could be. He

Mack's chief winemaker, Otto Selig, left, had a genius for creating popular fruit flavors of Richard's Wild Irish Rose.

To push sales, Marvin and Mack came up with all sorts of promotions, including a contest featuring as a grand prize a brand new Bentley. When the winner was named, they practically had to pry Mack out of the driver's seat.

couldn't even use a screwdriver. And he had several accidents in the winery. One day a hose got away from him, and he held onto it and it pulled him off the top of a tank. He broke his shoulder. Another time he stood up on a jack to tighten up a tank, then he slipped off and broke his leg. Another time he came into the winery one morning and a tank had overflowed with foam. We were making pineapple wine at the time, and Otto stood there and it frightened him so much he slipped and cut his hip. But he was another guy that just wouldn't quit. He ended up getting married and he had two nice daughters."

There are many stories about how Mack would growl and bellow at Otto, but beneath that bluster Wink says that Mack had a deep affection for Otto, just as he did for everyone else working with him in Petersburg. "Listen," Wink says, "here's a guy that had to be very frugal; there was a time when he didn't have anything. He learned that you just have to put your nose to the grindstone and watch where every penny goes. He didn't waste anything. So he was demanding, yes, but let me tell you this about him: Mr. Sands was always fair. For instance, let a clerk make a mistake in billing, oh, man, he would hit the roof. But if a pipe-line broke and we lost 10,000 gallons of product, it didn't faze him. An accident is one thing but for somebody to make a mistake on an invoice, well, that just wasn't acceptable."

There are a few more stories that Wink likes to tell about Grandpa Mack, and I can't resist sharing them with you. They tell you a lot about Mack – and about the character and values that are embedded in our company. "One day we were flying a Mooney and it was winter time," Wink starts in. "We were going up to Canandaigua and the Mooney was just a little single engine plane. It had no hot props or anything on the wings to knock off the ice. We were in a temperature inversion, and by that I mean warmer temperatures above, freezing below. Well, we were on the top – fat, dumb, and happy. I got the clearance for the approach and right there I made an error. I did not put the wind chill heat on 100 percent. When we headed down, all of a sudden it was as if someone had thrown white paint all over the windshield."

Wink and Mack couldn't see a thing, and they still had to land that plane in the thick of winter. "I knew what had happened and I knew the problem," Wink goes on. "So I imme-diately aborted the approach and went around and told the controller what had happened. He said, 'Okay, shoot another one.'" Wink's plan was to look out the side window so that he could see as he guided the plane down. He told Mack to monitor the instrument panel and when the gauges hit certain numbers, Mack was to give him a sign. "I said, 'Look, when you see the numbers, just hit me; don't try to talk to me, just tap my shoulder or leg. Well, we hit the numbers just right, and by the time we got up to the terminal, there was thick ice on the doors and we had to get somebody to put some water on the doors so we could open them up. None of this fazed Mack a bit. I mean, he was tough."

It was a good thing too. As I noted earlier, after all those years of smoking cigars, in the early 1970s Mack got throat cancer and the doctors removed his larynx in an operation called a laryngectomy. From then on, Mack spoke through a small tube in his throat and it made talking extremely difficult. Did that slow him down? For a little while, yes. To com-pensate for his inability to make himself understood, Mack pressed Wink into service as his voice pilot. "For about a year, when he was making business calls, I would stay on the phone with him," Wink explains. "He would write down what he wanted to say and I would pass it on to the person at the other end of the line. My arm got to the point where I couldn't straighten it out. I didn't have enough sense to get a little headset like you see people wear. So one day we were talking to a guy up in Michigan about a piece of equipment. His name was Lee. Mack was on the other end of the line and I said 'Lee, you've got a cold!' He said, 'No, I'm alive. I had a laryngectomy.' Well, at that time Mack had not yet tried to talk, and I looked over and saw tears coming down his eyes. So when we got through with the conversation, he started taking lessons on how to speak. From then on, you couldn't stop him."

There was no stopping Marvin either. Richard's Wild Irish Rose had generated a powerful wave, and Dad was determined to ride it as far as he could. But he did not suddenly turn into a daredevil. To the contrary, Marvin very astutely shied away from new markets where he felt Richard's could not be properly supported. There was also something that made him cautious: the American wine market was starting to shift. In 1953, dessert wines represented 75 percent of all the wine sold here. A decade later, that figure had dropped to 60 percent. The American consumer was discovering table wine, a trend that would only accelerate in the years to come.

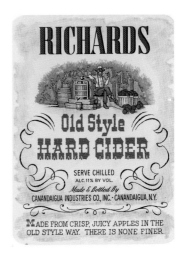

Throughout the 1950s, Dad also kept a wary eye on those two California giants, Gallo and Italian Swiss Colony, the lead brand of United Vintners. They were big, they were powerful, and they, too, were bold and inventive. Beyond that, the two companies were a study in contrasts. Gallo grew most of their own grapes and formed relationships with independent grape growers throughout the San Joaquin Valley. United Vintners, by contrast, was run by a cooperative of grape growers who had an ownership interest in the company. In the mid-1950s, Gallo pressed its advantage in fortified wines with a new product, a powerhouse concoction of white port mixed with lemon juice. It featured an alcohol level of 21 percent. The name? Thunderbird. I need say nothing more about it; it never out-sold our Wild Irish Rose. In this same period, United Vintners was pushing hard into the table wine market, on top of their strong positions in port, sherry, and muscatel.

Gallo and Italian Swiss both had national ambitions and strategies. Both were eager to move away from their bulk-shipped regional model for bottling and branding, and both, like Dad, were looking for ways to side-step the heavy costs of regulated shipping by truck and train. With that in mind, Bob Ivie at United Vintners came up with an ingenious idea: a wine tanker that would haul huge loads of bulk wine from northern California, out the Golden Gate Bridge, down through the Panama Canal, and then up to their bottling operation in New Jersey, from where they would serve their distributors on the East Coast. The upshot of Bob's idea was the SS Angelo Petri, a wine tanker that regularly made that run from 1957 to 1971, avoiding truck and rail costs and changing our industry in the process. Score one for United Vintners.

Not to be outdone, the Gallos went to the railroads and to federal regulators and argued for a new set of tariff rates, claiming that the existing rates put them at a competitive

I can't help but think that the top guns at Gallo and United Vintners looked at Marvin's innovations and growing revenues and muttered to themselves something along the lines of, "Why, that little son of a gun!"

RICHARD SANDS

disadvantage. Gallo secured several specific changes that they claimed would benefit the entire industry. In truth, though, those changes allowed Gallo to negotiate a deal with the railroads that no one else could duplicate because they were based on shipping a very high number of tank cars per year – a volume that no other wine group could match. On top of that, Gallo pumped huge sums into building a strong national sales force. Advantage, Gallo.

Dad did not have comparable means, but he worked hard to stay a step ahead of the big boys. Thanks to Dad's system of franchise bottling, delivered pricing, and his own freight company, Gallo and United Vintners found they were not able to compete in the East with our New York State wines. Dad, of course, was operating on a much smaller scale, but I can't help but think that the top guns at Gallo and United Vintners looked at Marvin's innovations and growing revenues and muttered to themselves something along the lines of, "Why, that little son of a gun!"

In the course of the 1950s, Dad also started making acquisitions. Cautious and methodical as always, Dad rarely went on buying sprees just to push growth or build market share; usually he was driven by a specific need or a problem that he wanted to solve. A case in point was his purchase in 1955 of the Mother Vineyard in Manteo, North Carolina. At that time, demand for Wild Irish Rose was exploding, and Marvin's and Mack's operations were struggling to keep pace. In Petersburg, Otto Selig had a constant fear: a shortage of Scuppernong grapes. Otto needed them for his blend of Wild Irish Rose and for his fruit wines – especially peach and apple – that were big favorites across the South. Mother Vineyard was the answer: it owned high-yield Scuppernong vineyards and its own popular brand, Mother Vineyard Scuppernong Wine. Once Dad had closed the deal, Mack, Wink, and Otto quickly melded those assets into their operation. A short time later, Dad bought another big grower of Scuppernong, the Onslow Winery in Holley Ridge, North Carolina.

In the late 1950s, there was another significant event in the history of the Sands family: the birth of my brother Rob. His arrival on June 10th, 1958, was a banner day for Marvin and Mickey, of course, but also for Laurie and me. We now had a new little sidekick to play with – and boss around! In the coming chapters, you are going to hear a lot from Rob. He is an amazingly gifted man: a first-rate lawyer, a skilled businessman, and an exceptional father. Rob also tells some rollicking stories about growing up inside the Sands household. I'll make sure he tells you a story or two about Marvin's prized Lincoln Continental Mark IV, just to make clear to you that Dad's challenges and headaches extended far beyond the world of wine.

PART III

Building To Last

As these tanks attest, during the 1960s Marvin built Canandaigua Industries into a strong, rapidly growing engine of the American wine industry.

CHAPTER 9

Our Greatest Treasure

In the business community of greater Rochester, Dad was surrounded by giants: East-man Kodak, Xerox, Bausch & Lomb, Birds Eye Foods. It was no different in the wine industry. Every year Dad and Mom would go to the annual meeting of the Wine and Spirits Wholesalers Association, and it was always a deflating experience. "No one would talk to Marvin," Mom recalls. "He was like a peanut in a big field."

At the start of the 1960s, Canandaigua Industries remained a very small family business. Dad had done a lot of building, but his only prominent success had been Richard's Wild Irish Rose. Still, even then Marvin was thinking big, dreaming big, and he was pursuing a clearly defined long-term vision: he wanted that small peanut to grow into an industry leader. "Marvin was driven to be the best and the biggest," Mom says now. "He didn't care about the money. But he wanted the success."

Today, Rob and I view Dad as a far-sighted architect and master builder, carefully design-ing and putting into place a sturdy foundation and the rock-solid cornerstones of long-term business success. And by the start of the 1960s, Dad and his team had made significant progress. They had:

Marvin taught us a lesson that guides us to this day: Your people are your greatest resource. The best are pure gold.

- Created a winning product and brand – Richard's Wild Irish Rose.

- Developed an innovative distribution system – franchise bottling.

- Devised smart, cost-effective logistics – Robert's Trading Company.

- Built a loyal and reliable supply chain – for grapes, glass, and beyond.

- Partnered with a first-rate bank – Lincoln First, now J.P. Morgan Chase.

- Enforced strict financial discipline – in every aspect of the business.

- Pursued opportune mergers and acquisitions – a strategy that Rob and I would later pursue with more vigor and much greater success.

Now if Dad were here today, he would study that list and say to me, in his quiet way, "Richard, you left out the most important thing: People. In any business, your greatest resource is always your people. The best are pure gold."

He's right. A winning brand, a strong distribution system, sound finances – these are all important of course. Still, you can't take your company to the heights of success with sound business basics alone. No painter ever created a masterpiece by starting with a paint-by-the-numbers kit, and Dad believed that the same is true in business. To build a strong company and make it into an industry leader, you have to start by recruiting good people. Then you have to motivate them, inspire them, and patiently cultivate in them a set of vir-tues that most business textbooks never even mention: Integrity. Commitment. Creativity. Passion. Discipline. Resourcefulness. And Pride. You also have to create an environment where people feel empowered, where they feel free to innovate, try new things, and even fail – provided they learn from their mistakes. And Dad also understood this: people want a deep and secure sense that they belong to an organization that respects them and truly cares about them and their families – and has the policies that prove it.

"Marvin was honorable. If he gave his word, it was his bond. So people trusted him."

MICKEY SANDS

How do you achieve all that?

Dad would answer with a single word: leadership. Dad's leadership philosophy and style had several different facets. Some of those came from what he had seen in the Navy, both good and bad. My brother Rob believes that Grandpa Mack played a critical role here, showing Marvin exactly how not to lead or empower. "Mack was irascible," Rob explains. "And he wasn't necessarily the most sensitive or the nicest person you've ever met either. Usually he spent the first 15 minutes of every conversation – regardless of who it was with – chewing them out, and many times for no particular reason other than to intimidate that person or to place himself in a dominant position. So instead of being diplomatic or dealing with people through persuasion, Mack usually dealt with people through intimidation."

Marvin, by contrast, led by persuasion. And in that vein he was blessed with an unusual set of gifts. "Dad had a way with people that very few people have," Rob explains. "He could garner people's respect and influence them almost in the manner of the greatest politicians. People always felt that he was 100 percent genuine, that he never had a hidden agenda, that he never was two-faced. People felt that Marvin possessed tremendous integrity. And he was forthright. But probably the quality that stood out the most is that he really loved people. Marvin liked to be around people and he was relatively uninfluenced by a person's station in life, which I think is one of the things that made him as genuine as he was and made people really like and respect him."

Marvin translated his personal warmth into company policy. "People today talk about having an open-door policy, about talking to anybody," Rob says. "Marvin truly had an open-door policy all day long. People were always streaming in, truck drivers, people from the plant. We would have events – years-of-service awards, events with people from the plant – and Dad truly enjoyed all of them. He loved going to the company party. And the company picnic. And having dinner with somebody who was retiring or talking to a plant employee whose wife had just had a baby. Marvin was the kind of person that everybody felt they could come to with their personal problems and tell him their life story."

Marvin also had another gift. "Anybody that you ask about Marvin, one of the things they say first is that he was a wonderful listener," Mom says. "That carried through in business. People in the community were always coming to him for help. When they came, Marvin talked very little. But they all had lots to tell him, and he was always processing everything that they told him. He had a great memory, he never forgot anything. Marvin was very smart. He was honorable. If he gave his word, it was his bond. So people trusted him. We called him 'The Godfather.' Everyone came to him with their problems."

There is a fascinating irony here. While Dad was willing to listen to anybody, he rarely shared his plans or his own problems with anybody inside the company – or inside the family. He was a leader who inspired trust – but he himself trusted very few people. "You would think of Marvin as somebody who would have a lot of close friends but he didn't," Rob says. "Being such a genuine and people-oriented person, you would have thought that Marvin trusted people. But Marvin, I would say, trusted no one. He kept his own counsel. He had two or three close friends over the years, but he kept a good distance between himself and even his close friends."

One prominent exception was George Bresler. George was the husband of Marvin's first cousin Dorothy, and he was a lawyer, an accountant, and a very savvy business advisor and financial planner. George became affiliated with our company in its earliest days, served on our board of directors, and was always one of our most trusted business guides. He died in 2006. "George was probably my father's very closest friend and confidant – to the extent that he ever confided in anybody," Rob says. "He was a very smart, very sharp guy, and he advised Marvin over the years on all sorts of legal and business matters."

In terms of leadership, Marvin set a standard that Rob and I often have trouble matching. We do have talents and skills that Dad didn't have, but when it comes to dealing with people, both Rob and I feel that Dad was in a class all by himself. "If I was going to contrast myself with Marvin," Rob explains, "I act more on a 'need-to-know' kind of basis. And I am probably not as inclined to want to have the same relationship with everybody. Marvin had a rare gift. He truly liked everybody and was able to communicate that in a very genuine and straightforward way."

As Rob is suggesting, our own leadership styles are very different from Dad's. That's only natural; we're not our father – and our company today is very different from the one that Dad was running four decades ago. Still, Rob and I cherish the values he instilled inside our company. We fully embrace his open-door policy, and we steadfastly support our father's guiding credo: Put People First. Empower them. Give them the tools and the support they need to succeed. When they win, you win. When they grow, your company grows.

In the 1960s and beyond, Dad hired and mentored a number of people who would play key roles in building Constellation Brands. Bert Silk comes immediately to mind. Dad hired Bert in 1965 and he proved to be a wonderful addition to our staff. Bert had wine in his veins: his father, Abe Silk, was a wine broker in Boston with extensive knowledge about what was happening in wine all across the country. Dad often spoke with Abe several times a week, to find out what wines were being sold in California, at what price, and what the forecasts were for the coming grape crops. This was critical information-gathering, a process that Dad felt was essential if you wanted to stay one step, or many, ahead of your competitors.

Bert was a powerhouse in his own right. He grew up in Massachusetts and then moved to California. He studied enology at Fresno State and then went to work in quality control at Italian Swiss Colony, in its Asti facility. When Bob Ivie came up with that ingenious idea of shipping wine from California to the East Coast by tanker, Bob sent Bert back east to manage the company's new bottling plant in Newark, New Jersey. Through Abe, Marvin kept a close eye on Bert's development, and he could see that this young man had a skill set that few people could match: he was expert in the chemistry of winemaking and the mechanics of production and bottling. He also understood systems and was a gifted organizer, innovator, and manager.

In 1965, Dad brought Bert onboard with a very specific goal: to replace Max Applebaum, who was getting ready to retire. Bert proved to be an excellent choice. For the next three decades and more, Bert built up our production side, constantly expanding and updating it to keep pace with the exploding demand for Wild Irish Rose and some of our other products.

Bert Silk, on the right, proved Marvin's point. Smart, resourceful, versatile, and creative, Bert for decades anchored our production side and served as Dad's most trusted troubleshooter. Together with Bert and Marvin in this photo, is Donna Buckingham, manager of the Widmer tasting room.

"Marvin was not just a good listener. He had an uncanny ability to filter, to perceive the problem that lay beneath the actual words."

BERT SILK

Dad had total confidence in Bert, and over the years he gave him many other challenges and problems to fix. In time, Bert grew into a senior statesman for our company, and he became a highly respected figure throughout the wine industry, serving at one point as chairman of the Wine Institute in California and representing us in many different venues both here and abroad.

Bert worked hand-in-glove with Marvin, and he has many insights into what made Dad such an effective leader. Dad's open-door policy was valuable, Bert says, but most important was what happened when an employee sat down with Dad and aired his thoughts and feelings. "Marvin was not just a good listener. He had an uncanny ability to filter, to perceive the problem that lay beneath the actual words," Bert explains. "Anybody could come in and complain – even if it meant jumping over his direct boss." Still, that policy did create headaches, especially for Bert. Our truckers were a magnificent team but those long, solitary hours on the road could make them awfully cranky. "For a long time all the drivers felt very comfortable in going to Marvin with any problems," Bert recalls. "As the person who inherited that responsibility, I can tell you it could be difficult. A driver would have some type of gripe – real or imagined – and when he arrived back at the winery, the driver would come back into the office and 'unload' – sometimes incoherently. Finally I was able to work out an agreement with the drivers whereby they would wait until the next day to come see me with their problems."

While Dad did listen to everyone, Bert says that Marvin was careful not to undermine or constantly second-guess his managers. In that regard he was the exact opposite of Grandpa Mack, as Bert often saw with his own eyes. "One time Mack was stuck with seven pallets of pretty mediocre product," Bert recalls with a sigh. "Mack told his sales chief, Irv Jarrett, 'You've got seven salesmen. Tell them to sell one each or they're through!'"

Bert came up with several important innovations for our company. In the 1960s, Dad and Bert realized they had to upgrade and expand our winemaking facility on Buffalo Street. Dad put Bert in charge of that. Bert knew we needed to install a new set of high-capacity tanks to manage our fermenting and storage needs, and he also knew that those big tanks could be extremely costly to maintain and regulate, temperature-wise, throughout fermentation. And Bert had another concern: managing high-capacity tanks in the often brutal winters of western New York State.

Bert found a way to use those cold winter temperatures to our advantage. He designed a system that would utilize huge stainless steel tanks – each several stories high – to be located out behind our existing facility. But here's the ingenious part: instead of constructing a huge building to house them – a very high cost in itself – Bert had a less-expensive, one-story structure built around their base, covering only the bottom 15 percent of the tanks. That left the remainder of the tanks open to the weather. That way, in winter we only needed to heat the bottom portion of the tanks. That kept the wine and valves from freezing but saved us hundreds of thousands of dollars a year in heating costs. Also, during fall and winter, we needed no additional refrigeration to keep temperatures down during fermentation – another important energy saving. Bert also installed an automated grape crushing system to replace our old crushers. The new system was able to accommodate a ton of grapes at a time, again saving us money while expanding our production speed and capacity.

Bert also redesigned the way we made Richard's Wild Irish Rose. At that time, Max Applebaum was making Wild Irish Rose with a blend of about 70 percent high-acid Vitis Labrusca grapes from New York State and about 30 percent lower-acid wine from California. Once the two wines were combined, Max would add a certain amount of sugar – in compliance with ATF regulations – to soften those acids and produce the desired color, flavor, alcohol level, and acid level. Bert combed through the ATF regulations and Max's procedures and soon found a better way. With two small tweaks to the process of amelioration – both lawful – Bert devised a new way to produce the exact same wine and save us $400,000 a year in the process!

Dad's business also profited from innovative, creative people on the advertising side. In 1955, when sales of Wild Irish Rose began to boom, Dad and Bob Meenan turned to Hutchins Advertising, a top advertising agency in Rochester. Over the next seven years, Hutchins developed ads and promotions for the major metropolitan areas where Richard's was most popular. In 1962, though, Dad spotted something new: a spurt in wines sales in suburban supermarkets and liquor stores. This was clearly a large, growing, and totally un-tapped market for Richard's Wild Irish Rose. Moreover, it was women, not men, who were selecting which bottle of wine to bring home, another important shift in consumer buying patterns. Could the Hutchins team find a way to capture this promising new market?

Like many other wineries in the Finger Lakes region, Widmer's Wine Cellars offered tours and tastings for wine lovers and summer visitors. Tour guides like this one added a little local flavor.

As a first step, the Hutchins agency brought together a crack team to develop a new campaign: Bob Wolf, executive vice president; James Morey, creative director; Brendan Wright, media director; and Joe McDonald, as account executive. Then they defined their strategic objectives: "win new customers in all economic, social, and intellectual strata, increase the consumption among old customers, excite distributors, and make Wild Irish Rose famous." In other words, expand the product's appeal to a much wider group of consumers, with suburban women leading the way. To do that, the Hutchins team decided there would be no more print or TV ads featuring soft sunsets over lush vineyards, no more seductive shots of wine being poured. Even in the early 1960s, those had become tired cliches. In their place, Hutchins brought in something new for the wine business: humor.

"This wine, with its funny name, funny square bottles and taste, needed a campaign that would be talked about," Joe McDonald explained at the time. "So we put together a campaign that would exploit the free-wheeling personality of a very unstuffy wine."

The centerpiece of the campaign was a bottle that laughs. In each TV spot, the cap on the decanter spins off and the bottle bursts into laughter. The Hutchins team put the laughing bottle into a series of amusing – and universal – human predicaments, each calibrated to touch a different segment of the buying public: a young couple trying to impress a stern boss, a suburban matron trying to impress her bridge group, a jaded matinee idol trying to woo a lovely young woman. In another, a 92-year-old woman tries and tries to blow out all of the 92 candles on her birthday cake. Then, in a fit of frustration, she opens the bottle and pours Richard's straight into her ear trumpet! The tagline drove home the underlying theme: "Buy Wild Irish Rose, the happy wine for happy people." The ads clicked; humor brought an entirely new face to American wine.

When Susan Read first came to us, she had no experience in the wine business and she only wanted a small part-time job. Forty years later, she's still with us, a valued member of our wine-making team.

The campaign succeeded at several levels. First, it dramatically increased public awareness of the Richard's brand. In its initial markets, it boosted sales by 15 percent. Then, it helped push a wave of growth that continued throughout the 1960s. There was a third payoff too: in November of 1967 Marvin convinced Joe McDonald to leave Hutchins and join our company as Marketing and Advertising Manager, reporting directly to Bob Meenan. Joe stayed with us until his retirement in 2000. When Sam's Club and Costco started to become major wine sales outlets, we gave Joe those big national accounts and he managed them with aplomb.

Hiring Joe was pure Marvin: when you spot exceptional talent, grab it; men and women like that are worth their weight in gold. Let me tell you another story that proves the same point. One morning in May of 1970, a young woman named Susan Read came to us looking for work. Susan wasn't looking for a full-time job. This was during the Vietnam War and her husband was off in basic training; Susan was just looking for something part-time to keep her busy while her husband was away. Susan had absolutely no experience in wine or in any other form of production. In college, she had studied some chemistry, but her work experience had been as a teacher of physical education. On paper, Susan was simply not an ideal candidate for us to hire. But something about her caught Bert Silk's eye.

"I was sitting out front," Susan recalls now, "filling out the application, and I was about half done when Bert comes out of the office and says 'Can you start on Monday?' I said, 'Yeah, I guess so.' And guess what? I've been here ever since."

Susan started out as a technician in our wine lab and quickly became a mainstay of our operation. Today she is in charge of quality control for the entire East Coast, and she can walk you through Buffalo Street and tell you the origin and capacity of every wooden tank, in what year we added our stainless steel tanks, and what spectrometer readings we use to ensure that the distinctive red color of Wild Irish Rose remains consistent from one batch to the next. Susan remembers how many tons of fresh peaches we used to haul up from Georgia in the early 1970s to make our popular peach wines, and in an instant she can list the other flavors we made: apple, pineapple, blackberry, cherry, and apricot. Susan Read is a walking compendium of our company's history and lore, and now she, too, goes to national and international meetings to represent our company and expand her knowledge.

To attract and keep people like Bert and Susan, Marvin paid his people well and provided generous retirement plans and medical coverage, benefits that were not yet common in either the wine industry or in the American workplace. "When I got to Canandaigua Industries, a full 15 percent of our earnings were put into a defined contribution plan," Bert recalls. "For every employee – not just the executives." With health care it was the same. Under the medical plan that Marvin put into effect, the company paid nearly all of it, and employees were left with only a small co-pay. Rob and I embrace that philosophy and provide a generous health care plan to our staff.

Great people produce great results. By 1968, with the success of Richard's Wild Irish Rose and the Hutchins ad campaign, our total sales hit $15 million, the best ever. Following the creation of Richard's in 1953, the company grew fifteen-fold in 15 years – an astonishing performance. Those results gave Marvin the confidence and the financial wherewithal to further expand the business. In 1965, he purchased Tenner Brothers Winery of Patrick, South Carolina. It was the oldest winery in the state, and though it was struggling financially, Tenner had two prized assets: a wine named Hostess that was very popular in the South – and the largest Scuppernong vineyard in the world, spanning over 300 acres. Tenner Brothers also made a popular peach wine, using thousands of tons of winery-grade Red Haven peaches. Mack and Wink Lanier integrated Tenner Brothers into our operation and used those peaches to make Richard's Peach Wine, which soon became a popular extension of our locomotive brand. The best acquisitions produce that kind of synergy.

In 1965 Dad also brought into our fold a true icon of American wine: Virginia Dare. Dad and Grandpa Mack could not have been prouder. They had both revered Captain Paul Garrett and his innovative spirit, and they had admired how he had turned Virginia Dare into what was, back then, the best-selling wine in America. We acquired the rights to Garrett's baby on a royalty basis from the Guild Wine Company. Virginia Dare then assumed a place of pride in our growing portfolio of big-selling brands: Mother Vineyard, Hostess, and, of course, Richard's Wild Irish Rose.

With the 60s in full bloom, Dad and Bob Meenan brought out a fun new product called "Aquarius," a light, carbonated "fruit punch" wine with a psychedelic label. The fabulously successful rock musical Hair featured a song heralding "the dawning of the Age of Aquarius," but our pop wine never achieved such exalted status. It had a nice run for five years but was then discontinued. In 1969, we added premium champagnes to our line via another acquisition: the Hammondsport Wine Company in nearby Hammondsport. Then in 1972 we bought the Eastern Wine Company of New York. Eastern Wine had a popular brand – Chateau Martin – but as with Tenner Brothers, its owners had not mastered the financial side of the business. So Dad was able to buy it an opportune moment and an opportune price.

An ad for "Aquarius," a light, carbonated fruit wine that Marvin and Bob Meenan launched in the late 1960s. It was not a glorious success.

To keep pace with this expansion, Dad took several important steps. In 1972 he brought the different entities of his company together under one umbrella and incorporated it in Delaware as the Canandaigua Wine Company. The following year he was ready for the next big step in his master plan: going public. He made the move on January 22nd, 1973, with an initial offering of 1,000,000 shares of common stock on the American Stock Exchange. (We later moved to the NASDAQ exchange in 1992.). Dad retained 80 percent of the stock. The timing was a little dicey; you might say we got in just under the wire. At that time, the Watergate crisis and a worldwide oil embargo were rattling the markets. Almaden and Taylor's had already gone public, at prices of 25-times earnings. We went public at 20-times earnings and were the last IPO before the big market crash of 1973.

Going public accomplished two interlocking goals. First, it put a very durable financial foundation under the Canandaigua Wine Company. Second, it gave Dad a huge measure of relief. The shocks he had endured when he first came into the business – 27 years before – were now a distant memory; the financial futures of his wife and children were now secure. As he approached his 50th birthday, Marvin could look back at what he had accomplished with a deep sense of pride and achievement.

But Dad was not about to rest. In 1974 he bought Bisceglia Brothers Winery, located in

California's fertile San Joaquin Valley. The Bisceglia family had deep roots in California wine. They began making wine in 1888 in San Jose, then they opened wineries in Fresno and further north in St. Helena, in the Napa Valley. Later they took control of the Yosemite Cooperative, a major operation in the Central Valley. Bisceglia Brothers was a good strategic fit for us. It was run by Bruno Bisceglia; he and Dad had been doing business together for years. Bruno supplied us with grape concentrate and high-proof distilled spirits, both of which we needed to produce Richard's Wild Irish Rose and many of our other dessert wines. Through Bisceglia, Dad also planned to diversify and bring out a line of California Chablis and Burgundy wines, to compete head-to-head with wines being produced by Almaden and Paul Masson, two of the leading California table wine brands. As Dad liked to do, we kept Bisceglia as an independent company, with Bruno still in charge but with a much stronger financial platform underneath him.

Like any master architect and builder, Marvin was also looking much further down the road. He wanted to ensure that the structure he was erecting was dynamic, resilient, and built to last. In his desire to turn his peanut into a giant, Dad still faced many difficult challenges ahead, and one of them promised to be especially daunting.

Me.

CHAPTER 10

Educating Richard

This may surprise you:

Marvin never pushed Rob or me to go into the wine business. He never set out to build a family dynasty, and he never tried to influence us or our sister Laurie in our choice of careers. Dad wanted us to be happy and fulfilled, and he wanted us to excel in whatever we chose to do, but he and Mom never laid out specific paths for us to follow. We always had the freedom – and usually their support – to follow our dreams and build our own futures.

"Marvin was very unusual as a father," Mom explains. "If the kids asked questions, he talked about business to them, but he never encouraged them. He really wanted them to pursue anything they wanted to excel at or pursue or enjoy. He wanted them to like what they were doing."

This approach to parenting was perfectly in line with the leadership model and philosophy that guided Dad at the office: Empower Your People. That model worked beautifully with his staff at the Canandaigua Wine Company, but how did it work with the three headstrong, high-energy kids growing up under the Sands family roof? To answer that, I'd better give the floor over to Mom. She was the one who caught the worst of it, having to contend with the three of us 24 hours a day.

"When they were growing up," Mom recalls, "I thought they were going to kill me, that I wouldn't survive them – all three of them – because it was very important to me that all three of them think for themselves and make decisions for themselves. Then," Mom adds with a sigh, "I hated everything they decided on."

Rob and Laurie and I were indeed a handful, but Mom and Dad managed to instill in us a strong set of values. Education was always their top priority, and in that domain both Mom and Dad were very demanding. It was fine for us to be outspoken at the dinner table or run a little wild on the playground, but they cut us no slack when it came to hitting the books and doing well in school. "None of them was easy to bring up," Mom says. "My daughter was never easy. Richard, you know, had the long hair, the whole nine yards. But through it all, all three of them did well in school. In fact, the crazier they got, the better they did in school."

Mom's right: we always did well in school, right up through our respective graduate degrees. "Marvin and I both felt that education was very important in our lives and for our children," Mom explains. "We were very conscientious parents. We were on top of them all the time. And I think we had some good luck too. They're very smart but also hard-working and concentrated. My daughter was a physician. Richard's a doctor in psychology, and Rob is a lawyer. And all three of our children graduated Phi Beta Kappa. Now they won't tell you that, but I will."

Laurie led the way. She was tiny, brilliant, and fiercely independent. "My daughter was very strong-willed," Mom recalls. "She was headstrong, and she was quite powerful; she had to feel powerful. I think she always felt that Marvin was more protective of her than he was of the boys and she did not appreciate it." At the slightest suggestion that Mom or Dad was being overly protective because she was "a girl," Laurie dug in her heels. And when she made up her mind to do something, nothing could stand in her way. For instance, one day Laurie announced that she was ready to get her driver's license. That she didn't know how

Richard Sands, right, has a Ph.D. in social psychology and initially had no interest in joining the family business. But then he came under the spell of a gifted and inspiring mentor, his father Marvin.

Like her younger brothers, Richard and Rob, Laurie Sands, above, was headstrong, ambitious, and highly intelligent. She became a prominent doctor.

to drive was only a minor impediment.

"She came home from boarding school," Mom recalls, "and said, 'I'm sixteen; I'm going to take my driver's test.' I said, 'You've never driven! You don't know anything about driving a car!' And she said, 'I can do it.' So I took her out and she must have hit every mailbox going down the street. We got to the examining place where the guy gets in the car with you. She's driving, he's in the car, and I'm in the back seat because she wanted me to come with her. I'm sitting as if with my foot on the brake, and she came to an intersection where people were crossing. Instead of stopping and letting the people cross, she stepped on the gas. The guy said, 'Pull over! Get out of the car! You fail!' Then he said, 'What made you do that?'

"'Well, it was a green light.'

"He said, 'People always have the right of way. You could have killed them!'

"'Well,' she said, 'I did have the right of way.'

"Laurie took the test three times and she finally passed. But she didn't want to take any lessons."

Then there was the time Laurie came home from college with some big plans for the summer. "She came home and said she needed a motorcycle," Mom recalls. "A motorcycle? And Marvin said, 'What are you going to do with that?' Laurie told us she was going cross-country with some friends. Marvin said, 'What friends?' and she said, 'You don't know them.' Well, of course Marvin said no. That sparked a big to-do. I tell you, she was something else."

Laurie found her calling in medicine, became a very successful internist, and married another doctor. Together they had two wonderful children, Abby and Zach. Abby started working for us in 2004, at the age of 23, and soon joined our business development unit. In many different ways, Laurie made a profound impact on our family and everyone who knew her, including the medical community of the greater Rochester area. A portrait of her hangs today in the new oncology center of the F.F. Thompson Hospital. In 1996, our sister was diagnosed with ovarian cancer. She died at the age of 47. We were all devastated, as you can imagine. "You know, doctors always take care of everyone but themselves," Mom says now. "By the time they recognized it, it was too late."

As with Laurie, no one ever accused Rob and me of being shrinking violets. Laurie and I both came of age in the 60s, and even today around Canandaigua you may hear stories about our escapades or see a yellowing photo or two of me with a long ponytail or at the wheel of my VW bus. Ah, the 60s; need I say more? Rob is seven years younger than I am, and in those days he looked at me and Laurie with a rather bewildered eye. Mom remembers it all too well: "When Robby was young he would look at his brother and sister and say, 'What's wrong with them? Why do they act that way? And then, of course, he did the exact same things."

Indeed he did. In high school Rob pulled off a stunt that Laurie and I could only stand back and admire. By then, Laurie and I were in our respective graduate schools, and Dad had given up any pretense of disciplining any of his three kids. That gave Rob enormous leeway. "There were no rules in our household for me," Rob says now. "No discipline whatsoever. Dad never punished me. Never. And he never could say no. He always gave me everything and anything I wanted, including a bright yellow Lotus Europa sports car. I was the epitome of the spoiled child."

By this time, too, Dad had put together the successful IPO and for the first time in his life he felt at ease financially. Up to then, Dad had been a ferocious penny counter at the office, and he had also been pretty frugal at home. In fact, he rarely spent much at all; Mom ran the finances at home and bought Dad whatever clothes or supplies he needed. That said, Dad always liked to splurge on cars. Every couple of years he would buy himself a new Lincoln Continental. One year when Laurie and I were off at college, but Rob was still living sat home, Dad bought himself a brand new Lincoln Continental Mark IV. The car was a beauty, leather seats, fancy trim, and it proved to be a temptation that young Rob simply could not resist.

Like Laurie and Richard, Rob graduated from college with Phi Beta Kappa honors. He then became a lawyer before joining the family business.

"Being in high school and being kind of a wild kid," Rob recalls, "one night I took Marvin's car out with a friend of mine to a party. The party ran pretty late, and my friend Scott was driving us home. Well, Scott went around one corner a little too wide and swiped the whole passenger side of Marvin's brand new Lincoln. I mean he literally flattened out the whole side of the car."

Now some teenagers might have slunk home, confessed their sin, begged their father's forgiveness, and promised to work hard to make amends. Not Rob. "I just didn't say anything at all about it," Rob confesses. "I took a lesson from Dad, which is basically: keep people on a strictly 'need-to-know' basis. Now I must reveal that Marvin was not always the most observant person in the whole world. So the next day he gets in the car and drives it to work. And he does that every day for a week. It just so happens that at the office he parked that damaged side of the car next to a wall, and it was also parked next to the wall in our garage at home. So literally a week goes by and I never hear boo about it. Then one morning about a week later I'm sound asleep and I hear him calling me, 'Rob! Come down here!'

He points to the side of the car and says, 'What happened to this?'

'Oh,' I said. 'Oh that. I didn't do it.'

'What do you mean you didn't do it?'

'I didn't do it. Scott did it.'

'What do you mean Scott did it? Weren't you driving?'

'Well, Dad, you see...'"

Laurie and I have no idea how he did it, but Rob somehow managed to escape that episode unpunished. And right then and there we knew that he would make a fabulous lawyer. If we had any lingering doubts, they were erased by another episode with that same Lincoln Continental Mark IV. "When I was about 17," Rob explains, "I had a girlfriend who practically lived with us. And this girl had a German shepherd. In fact, my mother had bought it for her. The girl was a year older than I was and she had gone off to college. But when she was home, she'd come over to the house and bring the dog with her....

"Now this dog was pretty ill-behaved. One night we took Dad's car down to the Colonial – a local dinner and drinking spot – and we left the dog in the backseat of the Continental.

Richard was a 60s idealist. He wanted to make a difference, change the world for the better.

We got finished fairly late, then we got in the car and drove back home. When I opened the rear door to let the dog out, I saw what he had done: he had chewed through the leather in the back seat. I mean, he had totally devoured it. Dad was not pleased, to say the least."

After high school, Rob spent a year at the University of Florida. But he soon became disenchanted with all the partying and where his life seemed to be heading. So he transferred to Skidmore College, in Saratoga, New York, and it provided a welcome change. His friends there put a real value on personal responsibility and academic achievement. Rob also had a lovely girlfriend there. "Rob really blossomed at Skidmore," Mom says, "and he did very well, graduating Phi Beta Kappa. In 1981, he went on to Pace Law School in White Plains, New York. Then he practiced law in Rochester for two years with a first-rate firm, Harter, Secrest & Emery."

When Rob married and had two children of his own, Lauren and Mackenzie, he was a much stricter father than Marvin ever was. One day his son Mackenzie asked his dad to buy him a fancy sports car. Rob was reminded of the shining yellow Lotus that Dad had bought for him, but here was one example from Marvin that Rob was not about to follow. "I bought him a pickup truck," Rob explains. "I thought it was unsafe to give a 16-year-old kid a high-powered sports car. Money's not even the issue. It's this: who would trust a 16-year-old kid with a car like that?"

Thanks, Rob. I had forgotten some of the details of your youthful adventures. And me? What was Richard Sands like in his early days? And how did I wind up taking the helm of the Canandaigua Wine Company? All that, I'm afraid, will take a bit of explaining.

I loved school. I started out in a tiny one-room school looking out on Canandaigua Lake, and after 3rd grade I went to Canandaigua's public elementary and middle school. For high school, I shifted to the Harley School, a rigorous private academy in Rochester. At Harley we had to wear coats and ties, and it was strict in its academic standards as well. I loved it. I loved studying math and physics. I loved solving problems. Even now I love absorbing information and tackling new realms of knowledge. "In high school Richard was valedictorian and president of his class," Mom is happy to brag. "He was always a mathematical genius. It ran in the family."

I did have my share of youthful misadventures. But apart from one crazy night when I landed in jail, I didn't cause Mom and Dad too many headaches and I never damaged Dad's Lincoln Continental; that distinction belongs entirely to Rob. "Richard was a fairly disciplined person when it came to his academics," Rob explains. "And that's part of the reason why Richard never had much discipline of any kind from Dad or Mom. Because he always did so well. He graduated No. 1 in his class and he got an 800 on his math SAT. He always did well in school, so there was never anything to be done with him."

When I was young, in the mid-1950s, Dad was very focused on solving his problems at the wine company. As a family, we would go snow skiing and water skiing and we'd take family vacations, but Dad was not the sort of father who was, for instance, active with Little

League. That was fine by me; I didn't like those kinds of activities anyway. Early on, though, I discovered that Dad and I had something in common: we both loved learning. And here I was extremely fortunate: he was a great teacher and I was a pretty good student. As I mentioned earlier, riding in the car he would give me math problems to solve, but what he really was teaching me was how to think, how to examine a problem in a calm, logical way, how to break it down into its component parts, and then how to solve it. He was helping me hone my analytical and problem-solving skills, in a tiny foretaste of what was to come.

I think that some of Dad's fathering was guided by the fact that his own youth had been somewhat curtailed by war, business, and marriage. When I was 16, I had a high school sweetheart that I liked very much. Things between us were getting very serious and we were planning to go to college together. But Dad offered me a word of caution: "It's too early for you, Richard. Go out and play the field. You've got plenty of time." I think he was trying to protect me from his own experience.

Still, being just as bull-headed as Laurie and Rob, I had to make my own mistakes and find my own way. After graduating from the Harley School, I went to the University of California at Berkeley. After the first semester, though, I transferred to Washington University in St. Louis to be with that same high school sweetheart. I wasn't happy there either. I was a math and physics major, but I wanted to branch out into something new. But I had no idea what. So I decided to take a year off to collect my thoughts, then maybe transfer to another school.

That proved to be a good decision. I spent the winter skiing, then I moved back to Rochester and made a little money driving a delivery truck. Major change was now in the works. That fall I entered the University of Vermont and there I found a brand new passion: psychology. I wanted to find out what truly motivated and inspired people and made them act the way they do. I loved the field and after my B.A., I went into a Master's and Ph.D. program in social psychology at the University of North Carolina at Chapel Hill. At this point, I saw myself happily headed into a career in academia, combining research and teaching in social psychology. I had no interest at all in the world of business.

Then something happened. At Chapel Hill, the Social Psychology Department was located next door to the Psychometrics Department, and the grad students there were working with a fascinating new tool: computers. This was the early days of computers – before PCs or spreadsheets – and right away I got hooked. Before long, I was working with the psychometrics team and creating computer models to analyze huge amounts of data. So while I finished my master's degree and then a Ph.D. in social psychology, I also learned matrix algebra and computer modeling. I had no idea at the time that these skills would later prove to be an enormous asset in our business, especially when we planned mergers and acquisitions.

During this same period, I grew increasingly frustrated with academia. The politics and departmental infighting were bad enough. But I also saw first-hand that it was not your intellectual capacity, depth of knowledge, or research that advanced your career; it was how much you published. A professor who published many small, rather meaningless studies would go further than a professor who really mastered a subject but only published one or

During this period, I grew increasingly frustrated with academia.

RICHARD SANDS

"Richard, you really should finish your Ph.D. Then, after you finish, come to work with me. You'll find it fulfilling."

MARVIN SANDS

two in-depth papers every few years.

The breaking point came in 1978. By then I was in my fifth year of graduate school and I was submerged in a very broad dissertation topic. My ambition was to show that personality is really situational in nature and that you could only define personality by a person's perceptions and behavior across a wide variety of situations. I planned to collect massive amounts of data based on thousands of people reacting across hundreds of different situations. From that data, I was going to define their personality types, using a psychometric model that I had already created for my Master's thesis. This was a monumental project, and I was getting nowhere fast.

That year I didn't go home for Christmas. I planned to buckle down and make real progress on my dissertation. Well, I sat there for two weeks and I still couldn't bring it under control. My theory confused me, my model confused me, and how the two were going to come together confused me even more. I was totally blocked. So I spent that holiday break building my parents a backgammon table. Then I called Dad and told him I was going to drop out of my Ph.D. program, live in the mountains, canoe, and lead a simple life. That was it. Academia, I told him, was just not for me.

Dad listened carefully and then offered me a few words of advice. "Richard, you really should finish your Ph.D. I know it's a strain but you're four years into it and one day you will regret that you didn't see it through. Maybe you can find a simple topic that you can complete by the end of the school year. Then, after you finish, come to work with me. You'll find it fulfilling."

My first inclination was to say no. I was very much the 60s idealist; I wanted to make a difference, change the world for the better, and truly improve people's lives. When I expressed that to Dad, he said, "Richard, what do you think we do in our business? Look at all the people we employ. They work, they grow, and they create better lives for themselves and their families. We do the same thing for our suppliers and our customers. Believe me, Richard, through business you will be able to make a very big difference in people's lives."

I was still not entirely convinced. Nonetheless, I followed Dad's advice, scaled back my dissertation, and thus was able to finish it on schedule. Then in 1979, with my Ph.D. completed, I moved back home to Canandaigua, ready to give the wine business a try. At the outset, I didn't see this as a lifetime commitment. I envisioned working in the company for a year, maybe two, to see if I liked it.

I started at the bottom. I felt it was essential to learn the wine business from the ground up. Production, bottling, shipping – I wanted to know how each department worked and how the whole process fit together. And I wanted to work side-by-side with the people in each department, see what problems they needed to solve and what their greatest frustrations and satisfactions were. To my surprise, right away I loved the work. I loved the interaction. I loved the concrete results that I could see every day. This was not some abstract doctoral topic; this was real, tangible, and yes, our work did have a big impact on people's lives. Even in those first days, I came home with a sense of achievement and fulfillment. Within a few short weeks I realized that I had found my calling, my own place in the world.

Susan Read was working in production and she remembers my first months on the job.

"When he was just trying it out to see if he liked the business, Richard had a small office downstairs and there he mapped out our whole production process. Step by step. What went where and how each step interacted with every other. That way he could visualize the entire process, absorb it, and make it stick in his mind. He did it on big sheets of rough paper pinned to the wall. It showed the whole process flow. Later, he would do something like this on a computer. From the get-go Richard was a statistical analysis person. That was clearly one of his strong points. And those big sheets of paper on the wall were his very first spreadsheet. Literally."

Now comes the best part. By this time, Mom and Dad were living in a large, lovely home a few steps away from Canandaigua Lake. My plan was to find a house and live in Rochester – I could have a better social life there than in Canandaigua, with its 10,000 people. But as an interim step I moved back in with Mom and Dad. It was a very agreeable arrangement and it led to an amazing experience. I'd come home at night, after a long day at work, and after dinner Dad and I would sit down in the den, a big, open room looking out onto the water. Then we'd start.

"So, Richard, what did you experience today?"

Dad wasn't asking me for a report on the health of our wine lab or whether our people there were working as well they should. He was finding out what I had learned, what I had gleaned and digested during the day. Then he would probe a little deeper with a question or two. The same patient Socratic method that he had used to teach me algebra in middle school he was now using to teach me about the wine business and the inner workings of our company.

Let me describe a typical session. Let's say I was working with Bert Silk in winemaking and I had learned that, by law, you can add up to 35 percent water and sugar to the grape juice, to increase the alcohol content and reduce the acid. I'd tell Dad that and then he would come back to me with a question: "If you had one tank, Richard, of juice at 1.1 grams of acid per liter, and you had another tank of juice at .5 grams of acid per liter, how would you ameliorate those two tanks of juice?"

As usual with Dad, there was a trick buried in the question. You see, in the ATF regulations it doesn't tell you that you can blend juice. It simply says "you can add sugar and water to increase the resulting alcohol and decrease the acid of the resulting product up to 35 percent of the resultant product provided you do not reduce the acid below .5 grams per liter." That's the rule. It says nothing about blending whole tanks of juice. Through his question, Dad was finding out – without asking me directly – if I had figured that out or if someone had taught me that you are allowed to blend tanks of juice. Dad knew how to elicit valuable information. At business meetings or meeting with our suppliers he did that by talking little and by asking very intelligent questions. As Dad was showing me, in business information is power, information is competitive edge.

Dad would then go on to the next lesson: understanding money. Once he had seen that I understood how to blend wines in the amelioration process, he would pose another question: "Let's say, Richard, that you didn't know you could blend tanks of juice. What would you have lost, money-wise, by ameliorating those tanks separately? And let's say each tank

I'd come home at night, after a long day at work, and after dinner Dad and I would sit down in the den, a big, open room looking out onto the water. Then we'd start.

RICHARD SANDS

Once in business, Richard made a startling discovery: far more than in academia he could now help people lead better lives and fulfill their dreams.

produces 8,000 gallons of juice..." Now my first task would be to recognize that to do that calculation I needed more information. So I'd ask him what price we had paid for the grapes in that tank. Then he'd come right back at me: "Okay, let's say we pay $200 for a ton of grapes and $75 for the added sugar to make wine. How many gallons of wine, Richard, do we get from each ton of grapes and what does each gallon cost?"

Assuming that I had been answering correctly or that I had learned where I had gone wrong, Dad would then take the lesson one level deeper. "Now, Richard, let's say that grapes are pretty cheap. On the average they cost $200. This year, though, there are extra grapes on the market and you can buy them for $175 a ton. You're going to have to make and store the wine for two years before you can use it, and you're pretty sure grapes are going to cost $200 a ton next year and $200 a ton the year after. Do you buy those available grapes at $175 a ton, make the wine, and then use it two years later – given that we have the tank capacity to do it and that the quality of the wine won't be affected?"

So now I know the cost of sugar, I know how much water and sugar I can add, and I can make the wine in my mind. My answer is that it seems cheaper to grab those grapes at $175 a ton. But it's another trick question. I failed to include the cost of money for holding the wine for those two years. The cost of money was not even in my concept. So Dad would explain to me that to buy those grapes and make them into wine, I would have to pay $175 for the grapes, plus another $75 for the sugar to be added and $50 for the overhead to crush and ferment the grapes into wine, for a total of $300 per ton. But if I'm borrowing that $300 from the bank for two years, I'm paying interest on that for the same two years. If, say, I'm paying 10 percent annual interest, that's $30.00 per year. Compounded over two years, the total cost of those grapes and interest would be close to $240 a ton. So step by step, Dad has shown me the answer: buying those grapes at $175 per ton would actually be more expensive than buying grapes, over two years, at $200 a ton. If we had bought those 5,000 tons of extra grapes we would have lost a full $200,000 dollars of value!

I loved learning this way. It was theoretical algebra come to life, with real-life consequences and opportunity. And this was far more appealing to me – and far more useful – than anything I had learned in psychology, statistics, or mathematical modeling. Moreover, Dad made everything clear and simple to understand. As the weeks and months wore on, we had these mentoring sessions every single night. I loved it and I know he did too. Still, I don't think Dad ever thought to himself, "I'm grooming Richard. I'm giving him the foundation to make a hundred-million or even a billion-dollar acquisition." I think Dad was just excited to share his knowledge and expertise with me and he was thrilled to see how much I enjoyed taking it all in. If this drew me tighter into the business, fine. But if I had told him that I was going to move to New York City and become a woodworker or a sculptor – two passions that I would cultivate later – I'm sure that I would have had his blessing to do so.

As time went on, I worked in every area of production: wine-making, bottling, shipping, warehousing, even the unit that processed the records we had to provide to government authorities. As I expanded my reach, Dad started teaching me marketing, sales, and finance, always via his Socratic method. "Richard, let's say I'm talking to Bob Huntington, our V.P. of marketing and sales, and a distributor has told Bob, 'Hey, look, I'll take two months' worth of Wild Irish Rose this month – if you give me a $.25 per-case discount.' Now, Richard, 25 cents sounds like very little, doesn't it? Wild Irish Rose was selling for $15.00 a case, so $.25 doesn't sound like any big deal. But over the course of one month he's going to take 20,000 cases instead of 10,000. But then next month he's going to take zero cases. So there's no change in the total size of his order, just the timing. So, Richard, my question to you is this: Is that a good deal for us? Should we grab it?"

Again, this is about understanding the power and complexity of money. Then, through more questioning, Dad would guide me to the answer: "Okay, Richard, all we're really doing is selling 10,000 cases worth of money one month early. And we're collecting $150,000 one month earlier. Now let's say interest is running at 12 percent per year. That's 1 percent a month. Now what is 1 percent of $150,000? Right: it's $1,500. So, yes, we are going to gain $1,500 by getting the money earlier. But wait: we are giving him a $.25 break on 20,000 cases. That comes to $5,000. So in reality we just lost a net $3,500! And the distributor just made an additional $3,500." From there, Dad would explain to me how we manage distributors and try to create for them the financial incentives that will encourage them to sell more of our products.

Through this process of mentoring, Dad made clear to me that to make money in the wine business you had to master the underlying financial algebra in every aspect of your business. You are dealing with constantly changing variables. So at any given moment you have to take into account every component of your costs. The cost of grapes, the cost of sugar for amelioration, the cost of shipping, the cost of fixed assets and storage, the cost of sales, the activities of the competition, and the cost of money. It's a complex equation and you can't look at any individual cost in isolation. Once you've mastered that, and once you've clearly calculated all of your costs, you can evaluate your pricing, your profit margins, and how much you can spend on advertising and the like to give your distributors greater incentives to sell your products. In other words, mastering the complete algebra is the only way to optimize your profits.

This was an extremely important lesson. And through it Dad showed me that the main reason why so many wine companies run into trouble is that their leaders have never really understood money and they have not mastered the underlying algebra of the business. That is a very significant truth about our business. And it is one that Dad used to his advantage – and so have Rob and I. When we began our expansive phase of mergers and acquisitions, we discovered that by doing our own in-depth financial evaluation of a target company – using sophisticated spreadsheets and computer modeling – we were able to understand the internal algebra of that company better than their own leaders and managers. And we were able to leverage that understanding not just to improve the terms of the deal but also to improve the performance of the acquired company. In Chapter Fourteen, I will show you exactly how that process worked when we acquired The Robert Mondavi Winery.

There was another dimension to Dad's mentoring: Dad began taking me on his business trips to California. To prepare me, on the flight out to California and on the car ride to whatever winery we were visiting first, Dad would give me my tutorial. "In California, Richard, the business is very different. The supply/demand cycle is different. The produc-

Dad showed me that the main reason why so many wine companies run into trouble is that their leaders have never really understood money and they have not mastered the underlying algebra of the business.

RICHARD SANDS

*Richard learned the wine business from the ground up, both in
New York State and in the vineyards of California, above.*

tion process is different. The end products are different. In a California winery, you only have grapes coming in, or products that come from grapes, such as raisins. And what do you have going out? You have wine, you have grape juice concentrate, and you have various forms of distilled alcohol – brandy or high proof. So there's a whole different algebra out here, Richard, and to run our business well, you have to learn it." Then Dad would teach me about proof gallons, about how to calculate Brix, and how to evaluate the cost of every end-product that comes out of a California winery.

On these trips, Bruno Bisceglia was always our most important port of call. As I noted earlier, Bruno was providing us with grape juice concentrate and grape spirits for our production back east, and with him we were developing our own line of table wines. Talking with Bruno was itself an education. He had grown up in the California wine business and he was just as knowledgeable as Dad. I loved watching the two of them discuss costs, plan different ways of doing things, and figure out ways to improve the quality of our products. Both men turned problem-solving into high art.

After seeing Bruno, Dad and I would make the rounds to our other suppliers. We'd wind through the San Joaquin Valley, from Lodi to Bakersfield. At every stop I got to see and study Dad's unique way of meeting with suppliers and negotiating to buy whatever materials we needed. Dad was never a schmoozer or a back-slapper. With our suppliers he was always quiet and respectful – and brilliant at asking the right questions and finding the right benchmarks when it came to supply and price. Everyone gave him slightly different information, so he was constantly processing, looking for ways to do a little better here, a little better there. In our business, Dad showed me, it is not only the devil that is in the details; so are the hidden costs and sources of profit.

Still, the most important value of these trips was that Dad introduced me to the many people who kept the California wine industry healthy and strong. I'm not talking about the Gallos or the corporate bigwigs of Inglenook, Heublein, and the like. I'm talking about the people who were on the ground, growing grapes, producing wines, and supplying them to those big brands – and to us. People like Fred Pirelli-Minetti of Pirelli-Minetti, Jim Lawrence of Giumarra Vineyards, Fred Franzia of Bronco Winery, Joe Borcia of California Products, Ramero Jimenez of Delano Vineyards, Russ Murray of Sunmaid, Bob Setrakian and Jeff O'Neal of California Growers and Golden State Vintners, Morris Katz from Paul Masson, Max Chodas of Papagni Vineyards, and Mike Nurry of Vie-Del down in Fresno County. These men were our California gold. Many of them were long-time suppliers to us, some came to work for us, and some we bought out but continued the working relationship, just as we did with Bruno.

During this period, I gained many insights into Dad's particular leadership model, and I could see that it had both strengths and weaknesses. I call his model "the hub and spoke." Dad was the hub of the wheel and his different departments functioned as the spokes. Through meetings and individual mentoring, Dad tried to teach the managers in each of the spokes what they needed to know to run their programs effectively. He also tried to keep them informed of what was going on in other departments and in the industry at large, so they could see the larger picture.

In the end, though, it was only Dad who had mastered the financial algebra. It was only Dad who knew the inner workings of every single department, only Dad who maintained close relationships with all of our department heads and with our biggest suppliers and distributors. So when it came to making a decision that drew together several different spokes, Dad was alone at the hub, and he alone could make the right decision. That leadership model was fine – up to a point. But I kept asking myself a very troubling question: what would happen if Dad got sick or was run off the road? What then? Who could step in and make the right calls?

As Fate would have it, that is exactly what happened next.

CHAPTER 11

Trial By Fire

When Marvin suddenly fell ill, Richard had to take the reins.

The diagnosis was colon cancer.

The year was 1981. Dad was 57 years old. We were all in shock, of course. Our first concern was that Dad's life was on the line. He had always been strong and robust, the unshakeable pillar of our family, and it was very hard for us to suddenly see him struck by disease, and at such a young age too. Losing him was downright unthinkable. At another level, though, we were also worried about the future of the Canandaigua Wine Company. At that stage, the company had been in our family for 35 years, and Dad had run it every step of the way. What was going to happen now?

Mom remembers that moment well. "Richard was still living at home and he had mastered his roles in production and learned about all the other parts of the business," she recalls. "When Marvin went into the hospital, he didn't know what was going to happen. So he put Richard in charge. Rob, then, was still in college."

Mom makes it sound so simple: "put Richard in charge." For me it was a little more traumatic than that. Yes, I had a Ph.D. in social psychology, and yes, Dad had been patiently mentoring me in every aspect of the business. Still, I was only 30 years old, I had less then two years' experience in business, and I had not spent a single day in the leader's chair. In my mind, I remained at the bottom of a very steep learning curve. Nonetheless, two weeks before he was scheduled to go in for surgery, Dad sat me down. "Richard, you're ready," he said. "You know everything there is to know about production, both here and in California. And I have given you the fundamentals of finance, marketing, and sales. All I have to do now is bring you up to date on our current activities in those areas. All of the V.P.s know you well and have respect for you. All you have to do is help them help themselves – and each other. You will be the leader while I am gone."

As a final preparation, Dad and I spent the next two weeks going over everything from accounting matters to current marketing and sales issues regarding our distributors. We worked almost 24 hours a day, right up to the day of his surgery. During this period, Dad retained the title of President and CEO. I had no title. But it didn't matter; I had Dad's blessing and the full support of his team.

At first, I assumed that I would be in charge only temporarily, until Dad recovered and came back to work. But it did not turn out that way. The cancer was serious and Dad was out of action, in the hospital and then at home, for more than six months. When he felt better, Dad chose not to reassume many of his prior responsibilities. In part, that was because he saw I was doing a pretty good job of running the company. And in part it was because, having survived cancer, Dad wanted to focus his time and energy elsewhere, mainly in spending more time with Mickey and working with the F.F. Thompson Hospital. When he was healthy again, he resumed his work as chairman of the Thompson board, a job that he would hold and cherish for the next 17 years.

When I stepped into Dad's shoes, we were a robust, growing, multi-faceted organization with 368 employees, and in terms of gallons produced we were the eighth largest producer of domestic wine in the United States. That year, 1981, we produced 9.2 million gallons of wine, about two-thirds of it dessert wines. But most of it was still Richard's Wild Irish Rose and we definitely needed another winning product to grow our business. The market was changing too. By then the migration of the American consumer from dessert wines to table wines and fine wines was accelerating, and competition in those arenas was fierce and growing. So I knew we would have to move strongly into those areas if we were to grow and prosper. But those were concerns for the distant future; I had much more immediate problems to solve, beginning with the pile of papers on my father's desk.

When I first saw that pile, I felt totally overwhelmed. I went through every piece of paper, but I didn't know what to file away and what to keep close to hand. So, like Dad, I just kept everything in one big pile on the desk. I couldn't process the information in my pile as quickly as he could and I was afraid of filing away anything that I might soon need. So my pile wound up being two or three times as big as his. Still, when people would come in or call, needing a decision, I was amazed to find that I did have the necessary information in my head or I could find it in somewhere in my pile. So, I thought, this is the first task of being the boss: managing all the stacks of paper on your desk and trying to keep all the essential matters neatly filed inside your head. Dad had made it look so easy; now I realized how gifted he was.

Still, I was lucky; I had a fabulous shepherd to guide me: Nancy Hadsell. Nancy was my father's assistant and an extraordinary asset. Nancy knew everything, including the status of every contract in the company. If we had a contract, say, with a supplier of the high-proof alcohol we used to fortify our wines, Nancy knew when the shipment was supposed to arrive – and whom to call if it didn't. Without Nancy, I never would have survived. That's not modesty talking; that's the plain truth. In my very first days, I was surprised to discover how many basic chores there were that Dad chose to do himself, rather than delegate. For instance, he did all the sourcing and ordering of that high-proof alcohol. It would have been easy for him to give that task to Bert Silk, but Dad always did it himself. Similarly, he personally managed all the banking relationships; those weren't handed off to the CFO the way they typically would be in a big company with multiple departments. With our advertising agency, too, Dad managed the core relationship. We had a strong marketing department, with good people. But if we were developing a new ad campaign, Dad would be at every meeting, to give input and keep the process on track.

Now I'm not suggesting that Marvin was a micro-manager. It was more complicated than that. In the case of our marketing managers, they were relatively new to the company; they hadn't been with us for 20 years like Bert Silk and others. So while Dad did empower his people, in certain key realms he stayed hands-on, in part to mentor the newcomers and show them how we do things and why. When it came to our sales team, Dad had an even more compelling reason to keep vital information to himself: to protect our trade secrets. With sales people who hadn't been with us for an extended period of time, Dad was especially cautious. He was concerned that they might quit and join our competitors, taking our trade secrets and future plans with them – a common occurrence in some corners of the wine business. Also, when they're out on the road, sales people from different companies frequently talk among themselves and to distributors, and Dad was afraid they might let slip some of our secrets. So when it came to his sales force, Dad adhered to the old Navy caution: "Loose lips sink ships."

Dad had made it look so easy; now I realized how gifted he was.

RICHARD SANDS

Ned Cooper, above, provided Richard with a lesson that would be key to the later growth of Constellation Brands: how to carry out a smooth, successful acquisition.

Then, too, there were the inherent rigidities and limits of Dad's "hub and spoke" leadership model. In Dad's operation, for instance, Bert Silk was in charge of East Coast production, and Bruno Bisceglia ran California production. Dad wanted clear boundaries between them, with only himself in the middle. So instead of letting Bert negotiate the different contracts we had with Bruno, Dad kept that function to himself. This system of management and the isolated silos it created later became a serious challenge for me. As our company grew and became much more complex, I simply didn't have the time to be so personally involved in every aspect of daily management. I can see, though, why Dad had maintained that model. It suited both his personality and the needs of the company at the time.

When I first sat down in Dad's chair, I didn't understand any of this, and at first I found the daily load of paperwork and decision-making a little intimidating. Still, in those first weeks and months I did learn how to handle it, and soon I was coming home at the end of the day with a satisfying feeling of accomplishment. Also, I was single at that time, so I could work from 8:00 in the morning until 10:00 or 11:00 at night, learning what I needed to know with nothing else impinging on my time.

While Dad was recovering, I developed a very good working relationship with Bruno Bisceglia. By this time, Bruno had launched a new stream of business: selling grape juice concentrate to big food and beverage producers like Welch's and Seneca Foods. Bruno saw a big market for blending California red grape juice concentrate into Concord grape juice concentrate, and he was already having some initial success. Concord juice was far more expensive than California juice and it was very foxy and fruity. So Concord producers like Welch's had started blending the two. Bruno and I talked a lot about this new business and how we could accelerate its growth. We agreed that I would start calling on potential customers both with him and on my own. The plan clicked: soon we became the largest supplier of grape juice concentrate to the food industry, selling about 10 million gallons a year – a niche leadership and profit center that continued throughout the 1980s. Even after Dad returned to work, he let me run the concentrate business; it was my baby.

During this same period, a wine company called Robin Fils ran into trouble. Robin Fils was a well-established New York State winery located in Batavia, New York, about 50 miles west of us, and it produced an array of very good sparkling and other wines. Dad and I had a great deal of respect for Ned Cooper, who was in charge of their production side. Ned was an able and very creative wine producer, and very cost-efficient too. But Ned had a problem: his sister's family owned the business and they were running their sales and marketing out of New York City. As a result, they were much too far away from their source of production and they were out of touch with their customers. From their expensive headquarters in the city, all those folks did was waste money and drive the business into the ground. In sum, like so many other wine companies – small and large – they had failed to control key aspects of their costs and they had failed to master the financial side of the business. The result was both brutal and sadly predictable: their creditors ran out of patience and forced them to discontinue their operations. The day it happened remains seared in Ned Cooper's memory: "One day the people who controlled the money called me, with no notice whatsoever, and said 'We can't operate any longer. Shut the doors – immediately. In the middle of the day!'"

Ned's first reaction was shock and anger. His second reaction was to pick up the phone and call Marvin Sands. "Marvin and I knew each other well," Ned recalls. "I used to buy concentrate from Marvin. He was one of the best businessmen I had ever known. I said to Marvin, 'I can make this into a very fine business, if you can buy it from the bank. I can make you at least $400,000 a year.'"

Dad called me right away. He told me about Ned's predicament and said it might be a good opportunity for us. At this stage, though, Dad was still recovering, and he was not well enough to manage a full-fledged pursuit or a thorough process of due diligence. So he sent me to meet with Ned the very next day. Now at this stage I knew next to nothing about how to put together an acquisition; I was once again at the bottom of a very steep learning curve. Still, I liked what I heard from Ned and I came back to my father with a very upbeat assessment. "I think we have an opportunity here," I told Dad. "We really should buy Robin Fils."

Dad, ever the mentor, then laid out a clear path for me to follow. "Yes," he said, "Ned is a great producer. And I'm sure we can straighten out their money and sales problems. Call George Bresler. Since it's a bankruptcy situation, there will be special issues that we need to be protected from. But I agree, Richard: go work it out." Then Dad laid down the three essential questions you have to answer in evaluating any potential acquisition: "See what you can buy the business for, what you think you can do with it, and how much money we can make."

As a next step, I took a hard look at Ned's operation. Robin Fils was doing $1 million in sales a year, and Ned was doing an admirable job of keeping production costs down. Ned didn't buy and crush his grapes. He bought juice from companies likes ours and concentrate from people out in California, and he made his wines and bottled them at the plant in Batavia. Ned was producing champagne, sparkling wines, fortified wines, and table wines, all of them from New York State. Robin Fils had a good brand in Capri Champagne and also a good private label business, selling wine to distributors and direct retailers. So the company had a very flexible manufacturing platform. Then I started to crunch the numbers. Dad and I calculated that if we could buy Robin Fils for $800,000, we could then take over the sales and marketing, clean it up, and indeed turn a profit of a few hundred thousand dollars a year – a very good return on our investment. George Bresler and I then met in New York with the lawyers and bankers of Robin Fils, and we worked out the terms. Ned Cooper was impressed: "Amazingly, in two days they had wrapped up the deal," Ned recalls. "We were back in business in three or four weeks."

Ned was also surprised by what happened next. I sent Bert Silk over to meet with Ned and see how we could best work together on the production side; finding the right synergies and making them work is one key to a successful acquisition. We also changed the name from Robin Fils to the Batavia Wine Company, but beyond that we let Ned run his own show. "They left me alone to do what I thought needed to be done," Ned recalls. "It was very difficult, but we built the business back up and even the first year was profitable. Slowly

Then Dad laid down the three essential questions you have to answer in evaluating any potential acquisition: See what you can buy the business for, what you think you can do with it, and how much money we can make.

RICHARD SANDS

From our positive experience with Batavia, I could see that mergers and acquisitions would be an important part of our future.

RICAHRD SANDS

we built up to $1 million in profits a year and by the time I retired, in 2003, we were making $8 million a year, before taxes."

Ned is exactly right. In line with Dad's preferred model, we kept Batavia as a separate entity and gave Ned the authority and resources to run it, including sales and marketing. When Ned retired, we integrated Batavia into our Widmer operation. We continued to sell their private labels and many original Batavia Wine Cellar brands. By any measure, Batavia proved to be a fine acquisition and an excellent addition to our portfolio. It also proved to be an important learning experience for me.

Thanks to what I had learned from Dad and from doing the Batavia deal, I now had a good template for doing a successful acquisition: Keep an eye out for struggling companies, do a rigorous study of their strengths, problems, and potential synergies, evaluate what we can do to fix them, then very carefully evaluate the purchase price and what kind of return and profit we can expect to make in the years ahead. In a merger or acquisition, we always start from a position of mutual respect. Then, once we've made the deal, we feel it's best to keep the acquired company intact, along with the best of its product lines and its managers and staff. We also try to keep intact the special spirit and corporate culture that built the company and made it successful in the first place. That's key. Like the wines and other products they produce, each company in the wine industry is unique; we never try to impose some standardized management model on the companies we acquire – or on the kind of wines they produce. Instead, we try to join forces as effectively as possible, sharing our expertise in sales, marketing, and distribution, and at the same time we put a stronger financial platform underneath their operations. This gives them the time and leeway they need to solve their problems, upgrade their products, and increase their profitability. There are some acquisitions that we did differently, but our experience with Ned Cooper and Batavia was typical of how we like to work, and you will see this same pattern repeated in many of our future acquisitions.

By this time, Dad and I were really running the company together and we were working in total harmony. By mutual agreement, we had decided that he would be the lead figure in certain areas – such as political and community affairs – but in other areas I was the lead person. In his realms, Dad never made a decision without me by his side and he would always say to me, "Richard, what do you want to do here?" Over the next few years, we worked side by side. By his words and deeds, though, Dad made it clear to everyone that I was now the person in charge and that I was the one who would be building the future of the company.

From our positive experience with Batavia, I could see that mergers and acquisitions would be an important part of that future, and in 1984 we added two new elements to our acquisitions toolkit: computers and spreadsheets. That year we were weighing the pros and cons of doing a leveraged buy-out of our own company, and I hired the accounting firm Arthur Anderson to make a detailed model of our business. I wanted to project, from the bottom up, our future earnings, brand by brand, and our future cash flows, balance sheet item by balance sheet item. The goal was to see if it would be better to buy our company back with a significant amount of additional debt, or would it be better to continue as a public company.

To help us answer that, the Anderson team brought in the first semi-laptop computers: big boxes made by Compaq with a keyboard that folded out. In the ensuing weeks and months, we spent huge amounts of time working on those computers, analyzing every aspect of our balance sheets and our profit-and-loss statements. This was when I first learned how to use spreadsheets to do detailed business analysis. From that moment on, I never returned to the old 13-column accounting paper; it became a relic of the past. Next, drawing on my own specialized computer expertise from graduate school, I created my own sophisticated computer models for evaluating a company's assets and performance. In the years ahead, those models would provide us with a wealth of valuable information and a real competitive advantage whenever we planned and executed an acquisition. In the end, those models helped us make the decision to remain a public company.

In the early 1980s, we also branched out in other ways. To extend the reach and popularity of Richard's Wild Irish Rose, we started advertising nationally with NFL football. Every Sunday Richard's took the field – at least in our ads. One of our ads featured a 40-member, all-female marching band – beautiful women strutting across the gridiron. That was a big hit with NFL fans, bringing us national recognition and a little up-market cachet. During this period, we also developed our J. Roget Champagne, a popularly priced brand that we had launched in 1979. Soon it became the second-largest selling champagne in America, after Gallo's André. J. Roget rapidly outgrew its home at the Hammondsport Champagne Company, so we added additional production capacity at our plant in Canandaigua. We also developed our Bisceglia brand, in an effort to compete with Almaden, Inglenook, Paul Masson, and Gallo in California table wines.

The results were strong. Our sales were growing at 15 to 20 percent a year and our profits grew in 1983 to $7 million, thanks to the growth of our brands and an exceptional California harvest. Our stock price quintupled in two years. In fact, the stock was so strong that Dad, George, and I realized that we needed to sell some more of the family stock. We just had too many eggs in one basket. So we did a public offering of shares – this was my first public offering and a real learning experience. We also went onto the American Exchange from the Nasdaq in advance of the offering, to have a better market. At that time, the Nasdaq exchange was not well developed, especially for consumer-package companies like ours. The AMEX was a real step up. Now I really began to understand what it meant to be a public company and, more importantly, how transparency and honesty were key to the security regulations and also key to running a public company. I also learned that it is essential to keep your shareholders properly informed. Dad, George, and our investment bankers at the time made it clear that we needed better investor communications. I took over this area and Dad left it up to me to make sure that we maximized our value and stayed within the reporting regulations at all times.

Then came Sun Country. This was an idea that Dad suggested but I brought to fruition. I want to discuss our Sun Country experience in some detail because it proved to be both a learning experience and a turning point for our company, one that helped define the future path of Constellation Brands.

A whiz at math, Richard brought something new to our business: computers and sophisticated spreadsheets.

The heck with buying the California operation; let's create our own wine cooler.

RICHARD SANDS

In 1981 a California start-up venture called California Cooler came out with a new creation, a zesty, lightly carbonated blend of wine and fruit juice called a "wine cooler." At first, this looked to be nothing more than a gimmick, but the coolers sold extremely well and many industry analysts felt it could become "beer for chicks," a market of enormous potential. Dad thought this was a big opportunity and I agreed. So in 1983 he and I went west to meet the folks at California Cooler and see if they might be interested in joining forces, via a merger or an acquisition. We told them we could put substantial cash in their pocket and thus minimize their risk should there be a slowdown in the cooler market. We also explained that with our strong sales, marketing, and distribution teams, we could really boost their sales and profits. The California group showed some interest in cashing out, but they wanted a huge amount of money, over $100 million.

On the flight home, Dad and I came to the same conclusion: The heck with buying the California operation; let's create our own wine cooler. We agreed that I would take charge of this new venture, from start to finish, and we set ourselves a very difficult challenge: create a new product from scratch and be ready to launch it nationally within six months. We gave ourselves a firm deadline for a national launch: May 1st, 1984. This was a colossal endeavor, one that would require all of our expertise and creativity, but the cooler market was getting hotter by the day, and we wanted our share.

And so it began. Back in Canandaigua I brought the team together – from production, marketing, and sales – and we worked out a game plan, complete with a detailed budget, benchmarks, and deadlines. We selected a manager for each aspect of the endeavor: Bert Silk was in charge of creating the taste and its supporting formulas. He was to duplicate the cloudy citrus formulation of California Cooler and, as always, keep costs as low as possible. Scott Rankin was in charge of installing new carbonation equipment and high-speed bottling lines. Howard Jacobson was brand manager, overseeing all the advertising and marketing, right down to the design of the labels and packaging. Then we got to work. Getting everything done was an enormous undertaking, but somehow by May we were ready for launch. We had even put the finishing touches on a national TV campaign to introduce to the world the Canandaigua Wine Company's new "Sun Country Cooler."

Well, be careful what you wish for. At the outset, we figured we'd probably sell one million cases over the first full year. Instead, we sold one million cases over the first summer! By the end of 1985 we had sold 5 million cases of Sun Country and we had become the No. 2 wine cooler in the entire country – almost overnight! The wine cooler market was growing at an explosive 30 or 40 percent a year – and our brand was growing just as fast. It was clear that a whole new category had emerged; there were 37 cooler brands in the market and Gallo was coming in with Bartles & Jaymes. Coolers had become a national phenomenon, and with Sun Country we truly had a tiger by the tail. To keep up with this explosion, we expanded our bottling capacity with new lines in Canandaigua. We also put wine cooler bottling lines in at Tenner Brothers in South Carolina, and we had to contract with outside bottlers as well. On the sales and marketing side, it was clear we were now in a merchandising war, so we recruited and put into place a 100-person merchandising force. Their job was to work the big chain stores, making sure we had huge displays and that our product was properly and prominently presented.

Wine coolers were a warm-weather, refreshment-type beverage, and in terms of demographics it skewed heavily female and young. With all that in mind, we really geared up for the summer of 1986. We were ready and able to produce 15 million cases, if sales continued to soar. We were also prepared to spend big dollars on national TV advertising. By this time, Seagram's had come into the cooler market and was spending millions on TV ads featuring Bruce Willis. Gallo, too, was supporting Bartles & Jaymes with a very costly ad campaign. We felt we had no choice but to follow suit and spend at a very high level.

By this stage we had left the Hutchins agency and were working with a New York City advertising firm named Towne, Silverstein & Rotter. For many years they had been doing our campaigns for Wild Irish Rose and J. Roget. For Sun Country, the Towne group now created a campaign that featured a delightful set of polar bears. During the spots, the bears would do something fun, and at the end one of the bear's heads would come off and viewers would see a prominent celebrity. The ads were a big hit and the polar bear became the mascot of our Sun Country coolers.

For three decades, Richard's Wild Irish Rose was the primary locomotive of our business. Then came Sun Country Coolers.

We had a great time innovating and pushing sales in 1986, and we succeeded beyond our wildest expectations: over the course of just two years Sun Country had become a $100 million brand. Our total sales jumped from $75 million to $175 million and we generated record profits of close to $11 million. The size of our staff jumped as well. On the wings of Sun Country, we were rocketing upward, and for the first time in our history we had a second engine powering our climb. The total sales of Sun Country were even surpassing those of Richard's Wild Irish Rose.

Now the press began to crow. "Sun Country Coolers Light Fire At Canandaigua Wine," read one headline in a Syracuse paper. "Hot for Coolers" was a headline from Detroit. I was elated of course. My early days of feeling overwhelmed were now long past; we had built Sun Country from the ground up and made into a roaring success.

At the peak of this activity, the financial community became very interested in our company, both in terms of our growth and as a financial investment. Wall Street knew we were a well-run company and our stock price was very healthy. So Dad and I sat down with George Bresler to plan our next move. We were well aware that the cooler phenomenon might not last, and we were determined to mitigate our risks should the bubble burst – and we were just as determined to capitalize on the Sun Country brand and its category if they continued their meteoric rise. To prepare for either movement, we began looking at various securities that combined debt and equity, and soon we zeroed in on a financial mechanism called a "subordinated convertible debenture."

These debentures are versatile tools. They are sold in a public offering and are essentially low-interest loans that can be later converted to stock at a significant premium to the current market price. At that time, many other companies were using subordinated convertible debentures as a way to mitigate risk. For us, the pros and cons of a public offering were very clear. If Sun Country continued to boom, three or four years down the road it might look as though we had sold equity cheap and diluted our ownership in the process. On the other hand, if the boom fizzled, we would have in hand a substantial pool of cash that would help

Sun Country became a galloping success and soon we were spending upwards of $30 million a year on glamorous advertising campaigns featuring cuddly polar bears and Beatle icon Ringo Starr.

us weather the downturn. With Sun Country being a $100 million brand, we set the bar at $60 million, then raised that same amount via subordinated convertible debentures. We felt that was a very comfortable level of protection. With that sum in hand, we felt prepared for any eventuality.

The success of Sun Country was an important milestone in the evolution of our company. It proved to Dad, to the wine industry, and to Wall Street that I could take charge of the Canandaigua Wine Company and lead it into a new era of growth and prosperity. Accordingly, in 1986 I was elected President and Chief Operating Officer. I was 35 years old. Dad kept his titles of Chairman and CEO, but in reality I was running the business. There was another dimension here as well: in 1986 Dad suffered a serious heart attack. Eventually he did bounce back, but then he had even less energy for the stresses of running a business. Instead, he focused more attention on the Thompson Hospital and his other outside activities. He made the transition beautifully and enhanced his standing as a highly respected figure in our local business and philanthropic communities. In 1982, our Chamber of Commerce gave Marvin its "Mr. Canandaigua" award. In 1984 he was named to the board of the Rochester Philharmonic. In 1987 the CPA's in Rochester named him "Outstanding Business Citizen" of the year. By the close of the 1980s, Dad had become a trusted ambassador for our company and the entire Rochester business community.

Simultaneous with the rise of Sun Country and before our public offering we started discussions to buy the Manischewitz wine brand, which was owned by Monarch of New York. We started talking in early 1986 and were very close to a deal when a competitor came in, unexpectedly, with a higher offer. We backed off and that proved to be a convenient move: The deal had to be dead for us to complete our offering of subordinated convertible debentures. As we expected, the rival deal for Manischewitz fell apart and the brand owners came back to see if we would do the deal that we had agreed to earlier. Our answer was yes. With the money we had from the offering, we closed the Manischewitz deal for $20 million, giving us one of the nation's best-known and most broadly distributed brands. Also in 1986 we purchased the historic Widmer's Wine Cellars, in nearby Naples, New York. Widmer's featured a number of good regional brands, such as Lake Niagara and Naples Valley, but it had another asset that we desperately wanted: excess production capacity. When we closed the Manischewitz deal, we promptly moved its production to the Widmer facility. That enabled us to smoothly integrate the Manischewitz operation and then focus on building its business. This was a different kind of acquisition for us; it was a full integration. Manischewitz became our fourth national brand, along with Sun Country, Wild Irish Rose, and J. Roget Champagne.

Just as we were closing the Manischewitz deal, we started talking to Heublein about selling us their wine interests, including the big Inglenook brand. Heublein wanted to focus its energy on its core strength, it spirits brands such as Smirnoff Vodka. Our talks progressed very fast and we were very close. At this stage, Rob had just finished law school and he was helping us negotiate with Heublein's lawyers. In fact, he and I were in a smoky conference room in Manhattan working feverishly to sew up the deal, knowing full well that millions of dollars were at stake. "It was classic negotiating all night long," Rob recalls. "Everybody was churning through documents and we got right down to the point where we were going to sign the deal. We did not have the financing for the transaction completely committed, and when we got down to the final blows, we had to tell them that the deal was going to have to be contingent upon us completing the financing."

We finally agreed on a purchase price, but Heublein's lawyers demanded a $10 million good faith non-refundable deposit as proof that we could raise over $100 million to buy the brand. We could afford it: we had $40 million left from the offering of convertible debentures. But I was nervous about putting up that kind of money. So we put in a call to Dad. He gave us the green light, but just as we were preparing to sign the agreement, I got the call: the deal was off. Heublein had been bought out by R.J. Reynolds, and their CEO Ross Johnson decided he liked the wine business and wanted to keep Inglenook. Despite the disappointing outcome, the experience provided Rob and me with marvelous hands-on experience in negotiating an acquisition. Handling their demand for a $10 million non-refundable deposit also provided us with a valuable lesson in how to weigh risk against opportunity. Through this and other ventures, we were also learning that in the wine business a failed deal can sometimes resurface; the Inglenook deal would come back to us a decade later.

Meanwhile, Sun Country continued its phenomenal roll. In 1986, we sold well over five million cases in the United States, and we started selling Sun Country around the world, in markets such as the United Kingdom, Canada, Japan, and Hong Kong. By this time, though, our brand had slipped to No. 3, behind Gallo's Bartles & Jaymes, whose down-home TV commercials had proved to be very effective. Still, coolers were continuing to grow at 30 to 40 percent a year and we wanted to build our market share. The advertising war would heat up again in the spring of 1987, and we would have to spend big on national advertising. But we had no choice; we had to spend to keep pace and improve our market position.

Now, though, coolers were changing. Our first wine coolers were a cloudy liquid, but then Gallo and Seagram's brought forth clear formulations and we felt obliged to follow suit. So for the summer of 1987 our big introduction was Sun Country Classic, a crystal clear cooler. We signed on Ringo Starr for over a million dollars to promote them; who better than a Beatle, we figured, to appeal to young women? We continued to add to the line, using different packages such as one-liter and two-liter bottles, something no one else had, and for Sun Country Classic we created big 20-gallon balls that functioned like kegs. We were ready for combat.

Then the bubble burst. Just as fast as it had risen, the wine cooler craze fell back to Earth – and we bounced down with it. We had spent a lot of time and some $30 million in advertising gearing up for big summer sales in 1987, but our sales proved to be disappointing. When we closed out our fiscal year on August 31st, 1987, our net sales had slipped from $175 million to $171.3 million. The plain truth is that our huge advertising expenditure did not produce the growth necessary to offset the expense. Worse, the company posted a net loss of $9.7 million for the year, down from a plus $10.6 million in fiscal 1986. It was our very first loss as a public company and it was definitely not the way I wanted to complete

Then the bubble burst...

my first full year at the helm.

Then our problems multiplied. When sales of Sun Country and other coolers declined, the retailers concluded that the cooler category would never live up to their earlier expectations. So in 1988 they pulled back on everything: the amount of shelf space devoted to wine coolers, the amount of space in the chiller, the promotional dollars, and the number of flavors and brands they were willing to feature. Since we were the No. 3 cooler, we were the first to be hit. Worse, anticipating that the cooler market would grow by 20 percent, we had increased our advertising spending by upwards of $20 million. But the market actually shrank by 10 percent, and all that advertising didn't generate a single dollar in extra sales. Our main cooler line was badly hit, and our Sun Country Classic line was proving to be a complete bust. It simply never got off the ground, Ringo or no Ringo.

The situation was serious. We were in a merchandising war and we were losing a lot of money. For me, every day was loaded with stress, and visiting our distributors was downright hellish. I and our sales force had to do a lot of pushing and negotiating to get them to put any resources behind our brand. Working with our suppliers was no picnic either. We had to be strong and resilient in a very competitive environment, and we were competing for every nickel and dime from our suppliers. Almost every meeting produced a knock-down, drag-out fight. The worst for me was the potential impact on our people. By then we had a payroll of 650 people – men and women with spouses and children. If Sun Country continued to fail, what would happen to them? That was always one of my greatest worries.

At one stage, when we couldn't stop the bleeding, I called my team together to assess the damage and discuss what we should do next. I told them, "This is not a good situation. We've got to cut back expenses because we can't go another year and have these types of losses." From there we all agreed that no matter how much we decided to spend on Sun Country, given the current market dynamics we were not likely to succeed. So then I put a few crucial questions on the table:

How do we develop a strategy to, in essence, milk whatever potential Sun Country has left and then let it decline? How do we let it die a natural death but build our business while it is declining? In other words, how can we maintain our sales at $170 million until the day comes that Sun Country is no longer a relevant piece of our business?

Those questions generated a lot of debate and creative input. Then we made some very tough decisions. The first was to put into place a series of crisis measures. We let go of our 100-person merchandising group. We pared down our general and administrative costs. We cut spending on advertising and promotion for Sun Country to minimal support levels. We scrutinized our production organizations to see where we could combine and cut costs. These measures, while necessary, provoked a hammering from the press. "Canandaigua Wine dismisses 130 due to slump," was the headline in Rochester's Democrat and Chronicle in November of 1988. "Sales of Sun Country coolers fall, causing losses; 20 percent of workers affected."

At that same meeting, we developed a plan to rebuild our sales – without relying on Sun Country to do any better. The plan was based on a three-pronged strategy: (1) Pursue organic growth of existing brands, meaning J. Roget, Wild Irish Rose, and Manischewitz.

(2) Boost new product development, building on what we learned in creating Sun Country and building it into a national brand. (3) Pursue more acquisitions. The Batavia deal had been small, only $800,000, but Manischewitz was a substantial buy. With it, we had proved to ourselves that we could pull off a major acquisition, integrate the company's staff and activities, and also take over its sales and marketing – all without missing a beat. So we decided to look for more companies to buy. And we also targeted something new: imported brands. We decided to look for hot imports to pursue, with the goal of securing the rights to import and distribute them in the United States.

Over the next four years, we aggressively implemented that three-pronged strategy. In 1988, we acquired Cisco, a strong, mildly effervescent flavored wine offered in gold, peach, red, and orange flavors. Also in 1988, as Zinfandel was gaining popularity with American consumers, we acquired a Brazilian-made White Zinfandel called Marcus James. We purchased important regional brands such as Chateau Luzerne and Tiger Rose. Then in 1990, we bought two well-known brands from California: Italian Swiss Colony dessert wines and Jacques Bonet sparkling wines. For new products, at Widmer we added a Sparkling Raspberry and a Sparkling Peach to its non-alcoholic lineup. We also came out with a flavored dessert wine line, Cool Breeze, and we created a product called "Perfect Mixer," featuring one percent alcohol so it could be sold in New York State liquor stores. One of our biggest new ventures was our own line of juice-added products for kids called "Flintstones Fruit Fizz." To expand our existing lines of J. Roget, we added spumante, almond, and orange-flavored champagnes, and we brought out new styles and flavors in Richard's Wild Irish Rose and added onto our Manischewitz Cream line. We were using our newly learned skills at using flavors to concoct new products for all of our lines. We also greatly increased our California concentrate business, coming out with deeper and more vibrant red concentrates for the food and juice industry and adding a white concentrate for the soft drink business; Pepsi used it in making Slice. Ned Cooper at our Batavia wine cellars continued to steadily grow his business, thanks in part to his new-found resources and responsibilities.

In terms of imports, we began an expansive period as well. In 1988, we took over the import agency of Mateus, a popular slightly sparking rosé made in Portugal, and Keller Geister, a very appealing white wine from the Rhine region of Germany.

We also continued our cost cutting, especially in production. We bought out our last franchise bottler, Consolidated in Chicago. We bought our own high-proof distillery, California Products, to control the production of high-proof from raisins, and we retooled our production methods to save pennies per gallon. This was really going back to the basic algebra of our business. The collapse of Sun Country had pushed us into a period of innovation and excitement as we applied everything that we had learned to date to dig out from the crisis.

These various moves achieved the desired result. From 1987 to 1991, Sun Country Cooler sales dropped by $80 million, but we still had $170 million in sales and by 1989 we were back in the black. By 1991, we were ready for another major acquisition. We still had money in the bank from our earlier $60 million offering in subordinated convertible debentures and we had recovered enough profitability to encourage the banks to lend us

"Sales of Sun Country coolers fall, causing losses; 20% of workers affected."

A HEADLINE IN THE ROCHESTER DEMOCRAT AND CHRONICLE

Many family companies run into trouble when it comes time to pass the reins from one generation to another. Here again, Marvin's wisdom came to the fore.

the money we needed to make our biggest acquisition yet: Guild Wineries and Distilleries of California, the seventh largest wine producer in the country. We closed the deal for just under $70 million.

Guild was an important addition to our company. It had deep roots in the California wine industry, and its leading brands included Cribari, Dunnewood, and Cook's Champagne. At that stage, André was still the top-selling champagne, but Cook's was No. 2, ahead of our J. Roget. Together with Guild's other sparkling wines, Cook's and J. Roget made us the No. 2 producer of sparkling wines in America, with a full 25 percent share of the market. Even with the decline of Sun Country, bringing Guild onboard boosted our total sales to nearly $250 million a year. At this critical juncture, the wisdom and strategic value of the $60 million that we raised via subordinated convertible debentures came into full view. That money gave us the cushion we needed to endure the decline of Sun Country, and it also enabled us to continue to invest in our brand and grow bigger through important acquisitions like Manischewitz and Guild.

Looking back now, I see Sun Country as a very valuable experience, despite its precipitous decline. It forced us to adapt and recalibrate our strategy. Without Sun Country, we never would have become as aggressive or as skilled at making new acquisitions. We emerged from the Sun Country crisis with a great deal of confidence. We were savvy, we were nimble, and now we were battle-tested. We had a deep and secure sense that we could absorb the inevitable shocks that come from investing in faddish products like wine coolers and then bounce back in a new and very expansive way. Even today, many of us who experienced "the cooler wars" refer to the important lessons we learned. One is that flavor proliferation is very dangerous to brand equity. At a certain point, the consumer can become more interested in the next hot flavor rather than in the brand itself. That lesson, too, is now burned into our DNA. In the vodka market today, for instance, we are determined to stick with vodkas with a strong base, like SVEDKA, instead of going in for new flavors and package sizes. The final proof of our resilience came in 1993: we let Sun Country Wine Coolers die quietly – and we barely felt the loss.

This was a period of larger losses and transitions as well. In 1986, Grandpa Mack passed on, exactly fifty years after he had started his original Car-Cal Winery. Three years later in Petersburg, Virginia, we closed down Richard's Wine Cellars, Grandpa Mack's second creation. It was truly the end of an era, bringing to a close both a colorful life and our family's first half-century in American wine.

When we look back now, Rob and I know how fortunate we were. With intelligence, bravery, and decades of work, through good times and bad, Grandpa Mack and Dad built a strong and durable foundation for our family business, and they did far more than that. By word and example, they shared with Rob and me their experience and their hard-earned wisdom about wine, business, and life itself. Then Dad did something more, something for which we will be eternally grateful.

As we all know, in a family business the process of succession can be a very difficult, even painful experience. Some families and businesses have been literally torn apart by the difficulties inherent in passing the baton from one generation to the next. In our case, though,

Dad made sure that the transition was as smooth and graceful as possible. After Rob came aboard in 1986, as our chief legal counsel, he and Dad and I would have lunch together in the office almost every day. We talked business, we talked family, we talked cars and golf and airplanes, and in this way Dad quietly continued his guidance and mentoring, always in a very subtle and self-effacing way, always behind us, never out front. In this way, Dad empowered us and gave us our wings. If we needed him, he was there. If asked, he would give us his advice and counsel. But he never interfered, he never second-guessed, and he never undermined our authority. And once he turned over the reins to us, he did so with no regrets. The teacher and mentor had finished his long and patient labor; it was now up to his students to prove that the best was yet to come.

CALIFORNIA

An outdoor ceramic at The Robert Mondavi Winery, Oakville, Ca.

Previous spread, A view from the prized To Kalon Vineyard at Robert Mondavi Winery.

Above, The barrel cellar at Opus One.

Opposite, A tasting and dining room at Franciscan Estates.

Above, Artwork at the Robert Mondavi Winery.
Opposite, The harvest, California-style.

Above, Stainless steel storage tanks at Blackstone Winery, Kenwood, Ca.
Opposite, California vines in September.
Following spread, The dramatic architecture of Opus One.

Old vine grapes at the Robert Mondavi Winery.

Above, A finishing touch at the Robert Mondavi Winery.
Opposite, Staircase at Opus One.

Above, The Simi Winery, Healdsburg, Ca.
Opposite, The storied entrance to The Robert Mondavi Winery.
Following spread: The new To Kalon wine-making facility at Robert Mondavi.

CHAPTER 12

New Energy, New Directions

In the 1980s, we saw the first buds of America's "Gourmet Revolution." Chefs like Julia Child and California's Alice Waters, above, were helping elevate American Taste in terms of both food and wine. We knew we had to adjust and move up-market.

Now Rob stepped to the fore.

When he first came aboard in 1986, Rob was 28 years old, and he brought to the company not only his legal training and experience but also a particular interest in the art of the acquisition. "At the law firm I was in the area of real estate, and I was making a decision at that time about moving into corporate," Rob explains. "But there were a lot of things happening in the wine company – we were considering making some larger acquisitions – and it seemed like an exciting time to leave the law firm and move into the family business and work with my brother and father. I wanted to have a hand in the acquisition strategy, as well as some of the other aspects of the day-to-day business that were extremely interesting."

Rob was just what we needed. He settled in as our chief legal counsel and rapidly became my right arm in running the company. By the time we planned and executed the acquisition of California's Guild Wineries in 1991, Rob was already shouldering major responsibilities – and he was ready for more.

By this time, we were no small peanut. We had about 100 different wine labels in our portfolio and, with the addition of Guild, we were the third largest producer of domestic wine in the United States. In our eyes, though, we still had a long way to go. Our total production represented only 8 percent of the U.S. market, while Gallo, the heavyweight champ, weighed in with a full 31 percent share. In other words, they were about four times bigger than us. So Rob and I knew that if we wanted to become a market leader, we still had a lot of work to do.

We could also see that the American wine market was in a period of tumult and profound transformation. During the 1980s we had witnessed the rise in popularity – and sales volume – of White Zinfandel; the rise and fall of wine coolers; and in the latter part of the 1980s we had seen the start of something new: a surge in the popularity of what were called "fighting varietals." These were inexpensive, cork-finished wines that were generally made from a single varietal and marketed that way, with the first focus being on the "noble" varietals: Chardonnay, Cabernet Sauvignon, and Merlot. This was an important development. More and more Americans were starting to enjoy wine, and many of them were young, well-traveled, and relatively affluent. The fighting varietals gave them an opportunity to drink good wine regularly and affordably. One company that led the way was Glen Ellen Winery, in Sonoma, California. Glen Ellen had been started in 1982 by Bruno Benziger, a New York transplant with long experience as a wine and spirits importer. Bruno knew his trade. In his first year, Glen Ellen produced 6,450 cases of wine. By 1987, riding the varietal wave, Glen Ellen was producing up to 1.5 million cases a year, and soon they would double that. The category was hot. In other parts of California and beyond, other wineries were scrambling to get in on the action.

"If you've noticed your friends serving a higher grade of white wine this summer – join the party," Fortune Magazine reported in 1988. "America's taste in wine, never especially elevated, is ratcheting up."

Fortune had it right: American wine drinkers were moving up market. They were buying more wine, learning more about it, and drinking better wines when dining at home, in restaurants and bistros, and even the corner tavern. We could see the impact right on our bottom line. At the start of the 1990s, in the category of dessert wines – which Mack and Marvin had made the foundation of our company – sales were continuing to shrink across the industry. Richard's Wild Irish Rose, our lead dessert wine and for four decades our most reliable sales engine, was not immune; in 1991 sales of Richard's slipped 11.4 percent from the year before. A large part of that drop we attributed to the imposition of a higher federal excise tax, but part was also due to the market's continuing shift away from dessert wines. Other sectors were also affected. Semi-generic wines, many of them sold in jugs as Burgundy and Chablis, were also in decline. That hurt several big American brands, including Almaden, Taylor, and Paul Masson. Most analysts believed that trend would continue or even accelerate.

"Inexpensive jug wines, made from lesser-quality grape varieties and blends, have always been the broad foundation of the U.S. wine industry," Fortune reported. "Now that market is shrinking." Fortune predicted that a major shakeout was coming in the industry and suggested that even the heavyweight champ might come in for a beating: "Perhaps the greatest challenge faces E.& J. Gallo Winery, which became America's largest vintner mainly by selling jug wines and may now be a victim of its own success. Gallo's low-priced varietals show only sluggish growth."

Faced with these seismic shifts, Rob and I knew we had some readjusting to do, and right in front of us we could see an entire landscape filled with both risks and opportunities. Then in the fall of 1991, another important event rocked our industry. The date will long be etched in the history of American wine: Sunday, November 17th, 1991. That night, with over 21 million people tuning in, CBS's highly respected news show "60 Minutes" aired a segment touting the health benefits of drinking red wine in moderation. The segment brought to the fore a phenomenon called "The French Paradox." How is it, CBS's Morley Safer asked, that the French can regularly consume enormous quantities of fatty cheeses, foie gras, and rich, cholesterol-laden sauces and still have an exceptionally low rate of heart disease, a rate much lower than ours? How can that be? Responding to his own question, Safer then lifted a glass of red wine and said the answer "may lie in this inviting glass."

The impact of Safer's report was both stunning and profound. He cited a wealth of studies and scientific data supporting the benefits of drinking red wine in moderation, and the very next day bottles of red wine started flying off of retailers' shelves. During the next four weeks, supermarket sales of red wine in the United States jumped by a full 44 percent! What a turnaround that was. Throughout the 1980s, sales of red wine in America had actually declined by 4.5 percent. Overnight, that trend reversed itself. In 1992, sales of red wine climbed by an astonishing 39 percent. And in terms of demographics, guess who was leading the way? Older, affluent consumers. Baby boomers. Men and women with education and money to spend – in other words, the makings of a powerful cultural and consumer vanguard.

What we were witnessing actually went far beyond wine: we were witnessing the surfacing of a striking, and in many ways historic, evolution in American Taste. Food and nutrition were moving to the center of the American stage. With baby boomers out front, Americans were discovering – and demanding – better food, made from better ingredients, and cooked

When Morley Safer, above, of CBS 60 Minutes, did a report on the health benefits of drinking wine in moderation, sales of red wine immediately soared. Our industry was entering a whole new era.

"To keep pace with the rapidly evolving market, Rob and I launched an aggressive new strategy of acquisitions and capital funding."

RICHARD SANDS

in healthier, more flavorful ways. This new trend was already flourishing in New York City, Chicago, and northern California. In the San Francisco Bay Area, for instance, chefs like Alice Waters and Cindy Pawlcyn had long been creating meals that featured fresh, seasonal fruits and vegetables – and they were supporting local growers who were farming in healthier ways. On her popular cooking show on PBS, Julia Child was showing chefs and homemakers the virtues of cooking in the French style – and how to enjoy good wines along with their food. Starting in the late 1970s, the Robert Mondavi Winery regularly brought in the leading chefs of France and America to teach the art of cooking and how to pair fine food and wines. In both Napa and New York, the Culinary Institute of America was enrolling legions of budding young chefs eager to learn a higher standard of cooking and new ideas about nutrition. By 1991, these seeds were starting to blossom and spread their pollen across the country. Soon many prominent writers began churning out articles and books about America's budding "Gourmet Revolution."

At Canandaigua Wine, we had to respond; we had to adapt.

We all knew that acquisitions would have to be one prong of our strategy. This required, first, some internal changes. I was still running the wine business, but Rob and I felt that we needed stronger corporate leadership in other areas, starting with financial public relations. This was an area that was essential if we wanted to maximize the value of our company and move forward more effectively with further acquisitions. We realized that while we could borrow money from the banks to make more acquisitions, as we had done with Guild, we would not be able to expand through more acquisitions until we had paid that money back. So we developed a new strategy: use our balance sheet and earnings power to borrow money to make an acquisition, explain the benefits to the investment community through a more muscular financial public relations strategy, and then when the value was recognized in the stock price, we could sell some company stock to pay down debt and expand our war chest. In February of 1992, we did just that. We went to the public market for $32 million to repay our bank debt.

So that I could focus on acquisitions, we decided to integrate the wine business under the sole direction of Guild's Chris Kalabokes. I remained the President of the larger company. Rob remained general counsel for both corporate activities and the wine business itself, which demanded increasing legal supervision. We then created a team that was a powerful blend of Guild and Canandaigua Wine executives. From Canandaigua, Howard Jacobson, became the V.P. of Sales and Marketing; Ray Bumpus was appointed V.P. National Sales Manager of the East; Paul Hetterich was appointed as V.P. of Marketing; Bert Silk became V.P. of Production, East and West Coast; and Lloyd Rockwell was named V.P. of East Coast production. From the Guild side, Chris Kalabokes led the way as President, with Doug Kahle becoming V.P. National Sales Manager of the West, and Mark Gabrielli becoming V.P. of West Coast production.

With that team in place, plus the new financial strategy, we were ready to execute an intensified acquisition strategy. Rob was thrilled; this was one main reason why he had chosen to leave his law practice at Harter, Secrest & Emery in the first place. By this time, Rob and I were working together as a very effective team. In this regard, I would say we were very lucky. Two smart, headstrong brothers working in the same high-pressure environment is not always a formula for peace and harmony. And our temperaments and personal styles are by no means the same. By nature, I tend to be exuberant and ebullient, and if I don't watch myself, I can push too hard and become bullish, impatient, and at times overbearing. Quick to anger? Yes, sometimes that too. Does all that sound familiar? "Richard has a temperament that is a lot closer to my grandfather than it is to my father," Rob says. "Richard has many of those same intensities. He has also been known to yell at people. Not in the same way that my grandfather did, but he does have a temper."

Rob is just as demanding and focused as I am, but he manages to keep his opinions and emotions more tightly tucked in. That's his basic temperament and I think his disciplined training in law made him all the more prudent and self-controlled. Whenever I get a little too exuberant, he has a way of reining me in. Like any fine lawyer, too, he is also extremely careful about confidentiality; he tends to keep his thoughts and plans close to his vest. Now who does that sound like?

"Mack wore everything on his sleeve," Rob explains. "He was an open book. You could always tell what Mack was thinking because Mack could never contain himself. My father was the complete opposite. Now I would say that I'm much more like my father or like my mother than like my grandfather. I'm really a combination of both my parents. Mickey, you know, loves to eat and to dine and to shop and to decorate – and I love all of those things in the same way that she does. With regard to my father, I'm probably not as good with people as he was. He had a way with people that very few people have. I'm not suave or smooth the way he was, and I don't have that same capacity to influence people. But I am very even-tempered, just the way he was. And like Marvin, too, I've gotten very involved with some of our local hospitals."

Our temperaments and styles are somewhat different, but throughout the late 80s and well into the 90s, Rob and I did almost everything together. We worked together, had lunch together, played golf together, and we and our families went on vacations together, usually skiing somewhere or to Florida where Mom and Dad had a second house and spent a lot of time during the winters. The result was a very close personal and working relationship, and while we had different realms of responsibility inside the company, Rob and I were very much aligned when it came to our core values and to our vision and strategies for the future.

In our approach to business, Rob and I also shared one fundamental quality that made us both exact opposites of Grandpa Mack: we never gambled. We never took unnecessary risks. We don't even like playing cards. Our game of choice, to be frank, is growing the business. We love it, we live it, we breathe it, and at that particular high-stakes table we can be daring and bold. We play to win. Even so, Rob and I never feel as though we are gambling. Even when we have had to make fast decisions, we always did exhaustive preparation and we always moved forward in a careful, deliberate way, always mindful of Dad's admonition that risk can quickly turn into ruin. Rob has it exactly right:

"We're not gamblers. I am definitely not a gambler. I don't even play bridge. Instead, I believe in the power of compounding. Someone has said 'Wealth is created through con-

"Rob and I were very much aligned when it came to our core values and to our vision and strategies for the future."

RICHARD SANDS

"We never risk the entire business on anything we do. You don't want to cross the street with your eyes closed."

ROB SANDS

centration and it is preserved through diversification.' I think that's right. I believe in concentration. I believe in diversification. Management is the key, good management. Given the preparation that we do, plus all the experience that we have, what we do really isn't gambling at all. What we have been all about over the years is increasing shareholder value, and that demands understanding the risks we are taking and making sure that those risks are always within an acceptable range. We never risk the entire business on anything we do. You don't want to cross the street with your eyes closed."

On those bedrock principles, Rob and I were determined to press forward with more acquisitions. We were especially interested in California wine acquisitions and, if we were lucky, finding the right way to make that difficult move up-market into the fine wine business. We had no illusions that it would be easy – fine wines are a very different business and the industry had us firmly type-cast at the lower end of the market. But with the evolution in American taste, varietals and fine wines were rapidly becoming the most dynamic and exciting part of the wine market, and we were eager to gain a bigger share. At that stage, we had no plans to move into beer or spirits; our sole focus was wine. But then something unexpected happened, an opportunity surfaced that was not in our original vision or strategy, but one that still looked extraordinarily promising – if we had the guts and the agility to grab it.

One day, at one of our Investor Relations get-togethers in Chicago, I was approached by a mergers and acquisitions investment banker. He asked me if I knew anything about a Chicago-based company named Barton Inc. Of course I did, but I just listened. The banker suggested that we take a look at doing something with Barton as it seemed to him that they were following the same strategy in imported beer and spirits as we were in wine. Little did we know what he really had in mind.

In truth, Barton had been on our radar screen for some time. Back when we had bought Manischewitz, Barton had bought Monarch's beer business, giving them the importation of China's popular Tsingtao beer. Barton, we knew, featured a very interesting and well-diversified portfolio of both spirits and beer. In spirits, its brands included Kentucky Gentleman, Ten High Bourbon, Northern Light Canadian Whiskey, Highland Mist Scotch, Montezuma Tequila, and Monte Alban Mezcal. In beer, Barton held the import rights to a rainbow of international brands: Germany's St. Pauli Girl, China's Tsingtao, Britain's Double Diamond, and, most important, Modelo's Corona Extra, at that time the No. 2 imported beer in the U.S. market. Those were very attractive assets, and while we had no plans to go outside the wine business, this struck Rob and me as a rare opportunity. So we agreed to meet the Barton team, in the company of the same investment banker in Chicago.

Going into the meeting, our ambitions were quite restrained. The plan was that Barton would tell us about their business and we would tell them about ours. Then we would see if there was anything that we could do in combination; no one came to the table with a fixed idea in mind. Many acquisition discussions start this way, and only in time do you find out what the real agenda is, since no one wants to openly admit they are for sale. So it was in this case. As the meeting unfolded, we learned that Barton was doing well and growing. But we also saw that it had gone through a couple of difficult years in the late 80s and early 90s when sales of Corona had actually declined for a period. That was it. We left the meeting wondering what Ellis Goodman, the CEO and owner of the business, really had on his mind.

Ultimately, the investment banker let us know that Ellis was thinking of selling Barton, but only under very special circumstances. He and his management team wanted to continue running the business but with no outside interference. Of course, Ellis also wanted to be paid a good price for the business he had built. We were definitely intrigued by the idea, and we had the same banker arrange more time for us to sit down and talk with Ellis. We needed to clearly see what his parameters were and we wanted to let him know that we were very flexible in the way that we approached these matters. To be specific, we wanted to tell Ellis that it was our custom to leave businesses independent, especially when their field of expertise was different from ours. Rob and I started thinking that this could be a great marriage. We could continue our expansion in the wine business and Barton, under Ellis's leadership, could continue its expansion in the beer and spirits business.

deserted island

Success in business is often a matter of seizing opportunity. That was certainly true for us when it came to Barton and Corona Beer.

We met in Chicago many times and we found Ellis to be a personable and capable manager and also very knowledgeable about his sectors of the beverage industry, both here and in the United Kingdom. He had a background as both an accountant and a financial planner and he had come to Chicago with the British firm that originally owned Barton. He had then purchased the company in a leveraged buyout. "Ellis told us that even though Barton was doing well," Rob recalls, "all of his personal assets were tied up in it and he felt this was the time to consider selling the business. We discussed the fit and how the two companies would operate. We were about $250 million in sales in 1993 and they were about $250 million in sales. So it was an opportunity to immediately double the size of the company. For us it was an opportunity to diversify into spirits and into imported beers."

So Rob and I decided to move forward with the deal. Despite its complexities, we were able to work everything out in only two months; we wrapped up the deal in June of 1993. I managed the financial and the relationship-building side and Rob handled the legal side. And we had skilled teams in place to work out the details and manage all of the follow-through. Everything clicked. We also built into the deal sizeable incentives for Ellis and his management team. Their success, after all, would be our success.

"Barton was not a synergy deal; it was an entirely new platform," Rob says. "Barton was being very well-managed and Ellis wanted independence. We were comfortable with that. It was actually an advantage, because it left us free to continue our pursuit of wine acquisitions. As part of the deal, we agreed to pay Ellis a consideration up front and then more as an earn-out over time, contingent on their achieving a number of performance targets, including the renewal of the importation rights to Corona. That was key to the economics of the entire deal. We also agreed to give Ellis's team sufficient independence to meet those targets and secure the earn-out. They continued to run the company very independently for a number of years and they exceeded those targets every year." Specifically, we paid the group $65.5 million in cash, plus one million shares worth $17 million and another $57.3 million over the next three years.

"Suddenly, Canandaigua Wine ranks as nation's No. 2 vintner."

A HEADLINE IN BUFFALO, NEW YORK

Once we had the basics of the deal put together, the Barton management team, led by Andy Berk, spent two months with our corporate acquisition team, reviewing operations, import contracts, and formulating the earn-out. In the process, we found that Ellis Goodman had put together a very strong team, with Andy Berk as President and Bill Hackett leading the beer business. Under Bill's management, and with the added resources we brought to Barton, we were able to build Corona into the No. 1 imported beer in the United States. At the same time, Ed Golden, in charge of spirits, proved to be a strong leader, improving the performance of Barton's spirits portfolio year after year.

In financial terms, Barton proved to be an exceptionally good buy. "We actually underestimated the return on that investment," Rob says. "From that point forward, the company grew at an astounding rate, primarily as a result of Corona. Today that company would be worth billions of dollars. Billions of dollars. And we bought it on the premise that it would grow at a modest rate."

In terms of the history of Constellation Brands, Barton was a landmark move. It was the largest acquisition we had ever done and it doubled the size of our business. It led us to diversify into beer and spirits and it helped us gain the financial strength, confidence, and credibility to pursue other opportunities in the beverage alcohol industry. "Some companies evolve from good to great with a slow, gradual momentum that builds over time," Rob says. "In many respects that has been true with us. Marvin built the foundation in a slow, methodic, very painstaking way. But there are two pivotal things in our history that really stand out. The first was when we created Sun Country Wine Cooler. That more than doubled our size and built us into a rising force in American wine. The second pivotal thing we did was acquire Barton. That one acquisition alone financed and enabled us to do many of the things that we were able to do after that."

In fact, as we were bringing the Barton deal to a close, a major opportunity in wine came back into our laps. Toward the end of the 1980s, the Seagram group, the spirits powerhouse headquartered in New York, had expressed an interest in selling its wine division. We were interested in buying. Seagram's portfolio included several brands of long distinction both in New York State and the history of American wine: Taylor, Taylor California Cellars, Paul Masson, Great Western Champagne, and Gold Seal. The meat and potatoes of the Seagram business was semi-generic wines, and even though the margins were thin and fighting varietals were gaining strength, we saw this as a good opportunity. So we examined a potential acquisition.

As usual, we went through our rigorous process of due diligence, evaluating their finances and looking for potential synergies and ways to improve the performance of their brands. In the end, we did make an offer, but our bid was really being used by Seagram to help establish the level for a management buyout. From there the Seagram wine division was sold to a team of its own managers, led by a man named Paul Schlem. The group was then renamed Vintners International. Schlem and his team did not have an easy time of it. They were struggling under a heavy level of debt and at the same time they were trying to change the nature of their business – move it up-market. That was proving to be a very difficult task. Rob and I, with our management team, kept a close eye on their progress.

"While they made some very good efforts," Rob explains, "and had in fact developed a brand that was very successful and that they saw as the future of the company – a brand called Deer Valley, their fighting varietal – that brand was nevertheless relatively small compared to the rest of their business and not big enough to hang the future of the entire business on." Also, their effort to move up-market had taken some of their focus off their two flagship brands and primary business drivers, Paul Masson and Taylor. "They really struggled," Rob explains. "By 1993, Vintners International was no longer in a position to sustain itself as an independent business. The banks were closing in. We approached Paul and he decided to sell the business – and we bought it."

Our purchase of Vintners International was major business news both locally and nationally. "Suddenly, Canandaigua Wine Ranks As Nation's No. 2 Vintner," was one headline in Buffalo, New York, above a national story from the Associated Press. A leading industry analyst was then quoted as saying of us, "They've gone from minor to major very quickly."

The acquisition was indeed a very significant step in our development. We paid $148.9 million for Vintners International, and we considered that to be money very well spent. At the time, Vintners was the fifth largest wine firm in the country; the acquisition made our Canandaigua Wine Company the second largest wine company in the country, though still a good distance behind Gallo. In this case, we did not follow our usual model and leave the acquired company as an independent entity. We felt we had no choice but to take over the entire operation and integrate it into our own infrastructure. In the process, we raised our market share in the hot varietal category from 7 percent to 11 percent of the U.S. market and we brought into our portfolio Deer Valley and their array of blue-ribbon New York State brands.

The assets that we had most coveted, though, were Taylor California Cellars and Paul Masson, despite their decline. "It wasn't so much that we were enamored of those brands or of those categories," Rob explains. "It was that we had an opportunity to create a tremendous amount of synergies in that division. Essentially, we are able to eliminate their entire organization and basically subsume the sales and marketing, as well as the management of their production organization, under our umbrella. The resulting cost synergies produced a very immediate increase in the profitability of the business, without having to rely on tremendous growth to make the investment a good return. In fact, we planned on some of those brands continuing to decline."

It is impossible to capture in words the hard work that goes into making a major acquisition, especially one like Vintners that took years to bring to fruition. This was truly a team effort. The team that we had organized, headed by Chris Kalabokes, took the financial models that I developed and the legal strategies that Rob had provided and used them as a roadmap. But the journey was far from easy. The process of doing financial and legal diligence, of fine-tuning our models, of negotiating and finally planning the integration – all of that seemed endless, and we felt like we were working 24 hours a day for weeks on end. We would fly back and forth from coast to coast, working feverishly aboard our plane to push the deal forward. We also tried to guard against some interloper messing up the deal. Later,

Our purchase of Vintners International was major business news.

Through Barton, we purchased 12 brands from United Distillers Glenmore, doubling our share of the distilled spirits market in the U.S. A bonus was ownership of this historic blending, bottling, and storage facility in Owensboro, Kentucky, now a state-of-the-art facility.

in the integration phase, we took great pains to make sure that the process of taking on new employees complied with our high standards of respect for our people and our customers.

With the added strength that Barton and Vintners International brought us, we were now positioned to accelerate our growth and our diversification. And we did. The very next year, 1994, we returned to Heublein and negotiated the purchase of its Mission Bell Winery, which brought into our portfolio two prominent American brands, Almaden and Inglenook, the nation's fifth- and sixth-largest selling table wines. That gave us four of the five leading brands in the high-volume end of the California wine market: Almaden, Inglenook, Paul Masson, and Taylor. Gallo remained on top. The Mission Bell acquisition brought us other significant assets. Mission Bell, located in Madera, California, was the world's largest multi-function winery, handling every phase of production and offering us a wealth of synergies on the production side. Mission Bell also had a cluster of smaller brands and a substantial grape juice concentrate business – another good fit for us. The following year we expanded our spirits portfolio. Through Barton, we purchased 12 brands from United Distillers Glenmore, doubling our share of the distilled spirits market in the U.S. to 8 percent. What also came in the deal was a nice bonus: a state-of-the-art blending, bottling, and storage facility in Owensboro, Kentucky.

While it was acquisitions that drove most of our growth, we also had some good success with organic growth and launching new products. One case in point is our Paul Masson Grande Amber Brandy. When we acquired Vintner's International in 1993, its Paul Masson brand family included a small brandy line positioned at the low end of the category. The line was declining in terms of profits. But here some good synergy came into play. Two years before, when we acquired Guild, we gained the services of a gentleman named Elie Skofis. Elie was a master in the art of making brandy. Also, Guild had been making brandy at its Cribari wine facility, so we had the production capacity close to hand. With those elements we set out to create a premium brandy with strong brand equity potential. The result was Paul Masson Grande Amber Brandy, and it has been a strong performer for us. In its first two years, we produced only about 200,000 cases, but in the year 2000 it had surpassed one million cases and it has grown every year since. Today Grande Amber is the 7th largest profit generator of our Centerra Wine Company.

Then there was Arbor Mist, another startling success story. This one flowed from our experience with Sun Country Coolers. In developing our Sun Country line, our winemakers had developed considerable expertise in blending wine and fruit, to achieve fresh, original flavors. Also, with the demise of Sun Country we were left with a lot of excess production capacity at our Canandaigua Winery. What to do? Innovate! Pioneer! We saw how well varietal-designated table wines were selling, led by white Zinfandel, so we wondered if there was some creative way to blend the attributes of the wine cooler category with the attributes of those hot-selling varietal-designated table wines. The result was Arbor Mist, a refreshing wine with a splash of fruit. Some of our flavors convey the feeling: Melon White Zinfandel. Winter Berry Merlot. Peach Chardonnay. Island Fruits Pinot Grigio. Cranberry Twist White Merlot. We launched Arbor Mist in 1998 and it caught on with consumers right away. We sold more than one million cases of Arbor Mist in its very first year. In 2006, we sold just under four million cases, making Arbor Mist the 6th largest profit generator of our Centerra Wine Company. And it was entirely our own creation.

Now, just ticking off all these acquisitions and new product launches doesn't really capture the frenzy or intensity of the 1980s and the early 1990s; the truth is we often felt we were caught in a whirlwind. Starting with our launch of Sun Country Coolers back in 1984, we had been on a decade-plus tear that had transformed us from a relatively small company in Canandaigua into an industry-wide powerhouse. We had become international too. By 1994, we were exporting to 70 different countries. For all of us in Canandaigua, it had been both exhilarating and exhausting. In our buying frenzy, we had spent over $100 million in cash to buy Barton, $150 million to buy Vintners, and $120 million to buy Almaden and Inglenook. Through Chase, which had become our acquisition financing bank, we started to access the Subordinated Debt market. So instead of selling our shares to reduce bank debt, we layered in $130 million of subordinated 10-year notes at a very attractive fixed interest rate of 8.75 percent. This enabled us to go to the syndicated bank market through Chase to make the Almaden and Inglenook acquisitions. But if we were going to make more acquisitions, we had to increase our overall borrowing capacity. So in November of 1994, we sold $96 million of equity to replenish our balance sheet. Of course, our stock price had nearly doubled over the past two years. And with our purchase of Barton's beer and spirits portfolio, analysts could see our great potential for continuing to build the three categories and, more importantly, to generate huge synergies by integrating our new wine assets into our existing portfolio.

Now, though, we had a lot of acquisitions to digest and we ran into trouble with the integration process. To get the best results from our acquisitions of Almaden, Inglenook, and Mission Bell, our team decided to integrate our operations from Guild and Vintners into Mission Bell. This would cost $20 million and was designed to save us $13 million a year in overhead. It was a monumental task, but one that I felt could and should be done within 12 months of the acquisition of Mission Bell. As it turned out, we were able to meet that deadline, but things did not go as well as we had hoped. We moved champagne tanks and bottling lines from Guild in Lodi to Mission Bell, along with still-wine bottling lines from the Vintners facility in Gonzales, California. Everything was supposed to be done by the beginning of the summer and running at full capacity as we entered the crucial pre-holiday selling period in September. For unknown reasons, though, those bottling lines didn't work the same way once they were moved and our production efficiency plummeted. As a result, by the end of August, 1995, we were a full month behind in shipments out of the newly integrated Mission Bell facility. We didn't think it was a disaster until we reported our results: we had missed Wall Street's expectations by a few pennies and our stock price plunged 38 percent.

Then things got worse. Our production efficiency did not improve as quickly as we had hoped and we struggled through the holidays simply to keep our product lines on the shelves throughout the country. In the meantime, Barton disliked closing out the financial year in August because it left the primary selling season for beer to the end of the year – and that meant a lot of unpredictability in their numbers. In many regards, August was not a

With the addition of beer and spirits, we were now becoming a broadly diversified beverage alcohol business.

This entire period was a time of important growth for Rob. What I saw emerging was not just Rob's increasing legal expertise in mergers and acquisitions, but also his increasing operational knowledge of the business. We made a formidable team.

RICHARD SANDS

good year-end for wine either, because you never knew where you would stand with the coming harvest. So we agreed to change our financial year-end to February. But there was a problem here too. We misjudged the impact of our wine LIFO reserves on our earnings and again we disappointed Wall Street, pushing the stock to new lows. Now Rob and I really had our hands full.

With so much to put right, we and our team in Canandaigua stepped back and entered a three-year pause with regard to making new acquisitions. Now we could again see clearly the value of our preferred acquisition model: keep the purchased company intact, respect its spirit and culture, keep the best of its leaders and brands in place, and then give them the independence and the financial and other support they need to be successful. That model – Dad's original model – was working well for us. And there was probably no other way to handle so many acquisitions in such a short period of time. That said, we were a big, diverse company now, and we had to retool our leadership and management models. We sought out various consultants for advice and tried different approaches. I won't pretend that the effort was easy or that we did everything right. We didn't. But I think we all learned a lot and grew in the process.

In fact, this entire period was a time of important growth for Rob. First, he really took charge of the acquisition process, making sure that we always did a thorough due diligence, financially, legally, and operationally. On my side, I would do the financial modeling and turn the results over to the team to verify and then decide how we were going to integrate and maximize the value of the new business, if we were able to buy it. But every step of the way, there were legal considerations, and Rob became, in essence, the quarterback for the entire process, making sure that all of the pieces were being properly handled. I usually led the negotiations, but he and I were constantly reviewing the risks, the opportunities, and the potential returns. What I saw emerging was not just Rob's increasing legal expertise in mergers and acquisitions, but also his increasing operational knowledge of the business. We made a formidable team.

By 1997, we had sorted out many of the problems we had encountered in integrating our wine operations. We had hired a new president of the wine business, Dan Barnett, a Nestlé veteran, to re-engineer our wine business into Accountable Business Units, or ABUs. Dan brought in Bill Newlands to run our table wines business and Bill Encherman to run our specialty business, including champagnes, dessert wines, and new products such as Arbor Mist. Paul Hetterich moved over to run our premium wine business, Riverland Vineyards, and Howard Jacobson became the leader of our customer ABU. We also hired two strong executives to join our corporate management team: Tom Summer as CFO and George Murray as head of human resources. We needed them; we now had a huge and complex organization to manage, with some 2,500 employees. Our marketing and sales force alone was 300 people strong. Our network of wholesalers was now over 1,200 people across the United States.

The entire nature of our business was changing too – and rapidly. Wine was only one part of our portfolio now, and the principal engine of our growth in sales was no longer Richard's Wild Irish Rose or Sun County Coolers. It was Corona Beer. Corona was outstripping all our expectations and holding its position as the No. 1 position in imported beer in the U.S. At the same time, our varietals were moving us steadily up-market in wine. Together, our imported beers and our varietals now accounted for more than 40 percent of our total sales. Just as Fortune had predicted back in 1988, the American wine industry had undergone a profound transformation – and we had transformed ourselves right along with it.

In the year 1998, Rob jumped on another opportunity: Matthew Clark, the U.K. beverage alcohol powerhouse. This was our first international acquisition.

At this stage, we decided it was important to signal that transformation to Wall Street and the investment community. Now that we had Barton and its big beer and spirits portfolio under our umbrella, we wanted to make clear that we were no longer just a wine company; we were a large, diversified beverage company with a portfolio of more than 125 brands and a sales and marketing network that reached out to 70 different countries. Accordingly, on September 1st, 1997, we brought our many different entities under a single umbrella and changed our name from the Canandaigua Wine Company to Canandaigua Brands, Inc. We liked that name, but we felt it still might need a little more tweaking down the road.

What ended our three-year hiatus in acquisitions? "One day I got a call from an investment banker I knew in London," Rob explains. "He said that we really ought to talk with one of the biggest beverage companies in the U.K., Matthew Clark. He had actually talked with us about Matthew Clark a few years before. The company had a fine portfolio of wine, hard cider, and bottled water, and at that earlier stage they had just done a big roll-up in cider. They had purchased several other cider companies and had become the second largest cider company in the United Kingdom. Cider is big business there and their stock price was flying high. They were about a billion dollars in sales and we were about a billion dollars in sales. So the banker suggested we talk to them about a merger-of-equals kind of transaction, with shared ownership. We thought about it and concluded we weren't particularly interested in that kind of relationship. We didn't see that Matthew Clark and its future prospects at that time were worth giving up control, potentially, of our own corporation through a merger of equals."

Now, though, the situation had changed. "They had not been particularly successful in their cider roll-up," Rob explains, "and some of the hot brands they had purchased had gone into decline. The company had come under a lot of criticism for having engaged in a flawed acquisition strategy. The management was coming under great pressure, with a lot of negative press. They did not own or control the corporation and the stock price had dropped dramatically. Our team then took a fresh look at Matthew Clark, to see what we could do. We found that it was still growing and still profitable, and its problems were really due to that failed acquisition strategy. So we decided to make a bid for the company. When we ultimately made our offer, I think the stock price had slipped to something barely over a pound. It made good sense for us to buy it at that price and we thought it would generate a good return on investment."

Matthew Clark was our company's first foreign acquisition and, with a purchase price of $475 million, it was our largest acquisition to date. It immediately made us one of Britain's leading producers of cider, wine, and bottled water, as well as one of the U.K.'s leading

Black Velvet, the Canadian whiskey, was an important addition to our spirits portfolio. So were its legendary ads featuring some of the most beautiful women in the world. And Telly Savalas too!

wholesalers of alcoholic beverages. The acquisition also accomplished far more than that, as Rob explains: "It was a good opportunity for us to establish a new platform outside the United States, which we could use not only to build their existing business but also for us to add onto through subsequent acquisitions. We could also use it as a platform to distribute our U.S. products and, potentially, to distribute some of their products in the U.S. market. That was basically the strategy behind that acquisition."

My brother Rob championed this acquisition and led the way, along with our CFO Tom Summer and George Murray, our head of HR. For six months, they flew back and forth to London, bringing together a U.K. team of lawyers, bankers, and acquisition specialists. Rob built the key relationship with Peter Aikens, the Managing Director of Matthew Clark. Again, we chose to keep Peter and his management team in place and we gave them broad leeway to execute their existing strategy. They felt their strategy was basically sound, but they simply had not had enough time to get it to work. Upon analysis, we agreed with them. Our purchase of Matthew Clark took them out of the spotlight that shines on public companies, and right away that gave them more room for maneuver. As Rob explains, "Peter felt that being part of a broader and larger group – and not being saddled with the expectations of The City, London's equivalent of Wall Street – would free them up to be able to manage the business in the manner they wanted – and be successful in doing it."

Again, the formula worked, and so did our larger business strategy. "Matthew Clark's business is much larger today than it was when we acquired it," Rob says. "It's actually twice the size. And we have been able to do essentially what we set out to do, which is use it as a platform that we could add different things onto. The best example of that came later with our purchase in 2003 of Hardy, the Australian wine giant. Hardy had a very large wine business in the U.K. and that wine business became part of Matthew Clark. Eventually, by a factor of way over two to one, we became the largest wine company in the United Kingdom. In 2006, when we acquired Canada's Vincor, they too, had a large wine business in the U.K. called Western Wines, and that came into our U.K. operation as well."

Now we come to the story of Black Velvet, a true icon in the world of spirits. It is a Canadian whiskey, 80 proof, with a strong, refined, velvety taste. It is also an advertising icon, with the "Black Velvet Lady" for years being featured in striking magazine ads, clad, of course, in elegant black velvet. She was first introduced to the world in 1969, and since then such world renowned models and actresses as Cybill Shepard, Christie Brinkley, Cheryl Tiegs, Kim Alexis, and Kelly Emberg have all been Black Velvet Ladies. Now, how did Black Velvet enter our constellation of brands? Not exactly with one knock on the door…

In 1998, when we were looking to buy additional spirits brands, we had convinced Diageo, which had purchased Heublein's spirits business, to sell us Black Velvet along with Christian Brothers Brandy and some other brands. This made sense to Diageo as they had decided to focus on the premium spirits category, while we were a popular-priced spirits player and these brands would help us move up our portfolio. We negotiated and agreed on a price with very little information at hand. Then, as we proceeded with our due diligence, it became clear that we could not pay the price that Diageo was asking; we needed to shave 10 percent off to make the acquisition work for us. At a meeting in their lawyers' office in

New York, we calmly explained our position. Their side asked for a recess, left the room, and did not return for a very long time. Finally, their head lawyer came back, alone. He said the deal was off and told us to get out of their offices within 30 minutes and leave behind every document, note, or other item connected to the transaction. He was actually quite rude about it, but we did as he asked. Over the next few months, we tried to mend fences with Diageo's management but with little success.

The following March, though, on a Thursday night, I received a call from an investment banker representing Diageo. His message was clear and to the point: "If you will still pay what you said you would pay on your revised offer – and if you can get the deal done in 30 days, with no ifs, ands or buts – you can buy Black Velvet. But there is one further condition: over the weekend you get your team in here to finish the contract and be ready to sign on Monday." My answer was just as clear and to the point: "No problem. We will be there tomorrow morning."

Black Velvet and the other labels would soon be ours for $184 million.

As you can see, the 1990s were a busy and exciting time for us. But Rob and I were also under enormous strain and at times it was very hard on our families, in my case especially. Directing our company and anchoring it throughout this whirlwind of acquisitions and growth was extremely difficult, to say the least. For a time, my marital experience was, shall we say, a little chaotic. Rob managed to keep his life on a more even keel. Nonetheless, his responsibilities at work kept growing. On the strength of his performance with Matthew Clark and other acquisitions, our board named Rob Chief Executive Officer for international operations. He also retained his post as our General Counsel. We all agreed that it was also time for Rob to get direct operating experience and that he should take over as interim President of the Canandaigua Wine Company, which at that time was under-performing. To clear the way, we moved Paul Hetterich and Howard Jacobson to the corporate team and Rob went to work at the wine company. His grooming was now entering a new stage.

One of the early lessons that Dad had taught us was now certainly proving its worth. As Dad had said to me, "Richard, someday you will see that your job as a leader will be about getting the right people in the right places and then giving them the right guidance and incentives." This is exactly what we were doing now. We spent a lot of time and energy getting the right people into the right jobs. By this time, too, we had developed, under the direction of George Murray, extensive annual incentive plans and lucrative long-term incentive plans using stock options for top management. The incentives were working. Our executives were doing well and meeting their targets. Their individual success fueled our collective success. By the end of 1999, our sales had reached over $2 billion and our earnings were over $75 million – what our sales alone were before we launched Sun Country. Also, our stock price had jumped more than fivefold from the period before the Guild acquisition to the end of the decade. We were working hard – and reaping the benefits.

For Mom and Dad, too, the 1990s were a very happy time. Financially secure and with more leisure time than he had ever had before – and no sign of a return of his cancer – Dad was determined to enjoy life to the hilt. He remained the chairman and elder statesman

As Dad had said to me, "Richard, someday you will see that your job as a leader will be about getting the right people in the right places and then giving them the right guidance and incentives."

RICHARD SANDS

As its chairman, Marvin helped build Thompson Health into the premier medical institution of the Finger Lakes region. He also endowed its esteemed cancer center, which bears his name.

of our company, and he and Mom enjoyed traveling together to many wine industry functions. They also did a lot of leisure traveling to Europe and beyond, often with Bert Silk and his wife Barbara. When they weren't traveling, Mom and Dad divided their time between their home on the banks of Canandaigua Lake and their winter home in Miami. They had good friends in Florida, and together they enjoyed golf, bridge, backgammon, and just being together. By this time, Dad had moved on from Lincoln Continentals; he was now driving a Bentley.

Mom was thrilled by their new life together. The many long years when Dad had been totally immersed in building the business had not always been easy on her. "If Marvin had a problem at the office, it was like you didn't exist," Mom recalls. "It was as though he couldn't talk about what was happening. It wasn't like he would come home and say, 'I have this terrible problem that I don't know how to handle and I really need to concentrate on it.' It wasn't like that. It was like a wall came down and shut everything else out." Mom did enjoy the security and material comforts that came with business success, but in those years she often wondered if all of Dad's work was worth the price: "My attitude always was, we have enough, we don't need to grow any more, what do you need to work harder for? What do you need more things for?"

Now, though, Mom saw the fruits of what Marvin had built. Financially, they were totally secure and at ease, and so were their children and so would be their grandchildren. Mom and Dad also had the urge and the resources to give back to their community and improve the lives of other people. They worked hard to develop and promote music and other cultural activities in Canandaigua and in the Rochester area. But when it came to community development and charitable-giving, Dad's first love and commitment was always to the F.F. Thompson Hospital, which is now called Thompson Health. Dad served Thompson's doctors, nurses, and patients for 30 years, first as their president and then as chairman of their board.

"Marvin really started the philanthropic aspect of what we do," Rob explains. "When he was building the business, Marvin was a very generous giver to several charities, but he was by no means one of the biggest givers around. In late 1998, though, he came to see me, as he often did regarding legal matters such as his will. Marvin told me he was contemplating making a gift to the hospital, to help build an advanced center for the treatment of cancer. 'I want to leave them several million dollars when I die,' he told me. So I looked at him and I said, 'Why do you want to leave it to them in your will? Why don't you do it while you're still alive? Wouldn't you get a lot more gratification by doing this now?' He thought about it for a minute and then said, 'You know, Robby, you're 100 percent right!'"

With Rob's help and legal support, Dad put together a multi-million dollar donation for an advanced cancer center. He announced the gift at the hospital's board meeting in March of 1999. By then his own physical condition had changed, and Dad also told the board that he was now suffering from stomach cancer. Linda Janczak, now the CEO of Thompson Health, was in the room. "Great men like Marvin only come around once in a century," she says now. "He was so dedicated to the community and to the economy and the well-being of our entire area. It wasn't just about him or his business. It was also about what he could do for others."

Six months later, on August 28th, 1999, Dad passed away. He was 75. It was the end of a remarkable and fulfilling life and a towering career in business. Starting with little, Dad had not only built a company, he had helped transform the quality and history of American wine. He had also helped build Thompson Health into a strong and thriving medical institution, serving our entire Finger Lakes region. When he died, we gathered together as a family and as a company and issued a statement that tried to express how all of us felt:

"Marvin was a visionary leader for more than fifty years and was the consummate gentleman in everything he did. His dedication to our customers and employees and his devotion to the community set an extraordinary example for everyone who knew him."

The Sands Cancer Center was dedicated the following year, and it is now a cornerstone of Thompson Health, treating thousands of cancer patients every year. Oil portraits of Marvin and our sister Laurie hang in the vestibule.

Even in death, Dad left us a lesson.

PART IV

Leaping to the Top

In California wine, Rob and I and our teams found two new sources of wisdom and inspiration. One was Robert Mondavi…

CHAPTER 13

Moving Into Position

Now we come to Agustin Huneeus.

In the world of wine, in the highest councils of our industry, and on four different continents at least, Agustin Huneeus Sr. enjoys a reputation as a master of the business of wine and also of the arts of viticulture and making fine wine.

As a winemaker, Agustin has been lauded as both a pioneer and an innovator, and he has created a number of fine wines that are deemed to be among the best in the world: Quintessa, Franciscan, Estancia, Magnificat, Mt. Veeder, Veramonte, and more. On the business side, he has run wine companies in his native Chile and also in Argentina, Spain, France, Italy, Germany, and New Zealand. In 1973, he moved to the United States and for a time he ran worldwide operations for the wine division of Seagram. Eventually, he and his wife Valeria, herself an expert in viticulture with a Ph.D. in microbiology, settled in the Napa Valley. In 1985, Agustin took charge of Franciscan Estates, in the heart of the valley, and later he and Valeria created their dream winery, Quintessa, set elegantly into a hillside off the Silverado Trail.

The other was Agustin Huneeus, the director and guiding spirit at Franciscan Estates. Both men helped us understand the essence and spirit of California's fine wine industry.

We first met Agustin in 1993, when we were looking to expand our presence in California wine. Marvin was still helping guide us at the time, and he and I sat down with Agustin and talked with him about his business and the possibility of doing something together. I thoroughly enjoyed meeting Agustin. He is a tall, very charming man, he speaks several languages and, both in his person and in the wines he creates, he has about him an air of Old World elegance and refinement. He struck me as a man of taste and breeding, but there was nothing about him that was showy or pretentious. Agustin is genuine. Real. And he's a very nice man.

I was also impressed by how knowledgeable, I would even say wise, he was regarding the business side of our industry. He knew, down to his fingertips, the stark differences that exist between the high-volume producers and the fine-wine producers. At one end of the spectrum, Agustin knew first-hand the market-share mentality and bottom-line demands of big corporations like Seagram or Heublein and, at the other end, he also knew first-hand the artistic spirit and the perfectionist demands that drive the smaller winery, where the individual winemaker will always be prepared to spend a king's ransom, provided it will improve, even by a nuance, the ultimate quality of what's in the glass. In the wine business, and in fine wines in particular, those two very different mentalities and those two very different sets of demands constantly collide. At their extremes, the artist is oblivious to cost, while the corporation counts nearly every dime. The artist bows only to connoisseurs and the dictates of his own palate; the corporation bows only to Wall Street. In Agustin's eyes, this constant collision is unavoidable. So success in the wine business is always a matter of clarity and balance. As the leader of your company, you have to be crystal clear about your needs and objectives and, especially in a fine-wine company, you have to balance both the artists in your house and the accountants. In our business, one side can never succeed without the other. Agustin understood that, and he helped me gain a deeper understanding of it as well.

As we talked, Agustin expressed an interest in selling Franciscan Estates. We were interested in buying. Dad and I liked what he was doing with his business, and Agustin liked

Agustin felt confident that we would maintain Franciscan's deep connection to its soil and vineyards. But the deal did not immediately come together.

our approach to acquisitions, in particular I think he liked our model of using our sales and marketing strength, but at the same time leaving the acquired company intact and independent, respecting the spirit and culture that had made it successful in the first place. Still, we didn't come to terms. I think that in 1993 Agustin was mainly interested in having us give him a valuation, so he would know what his company was worth. In his ownership of Franciscan, Agustin had partners in Germany, the Eckes family, which owned wineries and distilleries there, and I think his main interest was in either settling or restructuring his financial relationship with them. We understood. Having outsiders like us come in and help you determine the value of your company is something that happens quite often in our business. When you go out, like we do, and seek new acquisitions, oftentimes you end up doing months of work and you gain a wealth of understanding and knowledge, but you don't always end up closing the deal. In this case, we were fine with that. Meeting Agustin had been enriching in and of itself; we were able to learn a lot from him about how the fine-wine business works and how it differs from the high-volume end where we had so long been focused. I came away hoping that one day we could do something together; I knew I had much more to learn from Agustin. I also reminded myself that opportunities in the wine business have a way of resurfacing down the road, especially if you have built a good relationship the first time around.

That is exactly what happened with Agustin.

In 1996, we heard from Michael Tye, Agustin's national sales director, that Agustin might again be interested in selling Franciscan Estates. So again we sat down with Augustin and talked more about his business, how it had progressed, and where it was going. We also met his son, Agustin Francisco, who by now had come into the business. Again, I think that Agustin was impressed with our model and the way we conducted ourselves. He said he felt confident that we could bring our sales and marketing strengths to Franciscan without in any way compromising the deep connection that it had to its soil and vineyards in the heart of the Napa Valley. That connection to soil and vineyard – to what Agustin would call "a sense of place" – is the hallmark of fine wine and its primary attraction to upscale consumers, and we assured Agustin that we would respect it. We would not take the high-volume mentality and the fine wine mentality and try to homogenize them or meld them together. Still, when we priced it all out, our bid again fell short of his desired target. Or maybe he wasn't truly interested in selling yet. I can't say for certain. Either way, we didn't come to terms.

During this period, Agustin was busy building Franciscan's business and adding new parts to it. His portfolio soon included Franciscan, Estancia, Mt. Veeder, different vineyard interests, and their Chilean entity, Veramonte. Also in the Franciscan portfolio were the marketing rights to Quintessa, the small jewel that he and his wife Valeria had created. For me, Quintessa was a perfect illustration of how different the fine-wine business was from the high-volume side. Quintessa sold for about $100 a bottle, and its production, by design, would reach a maximum of only 10,000 cases a year – a level that back on Buffalo Street we could bottle and ship in just a few days.

Because of such dramatic differences in scale – and the business demands behind them

– many people in the industry believed that a company like ours could never operate in harmony with a company like Franciscan. But Agustin and I did not agree with that view, and even when we failed to come to terms a second time, that was not the sticking point; the purchase price was. We both believed that our model of independence and mutual respect would result in a fine working relationship. More than that, we and Agustin both believed that the character and core values that we shared were far stronger and far more important than any differences we had in terms of product line or output.

In 1998, Agustin brought in a new president and CEO: Jean-Michel Valette, a man with a pedigree that was ideally suited for fine wine, especially the international side of the business. Jean-Michel had been born to a French father and a German mother, and he had grown up in France, Germany, and the United States. At Stanford, he had earned a combined B.A. in German literature and economics, plus a Master's in Engineering Economic Systems. Then he did an M.B.A. at Harvard. Before joining Franciscan, Jean-Michel was a managing director of Hambrecht & Quist, the investment bankers, where his specific mandate was to study the wine industry and develop potential mergers and acquisitions. Jean-Michel quickly became an expert in the business of wine. In terms of the art of wine, he also did intensive study and became certified as a Master of Wine, an elite club of some two dozen experts in North America and 250 worldwide. We knew Jean-Michel well, starting from his days at Hambrecht & Quist, when he had been involved in our acquisition of the Guild Winery, our first major purchase in California. When Agustin brought him in as President and CEO of Franciscan, we called Jean-Michel to congratulate him and to remind him that, should Agustin ever again be interested in selling Franciscan, we would again be a very interested buyer. Jean-Michel politely assured us that was not the reason he had been hired, but that yes, should the time come, he would be happy to raise it with Agustin.

In May of 1999 I did receive a call from Jean-Michel. He told me, in essence, "Look, Agustin has received an offer he cannot refuse. The amount is well above his target and his partners, the Eckes family, are ready to liquidate their interest. So Agustin really has to sell the business, in deference to his partners of 20 years." But Jean-Michel also told me there was a tiny glitch in that deal: Agustin had serious concerns about what the prospective buyer would do to Franciscan. To put it bluntly, Agustin did not think the prospective buyer would be the best possible steward for Franciscan Estates and where he wanted to see it go. "Agustin wanted me to call you," Jean-Michel told us, "because he believes that what you would do with the business would be much more in keeping with the heritage of the business and where he sees its true potential." I got the message: Agustin wanted to protect his legacy, the quality of his wines, and the people who had so faithfully worked with him over the years. In sum, he wanted Franciscan and its spirit to remain intact.

That's the good news, Jean-Michel told me. The bad news is that if you want to come to terms, there are two conditions. First, you have to pay $250 million for the business and, second, you must complete the negotiations within one week. When I asked why the rush, he explained that the other party was willing to pay that amount, but they had yet to sign a final contract and, in fact, the other party had gone on vacation for a week. So we had

Agustin and Robert Mondavi helped us understand that in the world of fine wine, aesthetics and gracious living were essential components of image-building and commercial success.

In our company, "from father to son" is an ethos that extends beyond the Sands family. Charlie Hetterich, pictured above, worked for us at Widmer and his son Paul now leads our mergers and acquisitions team.

only a small window of opportunity to step in and seal the deal. Unless Franciscan had a matching offer and a signed accord from us by the end of the following week, they would be obliged to go ahead and sign with the other party. "No problem," I said. "We will be out there tomorrow."

And so it began: our third attempt to buy Franciscan and our third attempt to establish a prominent foothold in the upper echelons of California wine. I have to tell you, I loved the challenge. The stakes for us were high, and having a tight deadline really got the adrenaline pumping. I pulled together several key members of our top management group and told them to get ready. Rob couldn't make the trip. He was deeply involved in all of our acquisitions, but right then he was up to his ears in negotiating the deal for Matthew Clark and running our Canandaigua wine division, during an abrupt change of management there. So our team consisted of Paul Hetterich, who had been running Canandaigua's premium wine group but was now called to help us at corporate headquarters; David Sorce, one of our top corporate lawyers; Jim Locke, a long-term board member and our lead outside attorney; and Mark Gabrielli, who was in charge of grapes and vineyards for us in California. We worked that same night getting everything ready, and the next morning, a Friday, our team took off in our corporate jet. The race was on.

By this stage, Paul Hetterich had emerged as one of our most able, affable, and versatile executives. He knew the wine business inside out and we could turn to him to manage all sorts of complicated issues. Paul came by it quite naturally. His father, Charles Hetterich, had been a successful business executive, working much of his adult life for R.T. French, a Rochester-based consumer products firm best known for its flagship brand, French's mustard. At one point, R.T. French owned the Widmer Winery and Charlie Hetterich ran it for them. He later led a management buyout of Widmer and ran it until 1986, when he sold it to our Canandaigua Wine Company. Like his father, Paul loved the wine business. After college, he went to work for a Gallo distributor, then he joined his dad at Widmer for eight or nine months before we bought it. One afternoon in 1986, Charlie introduced Paul to me, and before long we had both father and son working for us. Charlie managed the integration of the Manischewitz production into our Widmer facility, and for the next ten years he handled many other executive tasks for us. Charlie passed away in 1996. Paul started out with us in marketing and brand management, then he headed up our premium wine group. In that role, he began gaining experience into what later proved to be his true calling: developing mergers and acquisitions. In May of 1999, when my team and I boarded our corporate jet to make our third run at acquiring Franciscan, Paul was onboard as one of my key aides and advisors.

"As soon as we got on the plane," Paul recalls now, "Richard handed each of us a big box filled with documents. Those were documents that the Franciscan team had faxed to us overnight, to help us prepare the groundwork for an eventual bid. Also in the box were instructions from Richard on what each of us, in our different fields of expertise, was to accomplish in the coming days. We knew exactly who had to do what. Then Richard spelled out the challenge: 'Okay,' Richard told us, 'we've only got 72 hours to complete the due diligence, okay?' This was the end of the week and the goal was clear: come Monday morning, we needed to decide among ourselves if we were we up for buying Franciscan and if we were up for buying it at that price of $250 million. That was our goal, our mission for the weekend."

Paul and the others knew how much we needed this deal. By that point, our company had tried to move up-market by developing our own premium table wine brands in California – the hottest section of the market – but we had not achieved the success we wanted. Quite the opposite. "We didn't get into the table wine business until the early 90s," Paul explains. "And we got in at the bottom end, the part that was starting to decline. We tried to buy businesses and build brands in the premium table wine arena, but we couldn't find the right formula. In truth, we had been failing miserably in developing any appreciable premium table wine business. But we thought Franciscan might offer us a better way, which was estate-linked wines and a separate sales and marketing group – without glomming it together with our other business and without a bunch of people on the East Coast driving the decisions. Franciscan was going to be a separate, stand-alone fine wine entity."

Once we landed in California, the operations part of our team went to Franciscan's headquarters in Napa, just north of Rutherford, while Paul and I and our legal and financial experts set up shop in San Francisco in the offices of Franciscan's legal team, Farella, Braun & Martell. There, we began reviewing all the information, putting together our acquisition plan, and doing our financial due diligence. That was not so hard, since we had already done this twice before in examining Franciscan. All we really had to do now was update our figures. But then came the hard part: sitting down with Jeff Newman, the lead lawyer on the Farella team, and working through the terms of the deal and the thorniest issues. "It was all-night negotiating," Paul recalls. "They were drafting contracts and negotiating the details of the deal."

In the end, we were successful. In the space of five days we studied their structure and answered all of the questions that both sides needed to answer. Those included what to do with their Veramonte operation in Chile – there we ended up doing a joint venture where we took 70 percent and Agustin kept 30 percent – and what to do with Quintessa. There Agustin and Valeria kept 100 percent ownership but we became their sales and marketing agent. In terms of the final purchase price, we managed to pay a little more than the other party had offered – a little over $245 million – and we were able to structure a deal that served Agustin better than the other deal did and also served the Eckes' interests better. Our way the Eckes got more cash and had less to pay in taxes. The result met the objectives that we always seek in an acquisition: that in the end, all sides feel satisfied that their primary needs have been fulfilled and all sides wind up with maximum value.

Agustin was very pleased with the outcome. He had been leery of taking the company public – fearing the relentless pressures of Wall Street – and he had been leery of selling to any number of big conglomerates, for fear that his fine-wine mentality and spirit would be devoured by a mentality that was "too corporate," too driven by bottom-line demands. One key here was the personal relationship that we and Austin had by now established. He knew us and trusted us. "Let me put it this way," Agustin explains. "I had seen the way many big corporations work when they enter the fine wine field. The approach of Richard and

When we finally did purchase Franciscan, Agustin Huneeus's son, Agustin Francisco, left, stayed on and helped lead Franciscan Estates into a period of dynamic growth and innovation.

Agustin Sr. confirmed Richard's understanding of the challenges of running both a fine wine business and a mass-market wine business under the same corporate umbrella.

Canandaigua was different. Very, very different. That made me feel very confident – it was really a personal confidence that I had in them. It was a matter of choosing corporations, really, and in that light there was nothing to compare with the Sands."

In Agustin's eyes, what does "too corporate" mean in relation to fine wine?

"Too corporate for me means that financial considerations, or Wall Street, or stock market performance take precedence over the product. Decisions are made based on factors other than quality," Agustin explains. "Apart from that, there is the marketing and imaging. I think that the consumer does not want to think that he or she is buying a corporate wine, a wine made by a corporation. There is an attraction of the consumer to the vintner or the winemaker or to the terroir that makes the wine unique. They want to think that the wine is something special. Wine is one of the few products that we consume on a daily basis that is based, in high percentage, on image. And that image is created by the winemaker himself or the place." Agustin is right. And before we closed the deal, he made sure that we understood that and would do nothing to damage that mentality and spirit.

After he sold Franciscan to us, Agustin took the title of Vintner Chairman but stepped away from daily operations to devote his full attention to Quintessa. We kept his top management team intact, with Jean-Michel Valette running the company and with Agustin's son Agustin Francisco directing sales and marketing. They were a powerful team. Jean-Michel was a scrupulous manager and strategic thinker, and Agustin Francisco was absolutely brilliant when it came to the sale and marketing of fine wine. They presented to us their plan for moving forward, we approved it, and from that point on we gave Jean-Michel and Agustin Francisco the freedom and the support they needed to execute their plan. "When I sold Franciscan, I was no longer involved," Agustin says now. "Obviously the Sands' team remained in very close contact with Jean-Michel and Agustin Francisco, and the relationship was very, very good, and very comfortable. There was a lot of mutual confidence."

Indeed there was. When we entered that hectic week of negotiations with Franciscan, we were also in negotiations to buy the Simi Winery, one of the oldest and most prestigious wineries in Sonoma County. Simi's history traces back to 1876, when two brothers from Italy – Giuseppe and Pietro Simi – began making wine in Sonoma, whose climate and rolling hills reminded them of their native Tuscany. In 1881, they set up operations in the town of Healdsburg and began constructing their first stone cellar. Tragically, both brothers died young, and Isabelle Simi, Giuseppe's 18-year-old daughter, took over the business. During Prohibition, Isabelle and her husband, a local banker named Fred Haigh, were forced to sell off most of their vineyards but they continued to make wine and store it in their stone cellars. When Prohibition was finally lifted, they were able to jump back into business with a large quantity of beautifully cellared fine wine. In 1970, at the age of 84, Isabelle retired, but by then her winery was on a very solid footing. In 1979, they brought in the celebrated Zelma Long as their winemaker and three years later, Michel Rolland, the noted French winemaking guru, came in as a winery and vineyard consultant – as he would later do at Quintessa.

We were very much attracted by Simi and the outstanding quality of its fine wines, and originally the negotiations were handled through our premium wine division, Riverland

Vineyards. Paul Hetterich had been organizing the deal. Right away, though, we saw that Simi would be a much better fit for the Franciscan team. We ended up closing both deals on the same day, June 4th, 1999, and immediately we put Simi into the Franciscan fold. From there, Paul became our chief liaison to Jean-Michel and Agustin Francisco. Paul's job was to make sure they kept their costs under control and maintained the highest quality of product lines and management practices. Paul made sure they also applied their sales and marketing creativity to the integration of Simi, as well as to developing their Napa brands. It was also Paul's job to keep Canandaigua corporate from overwhelming the Franciscan team with unnecessary work or outside interference. The formula worked. Thanks to those two deals and the proper follow-through, our company now had three prominent fine wine properties in California, one in Napa, one in Sonoma, and one in Monterey, along with smaller niche ultra-premium brands like Mt. Veeder and Quintessa. At last we had made a successful move into the upper echelons of California fine wine.

In 2000, Jean-Michel decided it was time to move on, and he was eager for Agustin Francisco to take the helm. We readily agreed. We parted ways with Jean-Michel on very agreeable terms and looked forward to working with him again at some point down the road. From that point forward, Agustin Francisco ran the whole of Franciscan, and he really developed and enriched the fine-wine vision that he and his father had so long been nurturing. Specifically, he changed the way Franciscan used its vineyards, to make sure that the best grapes went into the best wines. At his urging, we purchased new vineyards and built out the winery and its barrel-aging facility and hospitality center to accommodate the Estancia brand and develop Franciscan into a true estate winery. Under Agustin Francisco's leadership, we were able to grow Franciscan Estates and reposition Simi back to its original heritage as one of Sonoma's greatest labels.

Back at our headquarters in the Finger Lakes, this was also a dynamic period. By the year 2000, we knew that our rapid growth and the changing nature of our business demanded important changes. On the organizational side, we needed to give Rob greater control over all of our operations and bring him into full company leadership beside me. So we hired veteran attorney Tom Mullin to step in for Rob as our chief legal counsel. In this same period, Rob hired Jon Moramarco, a seasoned wine veteran from Allied, to replace him as President and CEO of our wine group, the Canandaigua Wine Company. Tom and Jon were first-rate additions to our top management team. Tom had a long background in both law and finance, and Jon had many generations of wine running through his veins. His ancestors had made wine in Southern Italy, and his grandfather had come to America and purchased a winery outside Los Angeles. As a boy, Jon had pruned vines, cleaned tanks, and stacked barrels. Then he earned his degree in viticulture at U.C. Davis. From there, Jon worked as an industry executive and became chairman of the American Vintners' Association and a member of the board of the Wine Institute. Few men in our industry are as skilled and respected as Jon Moramarco.

We also knew that we had to change our company name. Canandaigua Brands just wasn't working any more. Our beer and spirits chiefs at Barton wanted a new name that was in no way linked to the wine industry. And our fine wine chiefs wanted a name that

In making a fine wine, financial management, brand-building, and effective sales and distribution are all important. Ultimately, though, what's most important is the quality of the wine inside the bottle.

As a name, Constellation Brands was what we wanted. It was aspirational; it suggested we were looking up into the sky and pursuing big ideas and big dreams. It felt right.

was in no way linked to our high-volume roots in Canandaigua. We put George Murray, executive vice president and chief human resources officer, in charge of finding us a new name. George brought in a reputable outside naming firm and we gave them a clear line to follow: find us a name that is aspirational, a name that conveys that we are a company whose diversified divisions in wine, beer, and spirits are flowing together harmoniously and turning us into a significant force in the alcohol beverage industry. Well, the firm did its research and brainstorming and came back to us with a name that they thought was a sure winner: "Blue River." I had my doubts, but the specialists were adamant: "Look," they said. "We have to have this talk with every CEO. Trust us. It's a name that conveys different tributaries, all flowing together into a powerful river. If you can take this ball across the goal line, it's going to be touchdown. You'll win the game. Your job now is to go convince your operating people that Blue River really cooks."

I looked at George Murray and he said, "Richard, I think they're right."

"Okay," I said. "I'm going to give it a try. But I doubt our people will accept it. Of course I'm not going to let them know how I feel about it in advance. But I think I already know what we'll hear from them: they'll tell us we're crazy."

As promised, I ran Blue River by Jean-Michel Valette, Jon Moramarco, and Peter Aikins at Matthew Clark in London. Jean-Michel just laughed. The others struggled to contain themselves; they couldn't understand why I'd even consider such a name. So I went back to the naming group and said, "This is never going to fly. Forget Blue River – and any other concept you have like it. Come up with something that isn't going to cause these problems."

Ultimately, they came up with the name "Constellation Brands." For experts who prefer short, punchy names, that may be too polysyllabic. But Constellation Brands was what we wanted: it was aspirational; it suggested we were looking up into the sky and pursuing big ideas and big dreams. It felt right. So we had our logo redesigned and we began referring to our companies as individual stars, coming together to form a constellation. In December of 2000, we formally changed our name to Constellation Brands – and we all felt that we had taken another important step in our evolution.

Then we kept on building our constellation. In 2001, we added another prize to our fine wine portfolio: Ravenswood, a Sonoma County Winery best known for its exceptional red Zinfandels. The driving force for three decades at Ravenswood was – and is – Joel Peterson, one of the most gifted and interesting characters in California wine. Joel comes from a family with degrees in medicine and a passion for wine. His father had created the San Francisco Wine Sampling Club, and Joel started tasting there at the age of 10, unofficially of course. By the time he was a teenager, Joel was already a budding expert in European vineyards and vintages. After graduating from Oregon State University, Joel became a wine writer and consultant – while he also pursued research in immunology – then he began an apprenticeship with the late Joseph Swan, a prominent Zinfandel pioneer. In 1976, Joel became chief winemaker at Ravenswood and took it from a tiny, unknown producer of 427 cases of Zinfandel to a powerhouse producer of 800,000 cases a year, red Zin being his specialty. When we purchased Ravenswood, Jean-Michel Valette was again the go-between, and Paul Hetterich and Tom Mullin put together our side of the deal. It made a great addition to our fine wine estate concept and portfolio.

Personally, I was now getting a fabulous education in fine wine. And I had fantastic mentors. Agustin shared with me his passion and knowledge for vineyards and the concept of what the French call terroir, the unique spirit of place that comes from a vineyard's locale, climate, soil content, varietals, viticultural care, and of course from the character and passion of the winemaker and his staff. In my life in wine and in my apprenticeship with my father, I had never really been that close to the soil, so I found this exciting and illuminating. By teaching me about terroir, Agustin gave me a deep understanding of the roots of fine wine and the mentality and spirit behind it. Through Agustin, I developed a romantic relationship with the vineyards that I had never had before, plus a deeper understanding of how close to the ground and the vineyards you need to be to succeed in the fine wine business.

At the same time, his son Agustin Francisco was teaching me the differences in the marketing and sale of fine wine, and how important it is for a fine wine to have "a reason for being." In fine wine, Agustin Francisco taught me, you are not just selling a product, you are selling image, character, personality, and in the deepest possible sense, a winery's defining spirit and culture. In the Napa Valley, there are scores of wineries that feature elegant tasting rooms and sculpture gardens, and many put on concerts, art exhibits, wine and food pairings, even opera and theater performances. Corporate accountants may cringe at such indulgences, but in fine wineries the artists and the sales and marketing people understand that these are essential components of their winery's image and culture – and they do add tangible value when it comes to the price per bottle that consumers are willing to pay. During this period, I developed a warm friendship with both Agustin and Agustin Francisco, and it was with great kindness and generosity that they brought me into the spirit and ethos of fine wine. This was a whole new chapter of Educating Richard. I loved learning from them, and I continue to value their friendships to this day.

Joel Peterson, founder and winemaker of Ravenswood Winery.

In early 2001, we made two more substantial acquisitions. The first was Turner Road Vintners from Sebastiani Vineyards in Sonoma County. Turner Road was a collection of higher-margin wines led by Vendange, a very popular fighting varietal. The second was a group of Washington State wineries and labels called Corus Brands, which included the very popular Covey Run, the fine wine brand Columbia – crafted by David Lake, one of Washington's founding winemakers – and an Australian wine called Alice White. This gave us our first tiny toehold in Australian wine. Both of these companies were successfully integrated into our Canandaigua Wine Division, under the direction of Jon Moramarco.

Then came something even bigger. In the spring of 2001, a group of investment bankers approached us with a very tantalizing opportunity: Kendall Jackson. Known as KJ in the industry, Kendall Jackson was the creation of Jess Jackson, a true trailblazer in California wine. Jess was a big, imposing man, but he was also gentle, warmhearted, and down to earth. He had built a powerhouse company, with a wide spectrum of brands, including one

As time has taught us, wine-making is a unique meld of art, science, craftsmanship, and the miraculous hand of Nature herself.

When combined with Franciscan Estates in the Napa Valley, our purchase of the Ravenswood and Simi wineries in Sonoma County gave us a strong, diversified foothold in California fine wine.

of the first big-volume brands in the U.S. to sell at over $10 a bottle. Jess thought globally and was busy exporting to Europe and to the promising young markets opening across Asia. Jess was also a prominent force in the arts, education, and philanthropy of Northern California, a leadership role that had enhanced his stature and prestige in California wine. In sum, as we looked for ways to become more powerful in California wine, we saw few properties that were as attractive as Jess's beloved baby, Kendall Jackson.

The investment bankers who approached us said that Jess Jackson might be willing to sell KJ – but only if he got the right price. Of course we swung into action, taking our usual in-depth look at KJ's operation and at the potential synergies it could generate for us. We concluded that KJ was worth in the neighborhood of $1.2 to $1.6 billion – tops. But that was not enough. We were told that Jess Jackson had set the bar at $2 billion and would not take a nickel less. Our talks ended right there.

While we were eager to move into California wine in a much bigger way, in 2000 and early 2001 we were also keenly aware of a new development in the world of wine: Australian wines were suddenly on fire. In fact, they were the hottest item on the international wine market. And we were impressed. The Aussies had spent a lot of time and money investing in new methods of viticulture and winemaking, and they were producing an array of good wines that appealed to what I call the "new world wine consumer." These wines had fresh, fruit-forward characteristics and the Australians were able to market them at a very affordable price. Yes, we had to salute them. But we were also concerned that Australians were going to eat everyone's lunch, including our own. These hot Australian wines were already hurting our sales of Vendange, just as they were hurting the sales of Woodbridge wines, Robert Mondavi's line of premium wines. We needed to take a close look at the Australian phenomenon and find a way to get in on it – quick.

So in late 2000 we sent Paul Hetterich to Australia to see if there was any way we could secure a stronger position in this dynamically growing category. As Paul discovered, the lineup in Australia was pretty set. At that stage, there was Southcorp, with its lead brand Lindeman, which had merged with Rosemount. Southcorp was well positioned, especially in the United States. There was Foster's, the beer giant and one of the most powerful brand names in the beverage industry. And there was Pernod Ricard with Jacobs Creek, a strong brand in the Australian and U.K. markets. But there was another company that caught Paul's eye: BRL Hardy. Hardy was the volume leader in Australia and the No. 1 Australian exporter to the United Kingdom. Those were strong assets, but Hardy's wines were barely visible in the U.S. market.

Paul met with Steve Millar, the CEO of BRL Hardy, and together they began considering ways to structure a relationship that would make Hardy stronger in the U.S. market and us stronger in Australian wines. We saw a lot of potential synergy. Steve had built BRL Hardy into Australia's market leader with the same strategy and methodology that we had built Constellation: by putting together many different wine companies under a common umbrella. Hardy was also, like us, a public company. And Steve was very ambitious; he wanted, especially, to secure a powerful foothold in California wine, again just like us. It turned out that he, too, had made a run at Kendall Jackson – with an offer that was much larger than ours – but Jess Jackson had turned him down as well. So the upshot was clear: Hardy and Constellation Brands were two companies with similar histories, similar ambitions, and a common, expansive entrepreneurial spirit. In our eyes, this looked like a marriage that was meant to be.

In their initial discussions, Paul and Steve considered forming some sort of 50-50 joint venture. That seemed to offer both sides the most benefit. With our marketing and sales muscle, we could quickly expand the distribution of Steve's Australian wines across the United States. But Hardy already had its own distribution company in the U.S., and it turned out that Steve was looking for much more. He proposed, instead, that we join forces and purchase a big California winery, a strong California brand that would provide Hardy with real backbone and clout in the American market. Steve did not have a fine-wine brand in mind; he wanted something in the $7 to $11 range with a strong volume base, something akin to Kendall Jackson. One property Steve was eyeing was Ravenswood, but we had plans for Franciscan to buy Ravenswood, and we didn't want to put it into the joint venture with Steve. We looked at a few other properties that we might buy together, but when none looked suitable, we went ahead and set up a joint venture, Pacific Wine Partners, PWP. Its initial mission was to distribute Hardy wines in the U.S. and our wines in Australia. The Hardy portfolio included Banrock Station, Hardy wines, Barossa Valley Estates, and Nobilo from New Zealand. Pacific Wine Partners was established in August 2001, with José Fernandez, the head of BRL Hardy North America, as its President and CEO.

BRL Hardy has a long and proud history in Australia, tracing all the way back to the 1850s when Thomas Hardy, above, arrived from England and created the Tintara Winery in southern Australia.

Two months later, we expanded the mission of Pacific Wine Partners by purchasing for it the Blackstone brand. Blackstone was not a huge acquisition, but it was a hot brand, selling 400,000 cases a year and growing at 40 to 50 percent a year. That made Blackstone a good fit for Steve's larger ambitions. We felt that with our distribution strength we could really make Blackstone perform – and we did. But was Steve Millar entirely satisfied? No sir! And now we came to understand the full measure of Steve's ambitions: he wasn't satisfied with being the top volume producer in Australia; he wanted to become the biggest wine company in the world! In that light, Blackstone was a nice little step, but Steve wanted to make a much bigger acquisition, something that would bounce him right to the top of the world of wine.

The Blackstone Winery in California was another important addition to our portfolio.

At that stage, our goal for Constellation Brands was just as ambitious, but we had framed it in different terms: we wanted to double in size every five years. That was the objective that we had set for ourselves and our shareholders. Our top management team and our business development unit were constantly looking at ways to achieve that objective. As we moved forward with Steve Millar, though, we suddenly realized that there was a rapid and very efficient way of achieving that goal: by buying BRL Hardy. Instantly, that would give us market leadership in the hot, hot Australian wine business. Also, thanks to Hardy's strong presence in the U.K. market, acquiring Hardy would make us, at a single stroke, the largest wine company in the world. How sweet would that be? To grow, in the space of just two decades, from a small company in Canandaigua, New York, into the worldwide industry leader – yes, that prospect was tantalizing indeed. So we began to wonder if our initial 50-50 joint venture with Hardy, Pacific Wine Partners, could be turned into a much

"You know, we Australians are a very proud lot. So one of the things that we have to do is make sure that the board doesn't feel like the Americans are coming and taking them over."

STEVE MILLAR

bigger and far more profitable marriage down the road.

Over the next 18 months, we worked closely with Steve Millar and his team in Australia and in the United States. We liked Steve and his key people. We liked their approach to business and management. We felt we had built a strong and supple working relationship. So in 2002 we started exploring with Steve ways to bring the two companies even closer together, not in an expanded joint venture, but in a full-scale merger. In our preferred model, Constellation Brands would end up controlling the resulting entity, and BRL Hardy shareholders would receive a substantial pay-out and go away happy. Also, we would be delighted to have Steve run our entire wine business on a worldwide basis. Through a merger with us, Steve would achieve his ambition of running the largest wine company in the world. Still, we did not discuss that aspect of our plan with Steve, not until later.

Then something unexpected happened: The BRL Hardy stock came tumbling down. The stock had been selling at about $11 a share. But Hardy suddenly found itself with a negative cash flow. It had to bring in a huge crop in Australia and, at the same time, it was building out its premium vineyard holdings and building up its fine wine business. Seeing Hardy's cash crunch, the Australian stock market slammed them and took their share price down by 50 percent. So Steve had to run around the world, meeting with major investors in Asia, London, and the United States, trying to reassure them that the company was actually worth far more than its share price suggested. This was our opportunity. We never could have made a bid for Hardy when their stock was still at $11 a share. We couldn't pay the 30 percent premium their shareholders would demand to sell their stock. But with Hardy selling at $5 or $6 a share, we could step in with a generous acquisition offer, pay a significant premium to the shareholders, and make the Board of Directors and Steve into heroes in the process. Big heroes.

We laid out this scenario to Steve and he gave it a lot of thought. "Okay," he said finally. "This could be good – for all of us. For the Hardy Board of Directors, this may just be the right time." Whoever first said that "timing is everything" had it right. We could never have even considered this acquisition if the stock price hadn't fallen so precipitously. And we knew the truth: that fall in stock price was not based on any true structural weakness in the company, only on a momentary problem with cash flow – and a lot of bad PR. The fall in share price was based on false perceptions of the future – a phenomenon that I call a "dislocation of value."

Still, we had a steep hurdle to jump. Steve wanted to take our offer back to his board, but he knew he could face considerable opposition. "You know," he explained to us, "we Australians are a very proud lot. So one of the things that we have to do is make sure that the board doesn't feel like the Americans are coming and taking them over." We were sensitive to his concern. So I said, "Look, Steve, you know us well. We believe in keeping companies independent, maintaining their culture and heritage. Think about it: we're not taking you over. We're doing just the opposite. We're going to let you, Steve Millar and the Australians, run the world!" Steve thought about that for a minute and said, 'You know, that just might work!"

With that strategy in place, Steve went back, met with his board, and smoothed the way for an acquisition. We then flew to Australia to begin discussions. Our talks quickly turned into serious negotiations. We started the process in October of 2002, and on April 9th, 2003, we were able to close the deal. We bought BRL Hardy for $1.3 billion. Our initial 50-50 joint venture, Pacific Wine Partners, now became a wholly owned subsidiary of Constellation Brands. We renamed the Australian part of the business the Hardy Wine Company. Hardy now commanded 25 percent of the domestic Australian wine market and it exported to 60 countries. For Constellation, our new acquisition was a true jewel; Australia was producing excellent quality wine for the price. The Hardy deal also brought us another strong asset: Nobilo wines of New Zealand. This was a big plus: New Zealand wines were just starting to catch fire worldwide. Very soon Nobilo's Sauvignon Blanc would become the No. 1 imported Sauvignon Blanc in the U.S. market.

The transaction itself was very complicated. We basically were asking the Hardy shareholders to merge the two companies together and we offered stock in our own company as part of the deal. This gave the Australian investors and shareholders the feeling that they still had a degree of ownership. Publicly, we also stressed the point that Steve and members of his team in Australia, along with some U.S. team members, would be running our worldwide wine business. We also announced that Constellation's new worldwide wine headquarters would be located in Adelaide, Australia. Operationally, Steve now had several people and entities reporting directly to him: Jon Moramarco and the Canandaigua Wine Company, José Fernandez and Pacific Wine Partners, Agustin Francisco and Franciscan Estates, Richard Peters and Chris Carson on behalf of our team in London, now called Constellation Europe, and Brian Vieceli in New Zealand. Rob became the Chief Operating Officer, with Steve Millar and Andy Berk reporting to him. Steve was delighted by this outcome – and so were his shareholders.

We were pleased as well. At one stroke, the acquisition of Hardy made us far and away the No. 1 wine company in the United Kingdom, with a 20 percent share of the branded wine market, making us three times bigger than our nearest competitor. Moreover, with Nobilo we now had a foothold in New Zealand. Nobilo, the second largest wine company in New Zealand, was created by Nikola Nobilo, a Croatian winemaker of Italian heritage. What a marvelous family of artists, pioneers, and entrepreneurs we were putting together!

Oh, and there was something else: in volume terms, Gallo was no longer the largest wine company in the world. We were. The king had been toppled.

Still, putting together a huge acquisition like Hardy is one thing, integrating it into your operations is quite another. And so is running a company that has so rapidly become a global power. For Rob and me, these presented major challenges. And we were well aware of the minefield laid out in front of us. It's one thing to be the lean, hungry challenger, working your way up the ranks; it is quite another to be the market champ, with everyone studying your tiniest move or lapse in execution. And no one had to remind us of how merciless Wall Street can be at the first sign of a slip; Hardy itself was proof of that. So for Rob and me, closing these deals was the easy part; the real headaches were still to come.

As we moved forward with our expanded and very diversified portfolio, one of our primary concerns was maintaining that delicate balance that Agustin Huneeus had warned us

Agustin Huneeus played a quiet but very significant role in our next major move in California…

about, the balance between the art of wine and the business of wine. Could we succeed in both realms? Could we keep the artists and the connoisseurs happy, and keep the lions of Wall Street happy as well? That was going to be a big part of our challenge. And we knew that if we ever suffered lapses in that regard, our friend Agustin Huneeus or his son Agustin Francisco would be among the first to give us a gentle jab:

"Richard understands that in the fine wine business you have to make a special effort to protect the culture and legacy of companies that are successful," Agustin says now, by way of friendly reminder. "There is no question that Richard understands that. The only risk is this: does the larger corporation have a communications system – one that runs through its executive line – that can convey and protect that understanding? Does the chief financial officer, say, have the same sensibility as Richard? Can he? That's the risk. And that's what remains to be seen. So far, Constellation has done well. But as they grow and become more impersonal, the heart – the key to making fine wine – tends to be replaced by the head. The Sands brothers still have heart in their management of their fine wine business. But what about in the future? Will their next crop of professional managers have the same sensibility? That's the big question."

We hear you, dear Agustin. We hear you loud and clear.

CHAPTER 14

The Crown Jewels

In the history of American wine, Robert Mondavi stands alone.

From the first settlers who came here from Europe and vowed to make good wine, America has had many esteemed pioneers and champions of the grape: Thomas Jefferson. Benjamin Franklin. Father Junipero Serra. George Calvert Yount. Captain Paul Garrett. Charles Champlin. Jacob and Frederick Beringer, Charles Krug, and many more. Still, by the year 1966, no one in this country was making anything even close in quality to a world-class Bordeaux or Burgundy. French wines were believed to be in a class all by themselves, and no one in New York State, California, or anywhere else dared to dream that America could ever rival France when it came to the art and culture of making fine wine.

No one except Robert Mondavi.

Almost every step of his life, Robert was propelled by one over-arching ambition: to be, in his words, "The Best." His parents, Cesare and Rosa Mondavi, were born into poor peasant families living on a bleak hillside in Le Marche, a primitive and chronically depressed mining and farming region on the eastern side of Italy, south of Venice. Cesare and Rosa had little formal education, but they were smart, ambitious, hard-working, and they were both determined to leave Italy and create a better life for themselves and their children. With that goal in mind, they came to America in 1906 – in the same period when our great grandfather, Elias, brought the Sands family from Russia to America.

The Mondavis settled first in Hibbing, Minnesota, where Cesare worked in an iron mine alongside his older brother Giovanni. But when Giovanni was killed in a mining accident, Cesare said "Basta!" – that's enough for me. Entrepreneurial by nature, Cesare and a partner then opened a small grocery store in Virginia, Minnesota, serving the other Italian immigrants working in the iron mines. For added income, Rosa took in many of those same immigrants as boarders in their home. Rosa made traditional Italian meals for them and always put good wine on the table – that was the Italian way of life, whether in Le Marche or Minnesota: work hard but then relax around the family table with good food, good wine, and plenty of warmth and good cheer. La Dolce Vita, family-style.

Then came Prohibition. To utilize the loophole in the Volstead Act that allowed families to make wine at home, a group of Italian families and businessmen in the town of Virginia, Minnesota, asked Cesare to go out to California, buy good grapes, and ship them back, so they could make wine at home. Cesare did. But once in the Golden State, Cesare saw a much bigger opportunity and he soon moved Rosa and their children west to Lodi, California, in the fertile central valley where farmers grew good grapes in high volumes. There Cesare put down permanent roots and started a wholesale grape business.

The Mondavis had four children – Robert, Peter, Mary, and Helen – and even as a youth, their oldest son Bobby was determined to be the best. He excelled at school, he excelled at nailing boxes for his father's grape company, and despite his small size, Bobby excelled at football. His achievements earned him a place at Stanford University, where he studied economics and business and played on the rugby team. He was close to graduating when Prohibition was lifted in 1933. "You know, Bobby," his father told him, "wine's going to come back. I think you'd have a good future in the wine business. Go up to the Napa Valley. That's where they grow the very best grapes in the whole of California!"

Robert Mondavi, the lion of California wine.

Almost every step of his life, Robert was propelled by one over-arching ambition: to be, in his words, "The Best."

For some four decades, the Robert Mondavi Winery has been a symbol of excellence in the Napa Valley and a powerful magnet for winemakers and wine lovers from all around the world.

Robert followed his dad's advice. In 1936, the same year that our Grandpa Mack started his Car-Cal Winery in Greensboro, North Carolina, Robert moved to Napa and began a long apprenticeship at the Sunny St. Helena Winery. There, he and the crew made good table wines in big concrete tanks. But Robert wanted more. In 1943, he learned that the Charles Krug Winery was coming up for sale. Krug was located just up the road in St. Helena and it was a jewel, a magnificent property and one of the oldest in California. Krug had been crippled by Prohibition, though, and it had been mostly idle ever since. With Cesare's help, Robert and his younger brother Peter bought the Krug winery, and for the next twenty years the Mondavi brothers ran a nice little family business, making good, healthy table wines that were easy to drink. Life was good, though the Napa Valley then was a far cry from what it is today. There were only about 20 wineries in the entire valley, and none of them dreamed of making world-class wines. In terms of good eating, too, there was little to be had beyond steak and potatoes or a decent spaghetti, with or without the meatballs.

Then Robert went to France.

In 1962, Robert toured Burgundy and Bordeaux. He marveled at how well the wines married with France's elegant and flavorful cuisine, and he made special tasting trips to all five of France's celebrated First Growth chateaus, the absolute elite of the wine world: Château Mouton-Rothschild, Château Lafite, Château Margaux, Château Haut-Brion, and Château Latour. Robert was very impressed with the quality of those wines and he studied the wine-making techniques that produced them. From there, he came to a series of startling conclusions. First, that the quality of French wines was not due to any magic formula or any great technological secret; one key was to be found in the small oak barrels that the French used to age their wines, often for periods of two years and more. Those barrels, when properly "toasted," could enhance the natural flavors and accents of the fruit – provided those barrels were properly maintained. As Robert later explained in his memoir Harvests of Joy, even at some of France's finest chateaus he found "off characters and bacterial defects," due to the use of barrels that were too old or poorly cared for. In his view, oak barrels should not be used for more than three to five years. Moreover, using the best oak barrels, he found, was just as important as having first-rate soil, climate, vines and viticultural practices. The second conclusion that Robert came to was this: the primary difference between French winemakers and California winemakers was one of philosophy and culture. The Californians and U.S. winemakers in general treated wine, first and foremost, as a high-volume business; the great French chateaus treated fine wine as high art.

From those two conclusions, Robert came to a third: that he and other winemakers in California could make wines that were every bit as good as the best of France – and maybe even better! Yes, it would take time, patience, and lots of money, but Robert was absolutely convinced that America and the Napa Valley in particular could produce world-class wines. In a nutshell, they, too, could one day be considered among "The Best" in the world. But they had to get going – now. By temperament, Robert was not content to move quietly up the quality chain; he wanted to leap to the top in a single bound! To do that, he devised a plan that was simple and bold: bring together France's philosophy and devotion to fine wine as high art, plus the best of France's wine-making tradition and craft – starting with those French oak barrels – and wed them to the best in American entrepreneurial flair and technological innovation. That marriage, Robert was convinced, could stir a revolution in American wine – and maybe far beyond. And Robert was determined to lead the charge.

His brother Peter wanted none of it. By nature, Peter was quieter than Robert and more devoted to his family, and he did not share either Robert's passion or his all-consuming ambition to be The Best. "Peter wanted good grapes, he wanted quality," Robert later explained. "But I wanted more. I wanted to go to the top!"

Inevitably, I suppose, the two brothers had to part ways. What was not so inevitable was the way they did it: in a nasty fistfight around the family table. That fight shattered the Mondavi family, triggered an ugly lawsuit, and became a rather sad chapter in the history of American wine. Still, as destiny would have it, that same fistfight freed Robert to follow his dream and build his revolution – his way, with no constraints, no second-guessing, and no looking back.

From that point forward, Robert was on fire. He borrowed the money to buy the magnificent To Kalon vineyard in Oakville, in the heart of the Napa Valley – close to where our Franciscan Estates stands today – and there he built the Robert Mondavi Winery, the first new winery built in California since Prohibition. Robert imported oak barrels from France, rotary presses from Germany, and the best stainless steel-jacketed tanks that money could buy. In terms of wine-making equipment and technology, he wanted everything to be new and state of the art.

The influence of Robert and his Swiss-born wife Margrit extended far beyond the wine business. They used their winery to promote art, music, organic gardening, gourmet cooking, and international cooperation in wine, food and the arts.

The Robert Mondavi Winery was also the first in America to feature a distinctive architectural design and style that expressed – the way a great wine does – the character of its soil and vines, and the vision and artistry of the winemaker. Designed by Clifford May, the winery's signature Mission style was at once elegant, bold, and noble in spirit – like Robert himself – and it quickly became a landmark in the California wine and cultural landscape. It also became a beacon that attracted other winemakers to Robert's cause, as well as a number of entrepreneurs, artists, chefs, and wine writers, all of whom sensed a revolution was now in the making.

Robert had an eye for talent. In his first years out on his own, he hired two young winemakers who he felt had enormous promise: Warren Winiarski and Miljenko "Mike" Grgich. Warren had come to winemaking from a background in political science at the University of Chicago. Mike's father had taught him winemaking in his native Croatia, and he had trained under the legendary André Tchelistcheff, the French-trained dean of California winemakers, then creating wines for Beaulieu Vineyards.

Warren and Mike made wine for a few years at Mondavi, and then, with Robert's blessing, they both moved on in the Napa Valley – with exceptional results. Warren created Stag's Leap Wine Cellars, and Mike became head of winemaking at Chateau Montelena. By 1976, they had reached the top. In the celebrated Paris Tasting of 1976, it was Warren Winiarski's 1973 Cabernet Sauvignon that beat the best of France in the red wine category, and it was Mike Grgich's 1973 Chardonnay that beat the best of France among the whites. Robert's own wines had not been chosen for the competition, but in the achievement of Warren and Mike, Robert found both joy and validation. His vision had come true: Cali-

With the support of the Mondavis and many other vintners, the Napa Valley branch of the Culinary Institute of America teaches young chefs the art of elegant and healthy cuisine.

fornia could make wines that were as good as the very best of France – and, in this case at least, they were judged to be even better!

This was a golden moment in the history of American wine. In a blind tasting, with a panel of the very best French judges, these upstarts from Napa had whipped the very best wines of Burgundy and Bordeaux. This shocking "Judgment of Paris," as Time magazine called it, signaled to the world that America was now a rising power in the art of wine. The French trembled – and they were right to do so.

Today, there are no longer 20 wineries in the Napa Valley; there are more than 400, and scores of them are making world-class wines. Across the valley there are dozens of innovative restaurants and bistros of the highest quality, and each year over five million people – from all over the world – come to the Napa Valley to taste the wine and the food, to enjoy the spas, the vineyards, and the landscape, and to marvel at America's own sunny version of "The Good Life." In my view at least, every single one of them owes a grateful bow to Robert Mondavi.

"No one has been more closely associated with the California wine revolution than Robert Mondavi," wrote Frank Prial, the esteemed wine writer of The New York Times. "Probably because he started it."

Yes, with vision, clarity of purpose, raw energy, charisma, and a dogged determination to be, in his words, "The Best," Robert Mondavi changed the face of American wine and, in a larger sense, he helped catalyze what became known as America's "Gourmet Revolution." With Julia Child as one of his main allies, Robert and his second wife Margrit turned their winery into a showcase and learning center for young chefs and a parade of young painters and sculptors. They brought in the great chefs of France and exciting chefs from across America. They helped fund the Culinary Institute of America in Napa, and later they would spearhead the creation of Copia, the American Center for Wine, Food & The Arts, plus a stunning center for the performing arts at U.C. Davis. They also helped launch the Oxbow School, an innovative program for high school students from all over the country, each with a passion for the arts and creative learning. Culture, Robert believed, does not spontaneously grow from the soil; it has to be cultivated, like grapes, and Robert and Margrit were among Northern California's most determined cultural gardeners.

In 1978, Robert's rise in the world of international wine took a sensational leap: he joined hands with the Baron Philippe de Rothschild in the creation of Opus One, a fusion of the best of French and American wine-making, culture, and spirit. With Opus, many of Robert's dreams and ambitions were achieved; from their impoverished peasant roots in Italy, he had brought the Mondavi family into wealth and prominence, with a permanent place in wine's international aristocracy. As a crowning touch, on the label of Opus One, Robert's distinctive profile was now etched right alongside that of the Baron Philippe – the lion of American wine right beside the lion of French wine, fixed in perpetuity for all the world to see. What dreamer of glory in wine could dare ask for more?

Robert Mondavi was not alone in his campaign to bring wine to the center of the American cultural stage. The Gallos also played an important role. Ernest and Julio Gallo created the E. & J. Gallo Winery in Modesto, California, back in 1933, following the repeal of

Prohibition. Their starting capital was just under $6,000. From that humble beginning they built an empire, by developing close ties to their suppliers and customers, and in the process they, too, changed the face of American wine. In terms of wine advertising, merchandising, brand management, and product creation the Gallos were always at the forefront of our industry. As I mentioned earlier, they brought an array of innovations to the way wine was shipped and sold across the country. They were also the first to develop a significant sales force overseas, and for decades they were the dominant force inside California's influential Wine Institute, an industry organization that is a powerful voice on behalf of American wine. For our family, the Gallos were always our fiercest competitors, but ours was a competition of mutual respect and admiration. Rob and I were deeply saddened when Ernest died in 2007 at the age of 97. It was the end of a remarkable life and the closing of a glorious chapter in American wine.

There is another pioneer who needs to be mentioned here, a man who played a unique role in the evolution of American wine and taste: Marvin Shanken. The Mondavis and the Gallos built their wine empires with soil and grapes; Marvin built his with brains and ink. The son of a jeweler in New Haven, Connecticut, Marvin earned an MBA, and then did a stint in investment banking, specializing in real estate. As a partner in a small investment firm on Wall Street, Marvin was involved in the financing of several deals involving premium vineyards in Northern California. Right away wine became one of his passions and Marvin was off and running. In 1972, for only $5,000, he bought a small wine and spirits industry publication called Impact. Three years later he left Wall Street behind to publish Impact full-time. In 1979, he purchased a small tabloid-sized magazine called The Wine Spectator, and by combining his passion for wine with his well-honed business skills, Marvin turned The Wine Spectator into the most influential and largest circulation wine magazine in the world. Today it reaches over two million readers here and abroad. In the early 1990s, he replicated that success with Cigar Aficionado, an elegant and thoughtful lifestyle publication that is the dominant voice of the cigar industry, both here and abroad. Marvin also publishes Food Arts for food and hospitality professionals and Market Watch, essential reading for those of us in the wine and spirits industries.

Marvin is a business genius and a taste-maker of enormous influence and refinement. His family of lifestyle publications has helped make fine food and fine wine central to modern American culture. They also elevate everyone's standards and performance. Yes, Robert Parker is probably the most influential wine critic we have, but in the end I think Marvin's influence is far greater. He has shaped American taste, he has shaped our wine and food culture, and I think it is no exaggeration to say that Marvin has shaped the way millions of people around the world eat, drink, travel, and entertain.

In terms of the rise of American wine, there are scores of other pioneers who played important roles; it would take a whole other book to give them a proper salute. In terms of vision, ambition, and raw charisma, though, there was none that equaled Robert Mondavi. Nor did any enjoy the respect and stature that Robert commanded in other parts of the world. In Europe, Asia, Latin America and beyond, Robert was, pure and simple, the face of the Napa Valley and the face of American wine.

Robert and Margrit with Julia Child, another true American pioneer.

Robert Mondavi changed the face of American wine and, in a larger sense, he helped catalyze what became known as America's "Gourmet Revolution."

Robert and Margrit also spearheaded the creation of two unique cultural institutions in the Napa Valley. One is Copia, The American Center for Wine, Food and the Arts. The other is the Oxbow School, a creative program for high school art students from around the country.

Now, where does our family come into the Mondavi story?

In their early years in the wine business, Mom and Dad often bumped into Robert at various industry gatherings and functions. According to Mom, their meetings were always friendly and mutually respectful. And according to Margrit Mondavi, Robert always had the highest regard for Marvin. Still, Dad and Robert had very different styles and ways of presenting themselves. Dad was always understated and self-effacing; even in the early years Robert was the man who would be king. Later, Rob and I did meet Robert once or twice, but we had many more dealings with his oldest son Michael. We had also met Tim, Michael's younger brother, once or twice. We found both Mondavi brothers to be smart and very engaging; Michael was more focused on the business side, while Tim was more focused on the winemaking. That said, despite their huge success, I never envied either Michael or Tim. They had a tough road to travel. Robert was a gigantic figure in American and international wine and he absolutely adored being center stage. Living in that kind of shadow is not easy for any son, and Robert never struck me as a man who would patiently mentor and nurture his sons, to pave the way for a graceful succession. Indeed, in 1993 when the company went public, his sons were ostensibly in charge. But it was Robert, at the age of 80, who still commanded all the attention. The sons remained in his shadow.

Throughout the 1990s and into the new millennium, our business development team kept an eye on how the Mondavi corporation was performing, the same way we track dozens of other leading wine and beverage alcohol companies here and abroad. To be honest, we were somewhat perplexed by many of their business decisions. While we were struggling to take our company up-market into the highest echelons of fine wine – the very realm where Robert was king – the Mondavi company was eagerly moving down-market, putting more emphasis on their high-volume Woodbridge line of wines, selling at $5 to $7 a bottle, than on their high-end wines, some selling for upwards of $150 a bottle. Sure, Woodbridge sales accounted for some 60 percent of the company's income, and Woodbridge had brought high-quality wines at everyday prices to the American table – a very important evolution for the American wine industry. Nonetheless, it had been Robert's relentless drive to be "The Best" in fine wines that had defined the company's culture, spirit, image, and sense of mission – and its many decades of business success. Mindful of Agustin Huneeus's caution about the dangers of running a high-volume business and a fine-wine business under the same corporate umbrella, we wondered if Mondavi could compete with Gallo and others at the high-volume end of the market without damaging the high-quality image that had made Robert Mondavi so successful in the first place.

As it turned out, their move down-market did create some problems – and some bickering inside the Mondavi family. First of all, the move confused some consumers. Many prestige wineries bring out a second, lower-priced, lower-quality label, but they are careful to keep their names off the label and off the supporting sales and marketing materials. The Mondavi company, by contrast, eagerly put the name Robert Mondavi on its lower-end Woodbridge line and on its mid-priced line, Robert Mondavi Coastal, which later became Private Selection. What did the Mondavi name stand for? Wines that were truly The Best? Or wines that sold at $7 to $9? Or both? Robert Parker compounded the problem. He gave withering reviews to some of Mondavi's high-end wines, heightening the public perception that something was terribly amiss inside the house of Mondavi. That perception only deepened when Mondavi's chief winemaker, Tim Mondavi, was later put on an unexpected six-month leave.

The timing of the turmoil inside Mondavi did not help either. In 2001 and 2002, the attacks of 9/11 were hurting the economy and, at the same time, an unusual worldwide wine glut was depressing prices. On top of that, we saw the rise of "Two Buck Chuck," the Charles Shaw line of wines selling for $2 or $3 a bottle at Trader Joe's and other big outlet stores. The entire wine industry was in a recession, but Mondavi was among the hardest hit. "Woodbridge is being decimated by Two Buck Chuck," Bud Leedom, an equities analyst with Wells Fargo Securities told the Los Angeles Times. "They are at the worst price point you could be at in this market."

Sales slumped. In the third quarter of 2002, Mondavi posted a loss of $1.6 million, with a drop in revenues of 12 percent. To raise cash, Mondavi was forced to sell 10 percent of its vineyards and lay off 10 percent of its workforce. Wall Street bit down hard. By June of 2003, Mondavi's share price had fallen by 30 percent. Now the long-festering problems inside Mondavi were plain for everyone to see. And guess who was the harshest public critic of the company's many errors in strategy and direction? Robert Mondavi, still roaring at the age of 90.

"We made mistakes in our public relations and marketing," Robert told Frank Prial of The New York Times. "We concentrated too much on Coastal and Woodbridge. Now we're known for wines at $7 and $9 a bottle. We've got to get our image back."

Three months later, in October of 2003, the Wine Spectator ran a cover story entitled "Mondavi At The Crossroads." And their Napa-based writer, Jim Laube, did not mince words: "Speculation is rampant that the company is ripe for a takeover. Some analysts believe the current price for RMC stock on Wall Street already reflects a built-in premium in anticipation of a sale. Would-be suitors include Constellation, Beringer-Blass, Brown-Forman, Diageo, or even a long-shot from outside the wine business, such as Anheuser-Busch, the nation's biggest brewer."

Paul Hetterich, our mergers and acquisitions specialist, Tom Summer, our CFO, and our development group all watched the slippage at Mondavi with astonishment. With them in the lead, we took a long, hard look at the numbers that Mondavi was generating, and we examined different scenarios and potential synergies that a merger or acquisition of Mondavi might generate. In 2002 and even in early 2003, though, we saw no way to make it happen. Even with the dramatic drop in share price, none of us truly envisioned Mondavi winding up in our portfolio. "We had resigned ourselves to the idea that Mondavi would never be for sale," Paul explains. "They were making less money, but the family still retained total control through their super voting shares."

Nonetheless, in the summer of 2003, when nothing at Mondavi seemed to be improving, I put in a call to Michael Mondavi. My intent was straightforward, and I had no clear plan to propose. I just wanted to sit down and talk with him, to explore ideas. Rob and I felt strongly that with our family's entrepreneurial culture and with their family's entrepreneur-

"None of us truly envisioned Mondavi winding up in our portfolio. We had resigned ourselves to the idea that Mondavi would never be for sale."

PAUL HETTERICH

"Michael politely but very firmly rebuffed my advance."

RICHARD SANDS

ial culture, there must be something we could do together to create mutual benefits for both families and for our respective shareholders. As public companies, our first responsibility is always to our shareholders. So I thought maybe there was a way that Michael and I could make 1 plus 1 equal 3 – for their shareholders and ours. "Let's sit down and explore what we can do together," I suggested to Michael, or words to that effect. "Maybe we can find a formula that will increase value for your shareholders and ours as well."

At that stage, I was not envisioning a total acquisition. But I felt there must be some way to protect Robert Mondavi's towering legacy and vision by permanently embedding them in a larger business entity, so they wouldn't be hostage to all of the merciless short-term expectations of Wall Street. I envisioned the Mondavis being able to maintain their family's involvement, including family ownership of at least some of the assets. But this was only an idea, a feeling.

Michael politely but very firmly rebuffed my advance. The Mondavi Corporation, he said, was not for sale, nor was it interested in any sort of merger or partnership, with us or anyone else. I hung up feeling, well, that's that. At least we tried. After that, Rob and I concluded, as Paul Hetterich had, that this was a marriage that was simply not meant to be.

Then, in 2004, events started to cascade – downward. There were continuing reports of a rift between Michael, on one side, and Tim and his sister Marcia on the other. There were also reports of tension between Robert and his sons. We assumed that someone would step in and sort it all out; the future of the entire company was now at stake. Then early in 2004, with the approval of Robert the aging patriarch, they brought in an outside consultant named Ted Hall as chairman of the board. Ted Hall was said to be an experienced business hand, he was a wine grower himself, and he was purported to be a very savvy turnaround expert. We all waited to see what he would do. The following August, Hall and Greg Evans, the President and CEO of the Mondavi Corporation, announced their plan of action. It had three components that we studied very carefully. First, the plan called for the Mondavi family to increase its holdings from 36 to 39 percent of the company stock. But, at the same time, the family's voting control would be cut from just under 85 percent to just under 40 percent – a major weakening of the family's control – as they converted their super voting shares to regular voting shares at a 16 percent premium. Stripped to its core, that meant the unthinkable could now happen: the Mondavi family, if they didn't stick together, could lose control of the Robert Mondavi Corporation.

Second, Hall and Evans planned to restructure the operational side of the business, to separate the high-end luxury wines from the lower-end "lifestyle wines," as they called them. "It has become increasingly clear in the new wine environment that $50 Napa Valley cabernet and $6 premium wines require different business models," Greg Evans said in a statement. "Therefore, our board has directed management to develop separate operating plans for each business." Evans said there would now be separate directors and separate divisions for their fine wines and their every-day wines.

Again our jaws dropped. This was 2004; were they really just figuring out that fine wines and table wines required different business models? Grandpa Mack could have told them that 70 years ago! The third element that we zeroed in on was this: Greg Evans said in his

August statement that they would soon announce a restructuring plan, to give them some financial leeway to manage the crisis and get Mondavi back on an even keel. We were very curious to see that plan. A few weeks later, Hall and Evans unveiled what they thought was a strategic masterpiece: the company would hold onto its high-volume, lower-priced wine business and sell off the original Robert Mondavi Winery in Oakville and their other high-end ventures. We were shocked: they planned to cut the Mondavi dynasty in two! Their business strategy, their way of fixing all of the problems, was to dismantle Robert's empire and his legacy.

Michael Mondavi denounced Ted Hall's grand plan in a very public way. Right away Hall and his allies asked Michael to leave the board of directors, purportedly for breaching the confidentiality of their discussions. Now what? The Mondavi family no longer had voting control and now Michael, the business anchor of the company, was off the board. Moreover, we agreed with Michael's assessment: Ted Hall's plan would spell the end of everything that Robert Mondavi had built. We were mystified. Splitting the Mondavi brand defied all logic and business sense. Selling the luxury side of the business – the original Robert Mondavi Winery, the icon of brands, the umbrella that created a golden halo effect over the entire company – we felt that was a travesty, pure and simple. It certainly did not protect the spirit and legacy of Robert Mondavi – or the financial interests of the Mondavi shareholders. How could smashing the crown jewel of the Napa Valley and the whole American wine industry ever be construed as improving shareholder value?

We had to move.

Our team rushed into action, analyzing Ted Hall's plan and trying to see if it made any sense at all. We concluded the answer was no. "We thought Hall's plan was the wrong way to go," Paul Hetterich explains. "They had tremendous assets. They had several strong revenue streams. And their problems really were not that hard to fix."

By this time, we had spent months following Mondavi, doing our usual financial and legal due diligence, looking at possible synergies, and getting ready for any eventuality. We had already been working too with an investment banker to see how we could make Mondavi's many assets mesh harmoniously with our own. In short order, we were ready to make our move.

In October of 2004, we made an unsolicited bid of $1.3 billion for the whole of the Robert Mondavi Corporation. In announcing our bid, we stressed that we believed that it would be in the best interests of the Mondavi shareholders and our own to keep the Mondavi empire intact – and to keep the guiding spirit, culture, and image of Robert Mondavi intact as well. After all, those were what had made Mondavi so successful in the first place. Our offer and the philosophy behind it were, of course, by no means new for us. On the contrary, for four decades or more, this had been our acquisition model of choice, starting back with Dad and then reinforced with our purchase of Ned Cooper's Batavia Winery in 1981. With Mondavi, we believed, again, that this was the best course to follow – for all concerned. I said that exact same thing in a conference call with industry and Wall Street analysts:

"We believe the whole of Mondavi is greater than the sum of its parts. You have to

> *"In October of 2004, we made an unsolicited bid of $1.3 billion for the whole of the Robert Mondavi Corporation."*
>
> RICHARD SANDS

I spoke to Robert from my heart, and I told him how much I admired all that he and Margrit had created, and I assured them both that Rob and I and everyone else at Constellation Brands would do everything humanly possible to protect his name, his company, and his enormous legacy in American wine, American culture, and far beyond.

crush grapes to make good wine, but you don't have to crush a wine company to make shareholder value."

We thought that $1.3 billion was a serious and very substantial offer, but Ted Hall dismissed it out of hand. He first waved us off in a private telephone call. As Paul Hetterich recalls, "We called him at his office at 6:30 in the morning, California time, and we were just planning to leave him a message with the broad outlines of our plan. We had it all scripted out. But Hall actually picked up the phone; he was in his office at that hour. When we laid out our offer, right away he pushed back real hard, he told us there was nothing to talk about, and he insisted that his plan to restructure and recapitalize was going to turn everything around. He made it quite clear that he didn't want anyone coming in and spoiling his plan."

In our minds, though, Ted Hall had made a startling strategic blunder, one that we never expected from a business professional of his purported skill and experience. In announcing his restructuring plan, Hall said that the plan would bring the value of the Mondavi corporation up to $1.3 billion in the course of the following three to five years. When we heard that, we shook our heads in disbelief. "The fatal flaw of their restructuring plan was that it put a bull's-eye on their forehead by fixing that number," Paul Hetterich explains. "Hall was saying what the company might be worth in the context of the next few years – provided that everything went according to their plan and that the many possible risks were averted. But that number gave us the opportunity to go in and pounce. It enabled us to say, 'Okay, we'll pay you that exact number and more, right this instant, with no risk to your shareholders whatsoever.'"

Paul had it exactly right – and pounce we did. We upped our bid to $1.4 billion. Of course, this was more than the Ted Hall plan would yield to the shareholders and it came without any risk, since we would pay in cash right away. The family, I'm sure, did not want to sell to us or anyone else. But Hall's change in their voting stock had stripped them of control unless they stuck close together. That didn't happen. By this time, members of the Mondavi family were on different pages as to what to do. Divided, the Mondavi family ran out of options. On November 3rd, 2004, the Mondavi board of directors, with Ted Hall in control, voted unanimously to accept our offer. The following morning, The New York Times put the purchase into a very accurate light:

"The world's biggest wine conglomerate, Constellation Brands, has snapped up the iconic but struggling Robert Mondavi Corporation of Oakville for more than a billion dollars, saving Napa Valley's best-known winery from its own draconian plan to split in two and sell off its luxury brands piecemeal. The deal will keep all Robert Mondavi brands – from the $5 Woodbridge by Robert Mondavi to the $125 Robert Mondavi Cabernet Sauvignon Reserve – under the same roof instead of splitting them among multiple owners."

The crown jewel of American wine now belonged to us.

Rob and I and everyone else in our Constellation Brands family were elated. So was Mom. Thanks to our ambitious and nimble acquisitions strategy, we now had many jewels in our portfolio of wine, beer, and spirits, but none shone quite as brightly as the one created and polished by Robert Mondavi. Combined with Franciscan, Estancia, Ravenswood,

Blackstone, Simi, Hardys, Nobilo, and more, we now had a star-studded portfolio of fine wines. In Australia, Steve Millar was elated; he now had the backbone and flagship property he had dreamed of having in America. We had paid a hefty price for Mondavi, but in our eyes it was a very sound business decision.

For Rob and me, though, the acquisition of what Robert Mondavi had created held a much deeper significance. Our feeling for Robert and what he had accomplished in the world of wine went beyond respect; we were in awe at his boldness and the clarity of his vision. We were in awe of his business genius. We were in awe of how he had taken his grand dream and, step by step, built it into a shining reality. Robert had changed the nature, the quality, and the face of American wine. He had taken the entire industry up-market and to the heights of international glory, and in the process he had also helped change the culture and the way millions of Americans eat, drink, shop, cook, and think about health and nutrition. That was a legacy that both Rob and I were determined to honor, protect, and carry forward.

Robert Mondavi

After we made the acquisition, an interviewer asked me if I felt that we had "rescued" Mondavi. I paused to reflect and then said, that yes, in some ways the word "rescue" did fit the situation. But, I added, the word "rescue" did not fully describe our intentions or purpose. It suggested that we were looking only to protect the past or to preserve the status quo of today. No. When we stepped in and saved Mondavi from being dismembered, our main focus was really on the future. Rescue was only the first step, the easiest step. It was closing the deal. The more important step, the far more difficult step, was the future. We wanted to build on Robert's legacy, and build on it in such a way that Robert could be proud and, in a sense, live forever. That was our goal, our mission, our challenge.

To that end, Rob and I wanted, more than anything, for Robert and his wife Margrit to know how we felt and to fully understand our family's commitment to protecting Robert's legacy and even to advancing it in a proper manner, in line with Robert's own dreams and aspirations. To assure them of those intentions, I flew to Napa and had dinner with Bob and Margrit. We gathered at their magnificent home on a hilltop overlooking the entire Napa Valley. I would be lying if I told you the dinner was easy. It wasn't. Bob's son Tim and his daughter Marcia were there and they were very upset by how Ted Hall's grand plan had played out, and their unhappiness had clearly started long before we had come into the picture. Of course I understood. They were in terrible pain. A lot has been written about Michael and Tim and their role in what went wrong. I think that most of that criticism is misplaced. Michael and Tim are both smart, admirable, and very capable men. If they had any shortcomings, it was simply that they were not Robert Mondavi.

Then again, who else is?

Our friend Agustin Huneeus Sr. played a significant role here. He was a longtime friend, dinner companion, and unofficial adviser to both Robert and Margrit, and he explained to them how we had taken great care, in our acquisition of his Franciscan Estates, to protect his fine wine heritage, image, culture, and spirit. When I had dinner that night with the Mondavis, Agustin and Valeria were with us, and I felt that in many ways Agustin had smoothed the way for me. I spoke to Robert from my heart, and I told him how much I

The crown jewel of American wine now belonged to us.

admired all that he and Margrit had created, and I assured them both that Rob and I and everyone else at Constellation Brands would do everything humanly possible to protect his name, his company, and his enormous legacy in American wine, American culture, and far beyond.

By this time, Robert's knees were wobbly and he walked to and from the table with a cane. He had big hearing aids in both ears, and he leaned forward to make sure he caught every word I said. But his bright blue eyes were as lively as a child's, and I knew he could feel the depth of my sincerity and commitment. A short time later, in an interview with a writer and filmmaker in Napa, Robert, the godfather of American wine, gave us his formal blessing:

"I find that it is going to work out very well, much better than I'd thought," Robert said. "They're going to do exactly what I would have liked to do. They have the right spirit."

CHAPTER 15

Aligning the Stars

Now came the most difficult part, the riskiest part.

Acquiring the Robert Mondavi Winery and all of its assets was a relatively easy proposition; now we had to turn this high-profile acquisition into gold, we had to make this $1.4 billion investment pay off for us as a company and for our shareholders. The three steps we needed to accomplish were Integration, Convergence, and Alignment. In sum, we had to bring the Mondavi star comfortably and happily into our constellation of brands and companies, and then we all had to move forward together, all of the stars aligned and moving in the same direction, but each star still separate and distinct, with its own special glow. "Constellation Brands," you see, was not only our name. It was our guiding philosophy, our business model, our way of managing a large, broadly diversified group of stars and leading them to long-term stability and success.

Mondavi, though, presented special challenges and headaches. Before we made the acquisition, we made a careful study of its strengths and weaknesses, and we found it to be in a very fragile state. In many corners of the business, we found deep fissures resulting from misdirection and general deterioration. In broad terms, we perceived two sets of problems that we needed to address. The first I call "The Tangibles" – problems such as product quality, cost control, resource allocation, vineyard management, organizational structure, and debt load. The second set I call "The Intangibles" – problems of image, brand, and managing the perceptions of Wall Street and those of the consumer. To successfully integrate Mondavi into the Constellation orbit, we had to gain a deeper understanding of both sets of problems and then create a blueprint of what we wanted the result to look like. By this time, our teams were quite adept at managing every step of the integration process. We had a standard practice to follow. Nevertheless, no integration is ever easy – and Robert Mondavi was like no other company that we had ever touched; this was the crown jewel of American wine.

The risks for us were huge. Purchasing Mondavi had put us under close scrutiny from the press and from Wall Street and industry analysts. If we failed to execute a smooth integration, we were sure to get hammered, both in the press and in our share price. That had already happened to us, remember, with the Mission Bell integration. Moreover, many big corporations in the beverage industry had already tried their hand with fine wine – only to fall on their face. Very few, if any, had been able to successfully manage fine wines and everyday wines under the same roof. Many observers expected us to fail. So the upshot was clear: we had to do this right. We had to deliver results that were concrete, measurable, and highly visible. In an interview I gave at the time, I set forth the full range of our ambitions – and our fears.

"Our aim is to really bring Robert Mondavi to the world," I declared. "The Mondavi Corporation had been struggling with that, because of their size and because of the intense consolidation and competition that exists on a worldwide basis in wine today. We believe that because of our worldwide scale, we can take the wines that speak in Robert's or Margrit's voice to the world much more effectively than they could. We have the infrastructure, the distribution, and the scale throughout the world. If we do this right, acquiring Robert Mondavi will produce a halo effect over our entire enterprise. Having this wonder-

Acquiring companies is the easy part. The real challenge is bringing them into harmonious alignment.

At the Robert Mondavi Winery, even the barrels have a signature look. We worked hard to keep that guiding spirit intact.

ful brand, this iconic brand, can shine a positive light on all of our brands and on our total business."

Yes, that was our hope. But I also laid out the consequences of failure. "That positive light will only continue," I warned, "as long as we build on the voice, the vision, and the culture that Robert himself created. The moment we contradict that, that light turns off and we lose that wonderful benefit. So it's in our best interest to build on Robert's legacy, and for years to come to make sure that the Robert Mondavi Winery speaks loud and clear – with Robert's voice."

That was our guiding vision. Now we had to execute it.

As a first step, we needed to gain a deeper understanding of what had happened inside Mondavi: what they had done right, historically, and where they had gone wrong. We needed to fully understand the core values and business strategies that had enabled Robert to create the premier winery in America. Once we had a deeper understanding of that, we hoped to find ways to turn back the clock to Robert's original vision and values. We also wanted to gain a deeper understanding of the man himself, to see what we could learn about his character and his qualities as a leader. As Dad had taught us long ago, success in business always begins with effective leadership. What made Robert such a unique and inspiring leader? What core values and truths had guided him? What lessons did Robert have to teach us? In sum, what did we at Constellation need to understand and be able to communicate – to our own people and to the world at large – to help us preserve and then build on Robert Mondavi's legacy?

As we examined what Robert had built, one value stood out above all the others: Quality. In everything he did, Robert demanded quality and excellence, he wanted to be "The Best" – he was never content to settle for second-class or second-best. No matter where we looked, we saw evidence of that, starting with his To Kalon vineyard in Oakville, in the center of the Napa Valley. In our eyes, To Kalon was the perfect symbol of the values and quest of Robert Mondavi. It was a magnificent property. In terms of the richness of its soil, the virtues of its micro-climate, the character of the grapes it produced, even the visual splendor of its setting and landscape, there was very little in California or anywhere else that could match the quality of the To Kalon vineyard. That was especially true when it came to growing and nurturing Cabernet Sauvignon, the most treasured of California varietals, the echelon where Mondavi's Private Reserves sold in the range of $125 a bottle. To Kalon was the birthplace and foundation of everything that Robert had built. Still, Ted Hall's restructuring plan called for To Kalon to be summarily sold off, so that the corporation could focus all of its attention on its Woodbridge and Private Selection lines, back in the range of $5 or $7 a bottle. In our judgment, this was the perfect illustration of how far the recent managers at Mondavi had strayed from Robert's original vision and values. To us, selling To Kalon was worse than business folly; it would drive a stake straight into the heart and spirit of Robert Mondavi – something we would never do.

To the contrary, as we developed our blueprint for the future of Mondavi, we realized that our first phase had to be one of "Restoration and Preservation." As a first step, we wanted to bring Robert himself back to the fore, to show everyone in the company and also in the industry that we embraced Robert's values and the clearly defined mission that had propelled him to success: to make great wines, wines that would stand proudly alongside the very best in the world. Robert himself understood our purpose and agreed to stay on as our special consultant and Ambassador of Wine. True, Robert's title and function were mainly symbolic; in his early 90s, he did not have the energy or wherewithal to play an active leadership role. Still, in dealing with "The Intangibles" of culture, image, brand, and outside perceptions, what more potent symbol could we have than Robert Mondavi himself?

We felt just as strongly with regard to Robert's wife Margrit. We consider Margrit to be a visionary in her own right. The work she had done in creating the Mondavi Winery's signature summer concerts, its great chefs programs, the Napa Valley wine auction, the Napa Symphony, the Napa Opera House, Copia, and the Oxbow School – all of these were important and highly visible expressions of the Mondavi values, culture, image, and brand. And they were all central to the Mondavi legacy. Naturally, we wanted Margrit to stay on too, to enhance those activities and to keep expressing the Mondavi culture in what we like to think of as "Margrit's voice." To our delight, Margrit agreed to stay on as our anchor and special Ambassador for Art, Music & Culture.

We found that same spirit alive and well at Chianti Ruffino, one of Tuscany's most celebrated wine houses and now our partner in Italy.

Behind that, we needed to make sweeping structural and organizational changes. First and foremost, we had to totally separate Mondavi's high-end wines from their everyday wines. We thought long and hard about how best to make that separation. We also studied the experiences of other large corporations that had tried to run a fine-wine business and an everyday wine business under the same roof. Our study only reinforced what we had already learned from Agustin Huneeus and our own experience: fine wines and popular wines are two dramatically different businesses. The terroir and the viticultural practices are different, the wine-making is different, the sales, marketing, brand-building, and distribution are different, and the financial planning and imperatives are also very different. In this regard, Ted Hall's analysis had been correct: you had to separate the two businesses. We just didn't agree with his plan for doing it. We didn't feel that he needed to break up the entire company to solve the problem – not, at least, if he had an organization with our expertise and our range of diversified assets.

Our solution was to create a new, separate division devoted entirely to our luxury wines. That took two steps. First, we placed Mondavi's high-end wines into our Franciscan group. Later, we created a new entity called, in a salute to Robert, Icon Estates. Jon Moramarco ran Icon Estates through the first stages of the integration process, and then, when Jon took over our European operations, Chris Fehrnstrom took the helm at Icon. Under the new structure, Icon was responsible for the sales, marketing, and distribution of Mondavi's Oakville wines. Icon also managed the other luxury wines in our portfolio: Franciscan, Estancia, Mt. Veeder, Simi, Tintara from Australia, and, later, Kim Crawford from New Zealand, and Ruffino from Tuscany, in which we acquired an equity position in the same period as the Mondavi deal.

We then took Mondavi's Woodbridge and Private Selection lines and put them into our biggest and most powerful sales and marketing group, the Canandaigua Wine Company, led by José Fernandez. We then changed the group's name to Centerra, to underscore the

Genevieve Janssens, above, is one of the most accomplished winemakers in the world. When we bought Mondavi, we were thrilled when Genevieve agreed to stay on and continue to craft Mondavi's marvelous vintages.

change in the portfolio to a more premium line based on California's unique terroir. This change meant that Centerra's wine portfolio included not only Woodbridge and Robert Mondavi Private Selection, but also big sellers like Almaden, Inglenook, Cook's, Vendange, Covey Run, Manischewitz, Taylor dessert wines, Arbor Mist, Alice White from Australia, and many more.

Our separation formula worked. In short order, our team at Icon Estates was able to re-establish Mondavi's Oakville wines at the high end of the market and return them to their iconic stature. At the same time, Centerra was able to leverage the Mondavi name and boost sales of Woodbridge and Private Selection lines to grocery stores, big box retailers, club stores and other retail channels at the popular end of the wine market, both within the United States and abroad. The tricky thing here was to separate the two businesses yet still use the Robert Mondavi name to our advantage at both ends of the market. That required a delicate balance in our PR and marketing tools and in our statements to the press. Stressing Robert's achievements and legacy was one good way to do it. "Robert Mondavi is the gold standard wine brand around the world," José Fernandez told a wine and beverage publication in the United Kingdom. "We understand what an important legacy that is and are honored to be the custodians of that legacy. Hopefully, three to four years from now the Mondavi family will be proud of what we've been able to do, taking the franchise and the incredible business they built to the next level."

José had it exactly right. But we had to back up those words with tangible results. One absolute essential here was restoring the quality of Mondavi's top-of-the-line Oakville wines. In the best of times, those had been the emblem of Mondavi's success and stature in the world of wine. Now we had to convince the industry – and the wine critics – that their quality was our No. 1 priority. Here we had some work to do, though much good work had been done already. First of all, when Tim Mondavi had left his post as director of winemaking, Genevieve Janssens, Tim's right arm in Oakville, took over as head winemaker. Genevieve is a master of the art of fine wine. Her family had been making wine for generations, and Genevieve had worked for many years at the top of the top, Château Mouton-Rothschild. She then came to Napa and spent several years helping the Rothschilds and the Mondavis develop Opus One. Then Tim enticed her to join Mondavi. We were thrilled to have her stay. As is our custom, we sat down with Genevieve, established our common goals, and then we gave her all the resources and independence she needed to make wines of the highest possible quality.

Here we also had another asset: Jean-Michel Valette, who had run Franciscan and had helped us buy Ravenswood and then Blackstone. Before we made our bid for Mondavi, Ted Hall had recruited Jean-Michel to oversee the preparations to sell Mondavi's Oakville Estate. Once we closed the deal, though, Jean-Michel agreed to stay on and help us with the transition. He then worked with Genevieve and others to eliminate the wines that didn't meet the quality requirements for the Robert Mondavi Napa blends – we were returning to Robert's philosophy of "The Best." Genevieve embraced our approach.

"The new owners of Mondavi have never interfered with the way we make wine," Genevieve says. "In fact, they have reinforced the principle that quality is the most important thing that we can deliver to the marketplace and to Constellation. Separating Private Selection and Woodbridge from the flagship has also been a positive development. Having the wines of Robert Mondavi Winery sold through a sales team that understands high-end placement has helped us to improve our image."

Genevieve's artistry – combined with our sales and marketing strength – produced handsome dividends. Sales of Oakville's Cabernet Private Reserves rebounded quickly – and so did the reviews and rankings by Robert Parker, The Wine Spectator, and other influential voices in wine. In 2007, Jim Laube of The Wine Spectator gave the 2004 Robert Mondavi Cabernet Reserve a 95 ranking, an achievement that made all of us extremely proud. Tim Mondavi deserved much of the credit here: the new wine-making facility at To Kalon that he helped design did much to improve the quality of Oakville wines. Over and over, we read gratifying words to this effect: "In fine wines, Mondavi is back at the top of its form." No one was happier about these developments than Genevieve: "I am very pleased that sales are strong again," she says. "Nothing makes a winemaker happier than knowing her wines are being sold and appreciated."

Our name, though, would not be Sands if we did not bring to Mondavi a much more rigorous approach to cost analysis and financial management. The previous managers, for instance, had spent upwards of $30 million on that new To Kalon winemaking facility, and we found that it was not being used in the most cost-effective way. In fact, parts of it were standing idle for long parts of the year. So we took several steps to boost its year-round usage and productivity, while in no way diminishing the quality of the wines that it was producing.

We also did a careful examination of Mondavi's vineyard ownership and management. This took us back to what we had learned from Dad and Bruno Bisceglia about the financial algebra that is specific to California wine production. What we found here was rather shocking. At one stage, when they were flush with cash, the previous managers had purchased thousands of acres of vineyard land along California's central coast, outside Monterey, to bolster their production of Woodbridge and the Robert Mondavi Coastal, which became Private Selection. We concluded that buying those vineyards had not been a wise investment. First of all, for that price point, you should not own your own vineyards. Second, we believed that the land they had bought was just too expensive for the quality of wine it was producing. If you're making fine wine in the Napa Valley, sure, own every acre of prime vineyard you can afford to own. But not on the central coast. Third, they were not getting the crop yields there that they had expected, there was more volatility in those yields, and the grapes had proven more expensive to grow than they had originally anticipated. By contrast, you could grow grapes further inland in the San Joaquin Valley, on much cheaper real estate, and they were just as good and produced yields of equal or even quality at about half the price.

We also discovered that the Mondavi managers were paying growers in various regions from 20 percent to 30 percent above market value for grapes. I don't know why. Maybe it was because they had long-standing relationships with those growers, or maybe they just didn't understand the relevant financial algebra. But this much was clear: the Mondavi

"Nothing makes a winemaker happier than knowing her wines are being sold and appreciated."

GENEVIEVE JANSSENS

Wall Street applauded our purchase of Robert Mondavi Winery. Here our team rang the opening bell at the New York Stock Exchange.

managers were steeped in the fine-wine mentality, not in the mentality you need to properly manage a high-volume business with very tight margins and fierce competition at home and abroad. We took prompt action. We sold $125 million worth of vineyards and, in the process, we increased our operating profit by $5 to 6 million. The reason was simple: the cost of buying the right grapes was lower than the production costs at those vineyards. So we generated money and increased return. Normally when you sell an asset, you lose a return. But those vineyards were a low-returning asset, in fact a negatively returning asset. In addition, we were able to use some of those profits to pay down debt. In another cost-saving move, in 2005 we sold two other Mondavi holdings – the Byron and Arrowood Vineyards and Wineries – to focus our energy on assets that were giving us a better return and to convert surplus assets into liquidity. In our minds, none of these actions was radical or brilliant. This was simply sound financial and brand management, with the intent of restoring a proper balance between the business of wine and the art of wine.

As we implemented these changes at Mondavi, we again saw the critical importance of effective communication. You have to communicate well internally, inside your company, and also externally, to the press, Wall Street, and your target consumers. In this regard, too, we had found a definite deterioration at Mondavi. Robert himself had been a master communicator – I think everyone on the planet knew that his mission was to see California make world-class wines; that was a mantra he repeated everywhere he went. I am not suggesting that his children, Michael, Tim, and Marcia, were poor communicators; they were not. I do believe, though, that somewhere along the line their message got muddled. As a result, their management team and many of their employees were no longer moving in lock step behind a common strategy or a clear set of business objectives. In sum, they had problems with Alignment. This is a common shortcoming in many companies, especially as they become bigger and, by necessity, more corporate. We struggle with that too. We spend a lot of time at Constellation trying to clearly communicate our values and strategy. Also, when we acquire a company, we try to respect and keep intact its existing values and business culture. Still, to make the acquisition work, we need to find common ground and common language regarding values, strategy, and mission. Those help Convergence and Alignment fall naturally into place.

Effective communication is also essential in dealing with Wall Street and other financial markets. Here, too, we found lapses at Mondavi. Specifically, we felt that the previous leadership had not managed Wall Street's expectations very well. I understand that it is very hard to do. You never want to let Wall Street run your business. But you still have to understand their short-term expectations, manage them, and then drive your business with the long term clearly in focus. In the wine business especially, you always have to anticipate short-term volatility, but at the same time you have to stick hard and fast to your long-term vision. That is much harder to do in a company like Mondavi with, at that time, $468 million of sales. It's actually much easier with a company like Constellation Brands. The reason is simple: any short-term volatility in, say, the fine-wine market, will be only a small part of our well-diversified beverage alcohol business. So we can afford to be patient, knowing that the ripples created by short-term volatility will be calmed by the totality of our business.

With a process as complex and challenging as integrating Mondavi, the most critical components are leadership and management. And here we were fortunate to have two strong anchors working in tandem: Jon Moramarco and José Fernandez. Jon, as head of Icon Estates, did a brilliant job of managing the operational side of the integration. With Jean-Michel Valette's assistance, Jon focused on strategic planning, organizational structure, managing public perceptions, guiding the separation of luxury wines from everyday wines, and generally making sure that everything went smoothly, especially when it came to protecting and promoting Robert and Margrit's original vision.

"One of Richard's strokes of genius," Jean-Michel says, "or at least great insights in building up the premium side of his wine business, going back to the time when he thought about how best to integrate Franciscan and Simi, was that running a fine-wine business and an everyday wine business conjointly, with a joint sales forces, for example, or with a joint production infrastructure, would probably lead to the ultimate failure of the higher-end part of the business. He's right. We've seen that repeatedly over the course of history in our industry, even with Robert Mondavi. It's really detrimental, if not fatal, to the fine-wine side of the business. Richard and Constellation were one of the few large companies operating in both groups to separate the two. That's why they were one of the few to be successful."

This brings me to José Fernandez, who now had Woodbridge and Robert Mondavi Private Selection in his portfolio. The challenge for José was stiff. Sales of Woodbridge had been declining 3 to 4 percent a year, and the Mondavi Corporation had been trying to prop it up with $10 million dollars in advertising and a lot of other promotional dollars. In José's opinion, we needed to get back to the basics of sales execution: let the distributor know our goals and vision and then – most important – hold them accountable for their results. Putting money into advertising campaigns won't do a bit of good if your team is not focused on the basic blocking and tackling of sales and brand-building. So José reduced the advertising budget, stopped the wasted promotional spending, and trained the Mondavi sales people who joined Centerra to be more effective in setting goals for the distributor and holding them accountable. The results that José achieved speak for themselves: he generated $15 million a year in cost savings and put Woodbridge back into the black and growing at 3 to 5 percent a year.

Did our integration of Mondavi come off without a hitch? To be candid, no. Of course not. The process of integration is always challenging, and each case is different. Yes, we had a blueprint of objectives to achieve, and a set of priorities behind that, but our integration team of course made some mistakes. However, they learned from those mistakes, made adjustments, and kept moving forward, always mindful that this would probably be a work in progress for a long time to come. And there was short-term pain. In the initial phase, we had to do some serious cost-cutting. We had to let a lot of people go, and we lost many wine industry pros. That's always a painful experience for us and for them. We also had to close down an entire suite of executive offices. On top of that, many of the people who had worked in the Oakville offices at the winery were now moved to new offices at Icon Estates, further north in the valley, and that left something of a void in the once-bustling corridors at Mondavi central. Many of the veterans told us that the old energy and spirit were simply

Did our integration of Mondavi come off without a hitch? To be candid, no.

RICHARD SANDS

Opus One presented special challenges. The joint creation of Robert Mondavi and the Baron Philippe de Rothschild, Opus One was designed to bring together the very best winemaking of the Napa Valley and Bordeaux. And we were worried: would the Rothschild family accept us as their new partners?

no longer there. We understood. And from our perspective this was not an easy problem to solve. How, after all, can you ever replace a leader like Robert Mondavi?

And that brings me directly to Opus One.

Under Ted Hall's recapitalization plan, the Mondavi half of the Opus One partnership was among the high-end Mondavi assets that Hall planned to sell off. Our intervention prevented that. Through the acquisition, that 50 percent stake in Opus came to us – provided Baron Philippe de Rothschild's family would give us their seal of approval. For us, the stakes here were again very high. Rob and I and our entire team felt strongly that for our acquisition of Mondavi to be fully successful, we had to hold onto our share of Opus; we had to preserve and honor this historic partnership. Opus One was not huge in terms of the revenue it generated, but in terms of those crucial Intangibles – image, culture, values, and brand – Opus was both important and symbolic. When it was first created back in 1978, Opus signaled to the world of wine that Robert Mondavi stood at the summit – right beside the Baron Philippe, the lion of Château Mouton. If we, too, wanted to be perceived as standing at the summit, we had to find a way to preserve Opus One and form a strong working relationship with the Rothschild family. In essence, we had to replace Robert Mondavi not just financially, but also in terms of our values and spirit, and in our commitment to the common vision that had brought Robert and the Baron together in the first place.

The task did not look to be easy. After the baron passed away in 1988, his daughter, Baroness Philippine de Rothschild, took charge of her family's side of the Opus relationship and she had been directing it ever since. We had casually met the Baroness but did not know her well, and we were not sure how she would view the idea of continuing the partnership with us. Yes, we were now the biggest wine company in the world, but in the Baroness's eyes, with her fine-wine heritage in Paulliac, that was not necessarily an appealing asset. And, of course, our last name was not Mondavi. So at the outset we were not at all sure that we could make the Opus marriage work. Moreover, our first talks with the Baroness's people had not gone well.

David Pearson, the CEO of Opus One, watched the process unfold from his sensitive perch between both partners. David's primary concern was preserving the partnership and all of its magnificent assets. "It was a bit of a roller-coaster ride from our perspective at Opus," David recalls now. "At times, the acquisition looked very good for us, but at other times the risks looked very large. The risks were the ones that you would expect: the exigencies and the obligations of large corporations – needing to create steady return and growth – have at times been incompatible with long-term, high-quality, capital-intensive luxury wine businesses like Opus One. And there are very few examples of large corporations that have been able to sustain iconic wines."

For all the people at Opus and for the Rothschilds, the real question came down to this: could we be the exception?

We continued to have talks with the Rothschild side through the end of 2004 and into the early months of 2005. And they did not improve; more than once Rob and Paul Hetterich felt that we might never come to terms. The Rothschilds had the same fear, as David Pearson recalls: "Baroness Philippine would frequently call me and say, 'David, please tell everyone at Opus that we are going to take care of them, we won't let them go.' It was a personal thing, rather than a business thing. It was very touching."

The sticking point, initially, was this: the Baroness and her people were insisting that Opus One be run totally independently of both mother companies, with virtually no input from us at all. We had problems with that. We certainly wanted to keep Opus's values and business intact, but we also wanted to make sure that the partnership maintained our usual level of financial discipline and we wanted to have a say in how Opus sales were handled. I wouldn't exactly say we were stalemated, but the Opus board of directors was set to meet in Miami on April 12th, 2005, and we knew that meeting would be crucial for both sides. In truth, the entire future of Opus One now seemed to hang in the balance.

"I flew to Miami," David Pearson recalls. "By then the parties had not been in discussion for awhile and there was some loose talk of taking it to court. When I got to the board meeting, I couldn't meet with the Rothschilds beforehand to get an update on the status of things. I was worried. Then, on the morning of the board meeting, I was told, 'Constellation has come onboard to the idea that Opus would be handled independently of the two and would be willing to move forward on that basis.' But we had no clear idea yet of how far Constellation would be willing to go."

David's right. Going into that board meeting, both sides had very difficult questions that still needed to be worked through. The issues were not just financial and operational; to make this marriage work, all the Intangibles also had to be right, starting with the personal chemistry between our side and the Rothschilds. And who could predict how that would play out? The Rothschilds had three executives on the Opus board and we had three; David Pearson was the seventh member. The lead player on the Rothschild side was Xavier de Eizaguirre, the polished and highly skilled Managing Director of Château Mouton-Rothschild. He was supported by Mouton's finance director, Pierre Guinchard, and his technical director for winemaking, Philippe Dhalluin. Our lead on the Opus board was my brother Rob. Backing him, we had two of our best people: Paul Hetterich and Jon Moramarco. They made a good first impression.

"That was the first time that I had met Rob Sands," David recalls. "All three of them were obviously incredibly competent business people who knew their business perfectly well and were entirely comfortable and confident in the board meeting. But when it got to talking about French wine and the French appellation system and history, they clearly did not know much about that. What I thought was most interesting, and absolutely true, is that they listened incredibly well. They just absorbed it. I thought, wow, that was really impressive..."

How proud Dad, the master listener, would be to hear that!

Still, the chemistry and the future of the relationship rode on this: Xavier de Eizaguirre and Rob Sands, face to face. "Both of these guys are tremendously demanding and challenging individuals," David recalls. "At one board meeting, earlier on, we had a very nice dinner before the actual meeting. The two of them swapped – almost like boxers, toe to toe, but there wasn't any boxing – tales and connection stories. You know, 'In this country I know so-and-so – do you know so-and-so in that country?' The two of them went at it for

As the Rothschilds came to understand, we had no desire to supplant Robert Mondavi or tamper with the success of Opus One. To the contrary, we were determined to honor and protect the legacy of Robert and The Baron for generations to come.

This photo is filled with meaning for our family. The Baroness Philippine de Rothschild and Rob Sands together in a ceremony at Opus One, marking the beginning of a new era in this historic trans-Atlantic partnership.

like half an hour. It was very amicable, but I had the sense that they were each taking the measure of the other. They both went all the way up, and then – oof! – it was over. They had passed each other's test. After that, they had total respect for each other."

In that critical board meeting, the rapport that Xavier and Rob had established earlier smoothed the way to full agreement. "We wound up having a terrific meeting," David says. "It was incredibly productive. In what was near-record time, given the complexity of what we had to do, we wrote the entire operating agreement, created a Limited Liability Corporation, and put onto paper the guidelines under which Opus One would be managed. The Constellation people were then true to every one of their words. They said the administration would be independent; it's independent. They said production would be independent; it's independent. And sales – which I thought might prove to be a source of conflict – well, that's independent too. We had a formal signing agreement in October of 2005, and our business has gone straightforward ever since. This may be the rare occasion where a large corporation has the intelligence to handle an iconic wine successfully, by keeping it at arm's length and letting us be ourselves."

David's right. Our experience with integrating both Opus One and the Robert Mondavi organization again proved the wisdom of our merger and acquisition model: bring our own strengths and financial rigor to our new partner company, but at the same time respect the people and special spirit that made that company successful in the first place. With both Opus One and the Robert Mondavi company, our job has been to help them succeed even further, and with care and effort our teams have been able to do that.

In May of 2008, though, our extended Constellation family experienced a profound loss. Robert Mondavi, the lion of the Napa Valley, passed away, a month before his 95th birthday. It was the end of a glorious, pioneering life and also the end of a glorious, transformative period in the history of American wine. I speak for all of us at Constellation Brands when I say, "Bless you, Robert. We all will miss you dearly."

THE WORLD

*Wine-making, no matter where in the world, is always
a blend of art, craft, science, and the hand of Nature.*

Above, From its ancient roots, wine-making today spans the globe.

Opposite, Grapes maturing on the vine.

Previous spread, Chianti Ruffino's Greppone Mazzi Vineyard in the Brunello region of Tuscany.

Above, Modelo brewing facility in Mexico.

Opposite, Hoddles Creek Vineyard, Yarra Valley, one of the coldest regions of Western Australia.

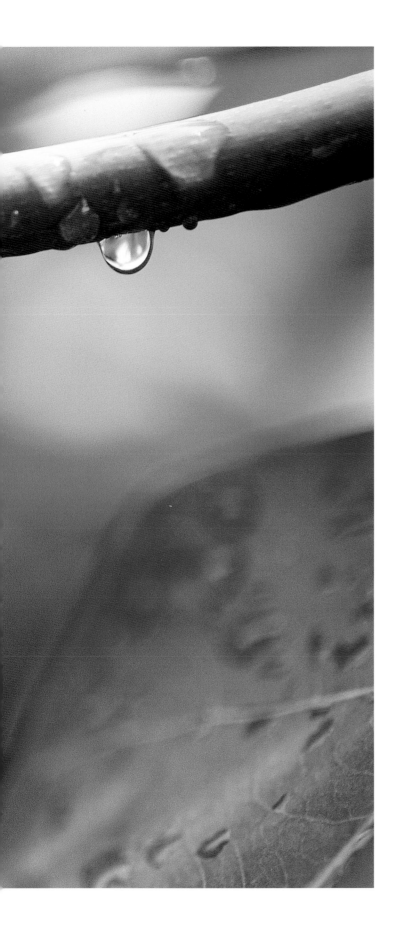

Above, Artistic hallway at Ruffino's Montemasso Estate in Tuscany.
Opposite, Nature's hand in wine-making.
Following spread, Storage tanks for beer at a Modelo facility in Mexico.

Above, Innovative fermenting tanks at the Drylands Winery in New Zealand. They tilt to facilitate the gentle draining into the press.

Opposite, Tending the barrels at Tintara, one of the oldest wineries in Australia.

Following spread, Dark Horse Vineyard in the Okanagan Valley, British Columbia.

Above, The late Jack Mann, the founder of the Houghton Winery and one of Australia's most influential winemakers.
Opposite, Spotless fermenting tanks at Chianti Ruffino.

Above, At the Barton Distilling Company in Bardstown, Kentucky, hand-crafted 1792 Ridgemont Reserve Bourbon quietly ages in the barrel.

Opposite, Nature and soil, the beginnings of wine.

Above, Stainless steel fermenting tanks, Jackson-Triggs Winery, Niagara Peninsula, Canada.
Opposite, Inniskillin's Bear Cub Vineyard, the Okanagan Valley, British Columbia.

Above, Detail from Mondavi Winery in California
Opposite, A man and his vines; the story of wine.

CHAPTER 16

The Best You Can Be

Wine speaks a universal language. So do beer and spirits. The accents may vary, the ingredients and local markets may vary, but when people in our industries sit down and talk, we are usually quick to find common ground. In one of the most enjoyable excursions of my life, I joined up with Agustin Huneeus and his son Agustin Francisco and we went around the world looking at many of the finest vineyards and wineries on the face of our planet. Our main points of focus were the "New World" wines: those produced in Australia, New Zealand, South Africa, Chile, Argentina, and Canada. The trip was an education unto itself. Wine, I could see, brought cultures together. No, it's more than that. Wine is culture. Wine is civilization. Wine – with its roots going all the way back to the ancient Egyptians, the Greeks, the Romans, the Mesopotamians, and the Chinese – brings together people of different cultures and different traditions of taste, art, and business. No matter what the country of origin, a good wine brings all of those elements together, in a unique meld created, ultimately, by each individual winemaker's own character, values, and spirit – all that in a single glass.

With that kind of outlook, I suppose it was inevitable that Rob and I and our top management team would be eager to keep expanding our international horizons. In 2004 we purchased a 40 percent interest in Ruffino, one of the most storied wineries of Tuscany. That same year we began importing Effen Vodka, a luxury vodka crafted in Holland. Loosely translated, "Effen" in Dutch means "smooth, even, and balanced," but what's in the glass requires no translation. In 2005, we marked the 60th anniversary of our company, tracing back to those days in 1945 when Dad finished his tour in the U.S. Navy and took command of Canandaigua Industries. Also in 2005, Decanter magazine named me the most influential figure in the wine industry. "Richard," I could hear Dad say, "don't take that sort of thing too seriously. Remember, the real credit belongs to all the people working behind you and Rob."

Richard grappling a log in his wood-working studio.

He's right, of course. Rob and I and our braintrust set the course, but then it is the more than 9,000 people in our Constellation family who make it work, day in and day out. Without their efforts and contributions, there could be no new initiatives, no sustained growth, no constant expanding of our horizons. And here's one of the best parts of it: as we have expanded, we have joined hands with many remarkable men and women, and they have shared with us their own expertise and spirit – and enriched our company culture in the process.

Take Don Triggs for example.

Don is a true pioneer. He grew up in Manitoba, on a cattle ranch and grain farm. Wine is in his veins. His mother used to make dandelion wine and chokecherry wine for their table at home. According to Don, it was barely drinkable, but his family would enjoy a glass or two to celebrate the end of harvest or a festive Sunday dinner. As a boy, Don went to a one-room country schoolhouse, then he studied agriculture at the University of Manitoba. After graduating, he did an MBA at the University of Western Ontario. A born marketer, Don started in business with Colgate-Palmolive, in product management. Then he moved into the wine business, managing John Labatt's wine interests in Canada and the United States. In the 1980s, Don ran the North American and then global horticultural business of

In spirit and vision, Don Triggs, above, is the Robert Mondavi of the Canadian wine industry. Don built Vincor into a powerhouse company, and along with his partner, Allan Jackson, Don built the Jackson-Triggs Winery and turned it into a model of innovation, creativity, and quality.

Fisons PLC. Then in 1989 he joined forces with his friend Allan Jackson in a management buyout of Labatt's Canadian wine interests. The new company became Vincor International. The two men then formed their own high-end winery, Jackson-Triggs.

Don brought together two big ambitions: he wanted to make great wines as Robert Mondavi had set out to do, and he wanted to become a worldwide force in the wine industry – like we had set out to do with Constellation Brands. Much like us, Don had used a strategy of mergers and acquisitions of smaller wineries to make Vincor into an industry giant, with a market share in Canada of over 20 percent. Moreover, Don had been able to succeed at both ends of the wine business. He took command of the popular-priced end of the spectrum but also, by creating brands like Jackson-Triggs and acquiring such high-end brands as Inniskillin, Don put together the best estate-based fine-wine business in Canada. He was also a major innovator in viticulture and enology, funding various university programs designed to educate other Canadian winemakers.

Few people realize it, but when it comes to winemaking Canada has some of the finest terroir and micro-climates in the world – and Don is helping in their development. The Niagara Peninsula, for instance, is a little Napa, situated some 15 minutes from Niagara Falls. There are a host of small wineries there producing top-quality Pinot Noirs, such as Le Clos Jordanne. Inniskillin, from our portfolio, is producing the world's best icewines. In addition, the Jackson-Triggs Winery on the Niagara Peninsula has one of the most advanced production facilities and hospitality centers in the world. Another prime wine-producing area is the Okanagan Valley in south central British Columbia, where Don and Allan started another Jackson-Triggs winemaking venture. In 2006, the London wine fair named their Okanagan Shiraz the best in the world, surpassing even the renowned Shiraz brands from Australia. I am also very impressed by Don and Allan's Bordeaux-style meritage blend Osooyos Larose, which I believe will be for the Okanagan region what Opus One was to Napa. One key to Don's success? He demands "The Best." He has found first-class terroir and has surrounded himself with first-rate winemakers, men like Allan Jackson, Donald Ziraldo, the co-creator of Inniskillin along with Karl Kaiser, and Mark Wendenburg, who created the many award-winning wines of Sumac Ridge Estate Winery in Summerland, British Columbia.

Don was also very astute when it came to the business of wine. He took Vincor public in 1996, and under his direction the stock soared. Then in 2000, with their eye on becoming a world power in wine, Vincor began an ambitious program of buying great brands. First they bought R.H. Phillips, a California winery that had hit it big with a very hot brand: Toasted Head. Vincor then bought two smaller wineries in Australia, Goundrey and Amberlay. To move into New Zealand's excellent Sauvignon Blancs, Vincor purchased the premier winery Kim Crawford, which Kim and his wife Erica had built from the ground up into a world-class brand. From there, Don and Vincor took the final step, purchasing Western Wines, a private label producer and importer in the U.K. which had struck it rich with Kumala, a brand they developed from South Africa. Kumala had become the fourth largest brand in the United Kingdom.

Needless to say, we had been watching Don and Vincor for a long time and with a great deal of admiration. We had long felt that Canada would be a great addition to our four core markets – the United States, the United Kingdom, Australia, and New Zealand. Canada had the key qualities of the greatest markets: growth and profitability. It was also a market where the consumer was trading up to more premium wines on a continual basis. Moreover, we thought that Don had made a smart move in buying Western Wines. In fact, we too had talked to Western Wines on a number of occasions, with the aim of acquiring them or, preferably, just buying the Kumala brand. In that transaction, as in others, we could see that Don shared many of our aims and ambitions, and we thought there might be an exciting way for us to join forces.

That said, when we did our close analysis, we saw a significant problem with Don's business. We calculated that Vincor had paid too much for some of its non-Canadian acquisitions – especially since they were generating few synergies for Vincor. Furthermore, each of the acquired companies lacked scale in their home markets. So keeping them competitive was requiring a heavy investment in sales and marketing. The results were plain to see. Vincor missed analyst expectations for five quarters in a row and its stock tumbled. The moment seemed opportune for us to move. For us, though, the question was two-fold: first, would Vincor be a good buy? That issue really came down to this: could we do better with their business outside of Canada than they could, by creating strong cost and revenue synergies? Second, could we convince Vincor's board and ultimately its shareholders to sell to us at a reasonable price? We had asked ourselves these same questions six months before, with Mondavi.

The first question was easy to answer: yes, this would be a good buy. We had scale in those countries that represented 50 percent of Vincor's sales but only 20 percent of their profits. So we felt confident that we could make a big difference in the bottom line and the future of Vincor's great brands. Moreover, the Canadian market was a real prize; Vincor would become another big jewel in our crown and Canada would become our fifth core market. Vincor also seemed like a good fit for our usual acquisition model: of course we would let Vincor remain an independent company. But could we convince Don, the board, and the Vincor shareholders to sell to us at a reasonable price? That was a much more complicated matter.

Don Ziraldo, above, is another Canadian pioneer. With his partner Karl Kaiser, Don created Inniskillin, Canada's premier icewine. What is icewine? It is made from grapes that are left on the vine well into the winter months. The resulting freezing and thawing dehydrates the fruit, and concentrates the sugars, acids, and extracts in the berries. That intensifies the flavors and adds complexity to the resulting wine.

As a start, we met with Don Triggs and his CFO, Richard Jones. We quickly realized that, like Mondavi at the outset, they were not inclined to sell to us. So we gathered together a team of investment bankers and lawyers, plus our own specialists, and prepared to launch the "bear hug." That's where you make a public offer, with the aim of putting pressure on the other company's board and management to either accept your offer or at least negotiate. We launched our bid, feeling very confident that we would succeed; we were offering a price of $31 per share, representing a premium of 40 percent above Vincor's trading price over the previous 90 days.

Now here I have to hand it to Don and his board. They did not succumb to the pressure. They quickly convinced their major shareholders to stand behind them, turning down our offer and ultimately turning down a tender offer at $33 a share – a $1.2 billion value. We battled for months but by December of 2005 our effort was dead; we were defeated. At

Carlos Fernandez Gonzales, above, has totally revamped Grupo Modelo and, with our Barton arm, has made Corona the No. 1 imported beer in America.

Constellation, we were very disappointed; we really wanted a strong base in Canada and we loved Vincor's fabulous brands from the rest of the world. But we figured that was that. Nearly four months went by and we did not exchange a word with Vincor. Ultimately, though, our patience and persistence paid off – and so did theirs. We finally sat back down and gave Don's side exactly what they wanted: $36 a share – and I am glad that we did.

Why? For one thing, Vincor had a first-rate management team. Jay Wright had been running Canada and was getting ready to run their entire international business, while Richard Jones was going to take over Canada. At the suggestion of both Don and Richard, though, we asked Jay to stay in Toronto with his team and grow Canada with the additional resources that we wanted to invest in that market. This suited everyone. Don and Richard were ready to leave corporate life. They had built one of the best companies in the wine business and they had accomplished every goal they had set out for themselves; it was time to move on. So Jay took the helm of Vincor Canada and we integrated the businesses that Vincor had purchased in other countries into each of our core markets. And for Vincor's home market, all I can say is, "I love Canada!"

I love Mexico, too, and it was there that I met one of the most remarkable people in our business, Carlos Fernandez Gonzales. Carlos is the Chairman and CEO of Grupo Modelo. He is the great nephew of one of the founders of the Modelo, and much like Rob and me, Carlos truly grew up in the business. He started at Modelo as an office boy at the age of 11. After receiving a degree in industrial engineering, he held posts in every area of the company. At the age of only 36, he was made CEO of the entire group. From there, Carlos brought many bold innovations to what had been a traditionally run Mexican company. For instance, he initiated a program whereby company executives meet, American-style, with their staffs on a regular basis, to make sure everyone inside the company understands Modelo's market position, mission, and strategy. He initiated production and quality control standards based on Japanese and U.S. "just in time" methods. In sum, Carlos was a forward-thinking leader and he was to play an instrumental role in the growth and development of Constellation Brands.

Since 1978, Barton in Chicago had been one of two U.S. importers of Corona and the rest of the Modelo portfolio. Barton had the account for 25 states primarily in the West, while a company called Gambrinus served the remaining states in the East. Ever since our acquisition of Barton in 1993, Corona had been a powerhouse driver of our business – and we were eager for more. On the face of it, the two-importer model was working well. By the year 2000, Gambrinus and Barton had been able to lift Corona into the No. 1 imported beer position in the United States. Still, there were problems with the two-importer model, and in our view it had outlived its usefulness. In fact, we felt it was now impeding the growth of Corona and the other Modelo brands in the U.S. market. By 2000, the Modelo portfolio represented 40 percent of imports, translating to 15 percent of all the beer sold in the U.S. This portfolio was driving the growth of the entire U.S. beer business, but we felt that as the sole importer we could take Corona to the next level and better service the distributors and retailers, many of whom spanned the country. Gambrinus was eager, however, to hold onto its share of the business. It was in this context, in the year 2001, that we sat down with

Carlos Fernandez Gonzales.

We had an astonishing meeting. Carlos only recently had been appointed CEO of Modelo, and Gambrinus also happened to be renewing its contract in this same period. So Carlos had important decisions to make. During the meeting, we got to know each other and made our case for becoming the sole importer of Corona and the Modelo portfolio. To our amazement, though, Carlos never gave us a direct response. Instead, he carefully outlined his vision for the future of Modelo. It was a simple vision but, as he explained, challenging to execute.

The core of the issue was this: Modelo was and is 51 percent owned by Anheuser-Busch, but it is controlled by the Mexican families that founded the company back in 1925. Making things more complicated, different families had been running different parts of the business. And a big business it was: Modelo was the exclusive importer in Mexico of Anheuser-Busch's entire line of beers. In Carlos' view, the Modelo company needed to be an integrated, collaborative team under one leader, more like Anheuser-Busch under an August Busch or like Constellation under me. That can be hard enough when one family controls the business; imagine how hard it can be when several families are involved! Carlos was a model of discretion, but reading between the lines we gathered that Modelo's decision-making was hampered by family silos, and we understood that 2001 was not the time to press too hard our argument in favor of the one importer model. Instead, as with Vincor, we decided to be patient, all the while being ready to help Carlos in any way we could.

Over the next three years, Carlos did a near-miraculous job of achieving his vision. With the consent of the many families involved, he brought forth new leadership from within the company to drive each key function of the business – but this time the leaders did not come from the founding families. Instead, he chose only accomplished business professionals. By 2005, Modelo was running like clockwork and Carlos had doubled the shareholder value. The following year, the Gambrinus contract was again coming up for renewal. (We had a slightly different contract: ours automatically renewed every five years if we met our sales quotas, which we always did.) With his position as CEO now solidified, Carlos made a decision that was both bold and surprising: he terminated the Gambrinus contract, effective at the end of their term: December 31st, 2006. He was ready to embrace the one-importer model.

We immediately saw this as a major opportunity for us – but Carlos was not about to hand it to us on a silver platter. It was clear that he wanted as much of the Gambrinus profit as before and maybe some of ours too; he was determined to hold onto all of his earlier advantages. To that end, Carlos made it clear that he would pursue many different options; therefore, we knew we had to deliver to him the best possible deal. We looked at all the possible equations. We were certain that Modelo could not run the Eastern United States by itself; with Anheuser-Busch owning 51 percent of Modelo, that would raise antitrust issues. But perhaps Modelo could find someone else who could run the East Coast business for them at a very low cost to Modelo – lower than us. So we really had to come up with a winning formula.

Within that context, we then began long months of negotiations – and they were among

"After this long, intensive push into new markets around the globe, we were all beginning to stop and wonder: where do we go from here?"

RICHARD SANDS

the most arduous negotiations we had ever had. Moreover, the stakes for us were extremely high: we were selling 75 million cases a year, representing more than $1 billion in sales and generating more than $200 million a year in operating profit. The business was also growing by nearly double digits nearly every year. Losing that business would be a terrible blow to our company. Now, by contract Modelo could not take the business away from us, but a brand owner can always make life very difficult for the importer. So we had to strike a very delicate balance. On the one hand, we had to negotiate hard to become the sole importer, but on the other, we had to be very sensitive to what Carlos was trying to accomplish for Grupo Modelo. After long months of discussions with Modelo, we finally came to the conclusion that we needed to create an entirely different business model, one that brought into clear alignment the common interests of all parties and the brand itself.

The result we agreed upon was a joint venture called Crown Imports, an independent entity much like Opus One. Crown Imports gave Modelo and us joint strategic control over the U.S. imports of Corona and the other Modelo brands. But it specified that Modelo could not determine pricing to the marketplace – thereby avoiding potential antitrust issues. More important for Modelo, they would get the Gambrinus profits plus 50 percent of the increased synergies that we were able to provide – a sum estimated to be close to $250 million the first year. This would bring Modelo a 20 percent increase in their base profit – a big win for Modelo shareholders. We also won. Our new importer entity, Crown Imports, was now the sole importer, and its interests were perfectly aligned with the interests of Modelo. This was very important: a serious misalignment can result if the brand owner chooses to raise his prices; that can squeeze the importer. Also, if the importer raises prices to the marketplace, that in turn can hurt sales volume. To avoid either possibility, we agreed on a strategic pricing formula that worked well for all parties. The upshot of these agreements was that our Barton Beers team, under Bill Hackett, was now independent and reported to a joint board of four Modelo executives and four Constellation executives. This enabled us to transition $1 billion of East Coast business from Gambrinus into our fold and to step up our development of the Corona brand all across the country.

The creation of Crown Imports and the acquisition of Vincor represented important steps in the evolution of Constellation Brands. When added to our recent acquisitions of Hardy of Australia and of course the iconic Robert Mondavi, we had a powerful, well-diversified constellation of affiliates and brands, reaching across the spectrum of the beverage alcohol business. During this same period, we also added a new star to our family, SVEDKA, an exciting premium vodka from Sweden.

In the course of 2007, we made some important executive changes as well. Steve Millar retired in early 2006, increasing Rob's responsibilities and control over the operating companies. Over the next several months, Rob realized that we had to revamp our organizational chart. In that process, Jon Moramarco was appointed the CEO for Constellation International, overseeing our wine business everywhere other than North America. Then we formed Constellation Wines North America, with José Fernandez as CEO. In July of 2007, when Rob assumed the Constellation Brands CEO role, Keith Wilson was named the company's first chief administrative officer, with global human resources, information technology, supply chain, and corporate communications reporting to him. These changes streamlined our team and resulted in a more efficient organization.

Then in late 2007, we made another important acquisition: the U.S. wine portfolio of Fortune Brands, Inc. This included such prominent fine wines as Clos du Bois, Wild Horse, and Geyser Peak. The purchase price was $885 million. "Clos du Bois is an iconic brand in California," Paul Hetterich says. "At its price point, apart from Kendall Jackson it is far and away the best brand in terms of size, consumer recognition, and a long history of consistent growth. Clos du Bois and the other wines are wonderful additions to our portfolios."

Paul is entirely right. During this hectic phase of our growth spurt, though, we were all beginning to stop and wonder: after all this phenomenal growth, after this long, intensive push into new markets all around the globe, where do we go from here? What were the next steps for Constellation Brands? Those were important questions – and we needed to answer them. At a personal level, I was starting to ask myself some probing questions as well, questions that refused to go away.

Throughout 2005 and 2006, I knew we were coming to a critical crossroads.

RICHARD SANDS

It was time to pause.

It was time to stand back and reflect.

Throughout 2005 and 2006, I knew we were coming to a critical crossroads. Our expansion had been proceeding at a pace that was, frankly, downright dizzying. Consider just a few basic facts. In 1984, before our big success with Sun Country Coolers, we were a $75 million company, with a few hundred employees, and our major base of operations was Canandaigua, New York. By the close of 2006, following the acquisitions of Mondavi and Vincor, we were a $5 billion company.

Beyond that, the Constellation Brands enterprise now counted nearly 10,000 employees, and we had major business operations in New York State, Chicago, Kentucky, California, Washington State, the United Kingdom, Continental Europe, Australia, New Zealand, and Canada. The "peanut" had become an international giant and an industry leader – and we all knew that we had to do some serious rethinking and readjusting. Rob and I and our executive management team had to be certain that we had the right vision, the right structure, the right people, and the right operating systems in place to move forward with confidence and vigor.

So we did the usual things. We launched studies designed to help us better understand our markets and the profiles of our consumers. We brought in outside consultants to help us evaluate our leadership model, our organizational structure, our staff-development programs, and also our approaches to internal communication, accountability, and strategic alignment. At our corporate headquarters in Fairport, New York, our top people asked many probing questions. Tom Summer, our CFO and a key strategist during our expansion, surveyed the wine, beer, and spirits markets and then posed this question: Given how big we have grown and given all the consolidation that has taken place inside the wine industry, how can we best pursue our goal of doubling in size every five years? Do we need to shift our focus or scale back our ambitions?

As I was writing about Robert Mondavi, all at once I gained a much deeper appreciation of the leadership qualities of Marvin Sands.

RICHARD SANDS

Keith Wilson, our chief administrative officer, asked this: in a corporation so big, so diverse, and so international, how can we make sure that our vast network of employees understands and embraces our guiding values? How can we help them understand that each of them is a vital part of our vision and mission? Michael Martin, our head of Corporate Communications, asked thought-provoking questions about Corporate Social Responsibility. In 2005, we donated substantial amounts to help the victims of Hurricane Katrina in New Orleans and for the victims of the tsunami that devastated Thailand and other parts of the Indian Ocean rim. Rob and I, following Dad's path, actively supported programs in hospital care, education for disadvantaged children, and in music, food, and the arts. But Mike pushed us to think about what more we should do. As a highly visible leader in the wine industry, for instance, should we do more to protect our environment, especially grape-growing lands, the very foundation of our company's richness and patrimony? Jim Finkle, our longtime liaison to our grape growers and many international organizations, asked important questions about our global presence and reach, pushing us to reflect on how we could work more effectively with industry and governmental bodies. Jim gave us eyes and ears and voice in many policy-making forums, and several times he spoke on viticulture and wine-related issues before the European Parliament.

As part of our reflection process, we also did something that was a bit more unusual: we started to look in a more deliberate way at our company's own history, values, and culture. We wanted to see if our past held any hidden clues about the best way to plan and build our future. Our corporate communications team spent months sifting through our archives, press clippings, annual reports, and SEC filings, and from those they drew together a detailed chronology of the evolution of Constellation Brands. Month by month and year by year, starting back in 1945, the team documented our growth and diversification, showing us the high points and also the low, and clearly setting forth the defining events and benchmarks in the life of our company. You can find an abridged version of that chronology on our website, www.cbrands.com. In this same period, we also set in motion the creation of this book. Our aim was to set forth, fully and accurately, the history of our family, our company, and our place in the history of American wine.

There is an ancient Zen proverb that says, "When the pupil is ready, the teacher will appear." In the course of writing this book, I saw again, in a very clear way, how true that had been for me, at every stage of my life in business. When I was finishing my Ph.D. and growing increasingly frustrated by academia – a young idealist eager to do good and change the world – Dad appeared. In his quiet, undemanding way, he opened the door to business, suggesting that I might find it challenging and fulfilling. He also showed me that by being a good business leader I could help a lot of people and do a lot of good. That was the start. Then, when I did jump into the world of business, determined to learn everything from the ground up, Bert Silk and Susan Read appeared. They taught me everything I needed to know about the process of producing, bottling, and shipping wine – and like Dad they showed me how to do everything in the most cost-effective way. Then in 1981, when Dad got sick and I suddenly needed to know how to run our company and push its growth, Ned Cooper appeared, giving Dad the opportunity to put me through a crash course in the fundamentals of carrying out a successful acquisition. The acquisition model he taught me during that period not only proved its value with Ned; over the next 25 years it would guide and propel our meteoric ascension in the world of wine.

There was more. When our company was working hard – but failing – to move up market and establish a foothold in fine wine, again the pupil was ready. And this time Agustin Huneeus Sr. appeared. Agustin showed me, with the patience and subtlety of a master teacher, how different, from the soil up, the business of fine wine was from the business of everyday wine – an illuminating lesson that would quickly prove itself to be pure gold. As we built our portfolio of fine wines, and when we acquired Mondavi and embarked on the tricky process of integration, it was Agustin's teachings that kept lighting the way. Then, with Mondavi now in our fold, we had new hurdles to cross, and again more teachers appeared. Margrit Mondavi taught us that in the world of fine wine, a commitment to art, music, and culture was not an ancillary extravagance; it was central to building an image and brand – and central, too, to building the necessary base of goodwill in a community such as Napa, which is ethnically diverse and economically split. Then, as if to put a final polish on Margrit's instruction, Opus One appeared and, like Quintessa before it, Opus taught us that in the world of fine wine, architecture and design are not empty bows to vanity; more than words can ever be, they are eloquent expressions of the highest standards in refinement and taste. More than any label, they are enduring testimony to the quality of what's in the glass.

Marvin and Mickey Sands were ardent and generous supporters of the arts in our community.

Then there was Robert Mondavi himself, providing his pupils with a wealth of lessons about leadership and character and values. Robert showed us that great leaders need a clear vision of where they want to go – and they need to have the passion, conviction, and integrity to inspire people to follow their lead. Robert also reminded us that the best leaders are not tepid and cautious; they are prudent in their planning, of course, but they are also bold and creative and fearless in pursuit of their dreams. Robert also highlighted for us the importance of demanding "The Best" – and never settling for less. When you do settle for less, Robert's experience showed us, the result is a double negative: it gives you a result that is second-best and it also tells everyone who works for you – or who looks at you from the outside – that second-best is acceptable. It's okay. It will do. If you want to build an organization devoted to being "The Best," and being the very best in the world, that is definitely not a message that you can afford, ever, to send out or approve.

As I was writing about Robert Mondavi and reflecting on his extraordinary leadership qualities, I also came to see Robert's weak points more clearly, and all at once I gained a much deeper appreciation of the leadership qualities of Marvin Sands. Yes, Dad. Robert was a master communicator, always ready and eager to speak his mind; he never saw a microphone that he didn't grab. Dad, by contrast, was a master listener, always keeping his thoughts and feelings to himself. Robert was ebullient and always insisted on being center stage; Dad was shy and usually shunned the limelight; for years he was terrified of taking a microphone and speaking in public. There was something else. Robert, for all his other virtues, never properly mentored his sons, Michael and Tim, and he never prepared the way for a smooth succession. And when he did hand the reins to his sons, Robert never

Now everything snapped into focus.

stood behind them; he stayed out front. With his sons, Robert's leadership model was not one of empowerment; it was one of dis-empowerment. And in the end, when their family company had run into trouble, Robert harshly and very publicly criticized his sons. Having constantly clipped their wings, he was now criticizing their ability to fly. Rob and I need to be eternally grateful; we had the wisest of masters showing us the way.

Now, too, I could see clearly what had been at the foundation of Dad's success as a father and as a leader: Humility. Dad never demanded; he suggested. Dad never ruled with an iron fist; he nudged with a velvet touch. Marvin's way, of course, was the exact opposite of both the traditional patriarch and of those "towering business giants" who so often get bal-lyhooed in the press. Think of a Donald Trump or a Jack Welch or a Lee Iacocca or even a Steven Jobs, and the word "humility" is probably not one that quickly leaps to mind. But "humility" is the exact word that best describes Dad and his unusual leadership model.

The more I reflected, the more clearly I saw it: now that we had grown into a huge global enterprise, a vast constellation of stars and products and divisions, we were obliged to re-think, we were obliged to make some adjustments. After all, keeping such disparate bodies aligned behind a common vision and a common strategy is never an easy task. Still, I now saw clearly that the model of leadership that Dad had shown us, by his word and example, was not obsolete or inappropriate for an enterprise of our colossal size and reach. Just the opposite in fact. What Dad had taught us was now more pertinent than ever. Yes, for all of the fancy studies that we had undertaken, for all of the high-flying consultants that we had brought in and listened to, and for all of the provocative questions that we had raised internally and tried our best to answer, I now saw that our very best source of wisdom and guidance for the future remained Dad himself. "Marvin's Way" was the way that we should proceed.

Now everything snapped into focus. At last I could see, fully and clearly, the unusual wisdom behind our father's teachings. All of the events and themes that I had been explor-ing in the writing of this book flowed together, converged, and came into alignment. Taken together, they formed a clear path for us to follow. If you want to succeed in business, if you really want to climb to the top, Dad had shown us the way. First, you have to take the time to understand the power of money and to learn how to manage it, down to the dime. Then you have to take the time to understand, in the smallest detail, the special financial algebra that is specific to your particular business. Those are the necessary first steps. On that foundation, though, you then have to learn how to master five different skills:

1. The Art of Leading. When we were growing up, Rob and Laurie and I were raised with few rules and no rigidities. We each had different natures and different temperaments, and each of us was encouraged to grow and develop our own special talents and our own special glows. Yes, we were expected to do well and meet our targets in school, but beyond that we were free to explore, be creative, and find our own pathways to success – as long as we stayed aligned behind the guiding values and culture of our family.

I think of this as "the good father model." For Mom and Dad, it had worked well in rais-ing their three headstrong, high-performing children, and it had also worked well for Dad in the early stages of building our business. Now I was absolutely convinced that this same leadership model could continue to work well for us as we charted the future of Constellation Brands. "To lead people, walk behind them," said the Chinese Taoist master Lao-Tzu, some 2,600 years ago. "Be the chief, but never the lord." Dad embodied that wisdom.

Still, in running an organization as vast and diversified as Constellation Brands, don't you sometimes need rules and certain rigidities? Dad would say no. "Richard," I can hear him say, "every situation is different. Be flexible. Listen. And then find the solution that fits the particular situation at hand." Dad would just call that good common sense. But I see it as invaluable business wisdom.

2. The Art of Listening. Dad was a master listener, and time and again he showed us how the best listeners achieve several goals at once: they show the most respect to their conversation partners, thus building rapport and gaining their trust, and they gain the most respect in return – and the most information. In any business, information is power, information is competitive edge. So if you want to maximize your business potential, start by learning how to listen. Also, if you want to initiate a successful acquisition, one based on mutual respect and where both companies feel their needs and ambitions will be heard and fully met, start by listening carefully and building the necessary rapport and trust. Those will always smooth your way.

Now, too, I could see how essential the art of listening is to directing a company like ours, a vast constellation of disparate stars operating in three different sectors of the beverage alcohol business. Each star or division has its own special needs and worries, each has its own markets to master and its own array of customers and consumers to satisfy. Listening patiently – at every level of the organization – is a vital first step in effective management. By listening to your people, you can allay their concerns and fears and also gain an early jump on anyone who isn't happy or is starting to veer off course. Listening promotes convergence and alignment, as well as mutual respect and harmony. As Dad showed us, the wisest leaders keep their ears open but their mouths shut.

3. The Art of Empowering. Dad often told us, "People are your greatest resource. The best are as good as gold." But he also told us that you have to give people freedom, independence, and support, so that they can learn to do things on their own and grow in the process. That is wise advice, and I think it holds true when it comes to raising children, or building a business, or even directing a vast constellation of stars. In each case, Dad showed us, imposing too many rules and regulations will only stifle initiative and creativity, and micro-managing from the top is always doomed to fail.

In terms of empowerment, Dad also presented to us what I think of now as a Golden Rule for Business: Your company succeeds when everyone inside your company succeeds at their own given tasks and responsibilities. Your company grows when your people grow in their personal skills and their individual powers. In other words, being the best you can be as a company depends on your ability to help your people and your teams be the best they can be. In sum, it is not enough to give your people a paycheck; the wise leader will

I saw that our very best source of wisdom and guidance for the future remained Dad himself. "Marvin's Way" was the way that we should proceed.

In business and in life, the learning never stops. And neither should the teaching.

RICHARD SANDS

also give them ongoing training, inspiration, and clear pathways to personal advancement. When they win, you win. That is the path to lasting success.

4. The Art of Creating Wealth. In financial terms, Rob and I learned from our own experience that consolidation and diversification are very potent ways for a company to create enormous wealth. Still, in teaching us the art of fine wine, Agustin Huneeus Sr. made us realize something more: that no amount of financial treasure is ever enough to create a beautiful wine. Money may help, but in the end it is not the money that generates beauty. It's the soil, the terroir, it's the quality of the climate and vines, and it's the skill and care that go into the viticulture and the winemaking. Ultimately, what creates the beauty of a fine wine is the unique blend of artistry, character, culture, and spirit that the winemaker can express – qualities that money alone can never buy. In business and in life, as in wine, true wealth is never weighed in dollars or gold. It's weighed in richness of character and generosity of spirit. And here Dad imparted to us one of his most illuminating lessons of all: that nothing equals the joy and fulfillment of giving to others and helping them succeed and generate wealth of their own. We learned that from the way Dad treated our family of employees and from his long devotion to Thompson Health. As the master Lao-Tzu expressed it, in words simple and pure, "The more you give, the more you have."

5. The Art of Teaching & Mentoring. As we have seen across these many pages, as a teacher and mentor Marvin Sands was second to none. The sustained success of any enterprise, from one generation to the next, always depends on how one group of leaders and managers mentors the next. Dad understood that. He lived it. He practiced it. And he passed that wisdom along to us. Dad also showed us, by his own quiet example, that a master architect and builder, when his creation is complete, feels no compulsion to crow from the rooftops or even to put his name on the front of the door. "A leader is best," Lao-Tzu tells us, "when people barely know he exists. When his work is done, his aim fulfilled, they will say: we did it ourselves."

In business and in life, the learning never stops. And neither should the teaching. By the end of this period of reflection, I had come to a decision: I was ready for a change. The company was ready for a change. And I felt entirely sure and comfortable that my brother Rob was ready to assume command, that he was the man best qualified and best groomed to build the future of Constellation Brands. On July 26th, 2007, we made it official: Rob stepped forward and become the President and CEO, and I remained the Chairman of the Board.

To make this passing of the baton a lasting success, of course I had a model in mind: Dad's. I wanted to be an active chairman, like Dad, and wherever my skills or expertise were needed and requested, I would of course be happy to serve, always working from behind and never out front. The reins were now in Rob's capable hands and, with the same respect that Dad had shown to me, I was not about to interfere or second-guess. Besides, I was ready to focus more of my time and energy on giving back, specifically in using what I have learned to help promote education reform and to help rebuild our inner cities.

Rob Sands

This is probably the biggest challenge of my life. The problems we face as a community and as a nation with regard to education and poverty are systemic in nature, and we need fresh thinking and real solutions. One essential step is to help the many children (and often their parents) who every day struggle to learn. To do that, we need to better understand the different ways that our children learn and go back to teaching strategies that focus on helping students develop their strengths, instead of pounding away at their deficits and weaknesses. The first approach promotes a student's self-esteem; the second destroys it. In this regard, and with the active support of my wife Jennifer, we helped co-found something exciting: a program called "EnCompass: Resources for Learning," headquartered in Rochester, New York. At EnCompass, our team develops innovative ways to help kids learn, grow as individuals, enrich their lives, and also give back to others. We started EnCompass by focusing on children in the suburbs, where many of their parents work for companies like ours. Then, when it became painfully clear that a community is only as strong as its weakest link, we extended our program to Rochester's inner city. This is a noble cause, and I am determined to help it succeed. But here is one of the best parts: As satisfying as it is to help children and impoverished families, I find I am also deepening my own knowledge in the process. As a teacher and mentor, I had not been as gifted or as patient as my father, and now I am seeing more clearly where I still have room to grow. "To act as if you know it all is catastrophic," the Tao teaches us, "and if you try to control it all, you will only stare into your empty hand. True nobility has its roots in humility."

Good luck, Rob. The future is yours. Keep us all reaching for the stars.

CHAPTER 17

The Path Forward

In July of 2007, Rob Sands became CEO of Constellation Brands.

Thank you, Richard. Thank you for everything you've done for our family and for Constellation Brands. You did a sensational job of steering our ship to prosperity and glory, for the benefit of our family, our many employees around the world, and for all of our shareholders. It has been my honor and pleasure to serve and learn at your side. Richard, I also thank you for doing such an admirable job of telling our family story, across three generations and in tandem with the rich history of American wine. Dad would be thrilled; he often dreamed of seeing our family story put down on paper.

Now let me cut right to the marrow of it. Richard and I may differ a bit in terms of temperament and style, but we share the exact same values and the exact same goals: to keep Constellation Brands robust and growing and to elevate our success to an entirely new level. Now, how do we achieve those goals? Let me set forth five areas where Constellation has to keep its focus and continue to advance:

Our Vision. Our plan is not necessarily to be the biggest; our plan is to be The Best. Yes, right now, in 2008, we are the biggest wine company in the world. But a year from now, or two or five, it may well be that somebody else is the biggest wine company in the world. That can happen for any number of reasons, many of which are beyond our control. Also, we feel strongly that being the biggest from a volumetric perspective doesn't make us The Best. Our vision is to create an enduring business model that incorporates the values that have made this company great up to now, then use those same values to elevate us beyond what we are today and make us the very best in our industry and the very best we can be. If we can do that, we will have created a company that will be sustainable, and one which will last and continue to create value for our shareholders for generations to come.

Our Values. We value people. We value quality. We value integrity and are customer-focused. And we value the entrepreneurial spirit. When those core values are aligned, and underpinned by a foundation of rigorous financial discipline, Constellation Brands can produce astonishing results. We've seen it. We've proved it. Our guiding beacon will always be quality. Throughout our history, we have always valued quality. When we have acquired or created or joined forces with high-quality companies in wine, beer, and spirits, we have empowered those companies to continue doing what they do best, providing them with additional resources and knowledge and routes to market that have enabled them to become even better than they were in the first place. That's the formula that has built Constellation's success – and that is the formula that will carry us forward. By being true to our values and by always putting quality first, Constellation has shown that it can enhance everyone's performance and results. Constellation has achieved what few believed was possible: it has proved that big can lead to better. Now we are out to prove that big can lead to best.

Our People. A clear vision and clear values are essential. But those alone do not build the future. People do. If we are going to achieve our goals, Constellation must recruit and retain the best people, make sure they understand our values and tradition, and we must keep them motivated, happy, and always eager to learn and grow. When they succeed, we succeed. In this regard, I see three areas where we must encourage our people to excel: first, in staying close to the ground and close to our distributors and retailers around the world; second, in staying creative and entrepreneurial; and third, in teaching and mentoring our people to be true leaders, at every level inside our constellation of companies and divisions. The best companies cultivate success, with every employee being an essential part of the process. We must do the same.

Our Spirit. In size and reach, Constellation Brands is a global giant, yet in spirit we remain a small, family-run company. So far, despite our size, we have been able to hold onto our small-company entrepreneurial flair and our crafted-by-artisans approach, while still being able to provide big-company resources, services, and scale to our constellation of stars. We must do everything possible to protect that small-company, family-run spirit; it has been fundamental to our success. Being big and corporate can dull your spirit and your senses, and it can make you think only in terms of numbers. Staying small in spirit makes you think in terms of people, your people, your staff, your distributors, your loyal customers, your business family. Consolidation has its dangers. However, like the Mondavis and the Gallos before us, we have been able to stay customer-focused by maintaining close personal relationships with our distributors and retailers. That cannot change. We always have to put the customer first – just the way smaller companies do.

Our Specific Strategy. At Constellation Brands, we will continue to focus on being broad in scale, both in terms of geography and in the range and depth of our product lines. Our customers in the beverage alcohol business have a wide array of needs and we intend to fulfill them, across all spectrums of taste and across the major categories of our industry: wine, beer, and spirits. We will also work hard to stay ahead of the positive trends in our industry and take advantage of those trends whenever and wherever we can. For instance, we are seeing more cross-category consumption. People aren't just drinking beer or just drinking Scotch or just drinking a good Cabernet. The days of the person who stuck to scotch on the rocks or drank only one particular brand of beer – those days are waning. People now are drinking across categories, meaning they are drinking beer on some occasions, wine on others, and spirits on others. That's the new pattern of consumption. Therefore, to be highly successful and create an enduring alcohol beverage business, we need to be well-positioned to satisfy evolving consumer preferences and tastes. We can do that with our scale and breadth of products.

Another trend we are seeing and will continue to take advantage of is what the industry calls "premium-ization." Simply stated, many consumers are moving up market, they are trading up to more premium products and brands. The trend is easiest to see in the wine industry, but it's not just wine. It's happening in beer and spirits as well. What is driving this trend? One factor is consumer aspiration. Another is price: beverage alcohol products are not fundamentally expensive. A bottle of wine or beer is not a Mercedes-Benz, yet it provides a lot of satisfaction to the consumer at a relatively affordable price. To take one example, it is simply not a big economic leap for a consumer to choose to buy a Corona instead of a Coors. For the vast majority of people in the United States and many other countries, moving to Corona will not break their budget. And as other nations around the world become wealthier and aspire to emulate Western European and North American consumption patterns, we will undoubtedly see this trading-up phenomenon elsewhere. We are already seeing the start of it in Brazil, Russia, India, and China. We intend to be ready.

In size and reach, Constellation Brands is a global giant, yet in spirit we remain a small, family-run company.

ROB SANDS

Richard, in the mold of his father, intended to remain "an active chairman," offering guidance from behind but never out front.

Working together as a family, yes, we can reach the stars.

We intend to go wherever the beverage alcohol business is healthy, vibrant, growing and will generate value for Constellation Brands. Historically, we have driven the growth of our portfolio both geographically and on a category basis, and we have done so through organic growth, new product development, acquisitions, and strategic business partnerships. We intend to build on that legacy.

Our Passion. On paper, business plans and strategies can sound rather dull and lifeless; implementing them never is. Richard and I took separate paths into our business, but once here we found the same thing: that building and leading a company like ours is an incredible personal experience. It's endlessly exciting, challenging, demanding, exhausting, exhilarating, gratifying, rewarding, and often fun. We love it. We have a passion for it. And I think building this company has brought out the best in both of us. I enjoyed practicing law. And I worked with many attorneys who truly love their work. Law is a very important profession. It's very cerebral and very interesting, and it certainly requires a lot of hard work and mental agility. But the mindset and spirit that you need for law are entirely different from what you need for business. As a lawyer, your objective – your duty – is to challenge, to be skeptical, to be critical, and to look at things on the negative side: what can go wrong with this contract or deal? How do we plug those holes? How do we anticipate future issues and problems? The law doesn't focus on the can-do; it focuses on the can't-do.

In business, it's just the opposite. The men and women who build successful businesses – Robert Mondavi is a perfect example – don't start out focusing on the negative and worrying about what might go wrong. Their mindset and spirit are positive and full steam ahead! They start with a dream and then they set out to achieve it, and they often charge forward with a blind faith and a total disregard for the minefields ahead, so strong, so clear, and so compelling is their vision of what they intend to create. In law, you rarely, if ever, get to feel that kind of passion or freedom. If I personally had stayed in the law, I never would have felt either that passion or the sheer unbridled joy of being entrepreneurial and creative. Nor would I have ever felt the deep satisfactions and sense of fulfillment that Richard and I have felt in running Constellation Brands and taking it to the top.

In business as in law, though, I think it's best to start at the bottom and learn everything from the ground up. Richard did that and so did I. I worked in the winery in Canandaigua, I cleaned tanks, I cleaned tank cars. So what about our kids, the next generation; will they follow in our footsteps? We won't push, of course, but the door will always be open – in line with Marvin's example. In the end, though, whether the management of our company remains in our family's hands will depend on the competency, experience, desire, and passion of the coming generation. Here again, Richard and I feel the exact same way: the name Sands is neither an obligation nor a birthright. It will be up to each of our children to choose their path and prove their worth. Richard and I rose to the occasion, but only because we had the training, the education, and the desire and passion to do so. What our children will decide, only time will tell. Either way, we'll have a plan in place and, thanks to Marvin, a map to follow.

Investing In The Future. Our vineyards offer us many lessons about business and life, provided we stop to listen and learn. You can't plant a new vineyard one year and expect fruit the next. No, it takes three or four years for a vineyard to start producing grapes, and the highest quality will not appear until many years later. It is usually true, too, that the oldest vines produce the richest fruit. So the vines themselves teach us to be patient and nurturing, to plant now what you want to see bloom in five years or ten, or even thirty or fifty. Like Marvin in his time, Richard and I are busy planting now, both inside the company and beyond. We are both deeply involved in many community projects, especially in the fields of healthcare and education. Richard has outlined his work as a founder of EnCompass. I've been pretty busy too. I served as President of the Harley School in Rochester, and I am now chairman of the board of ViaHealth, the second largest health care system in Rochester. Like Marvin in his work with Thompson Health, I see providing first-class medical care as a top community priority. And we have to find ways to do it better and in a more cost-effective way. In many places in New York State, as in many other parts of the nation, healthcare is a broken industry; it needs the help of businessmen and entrepreneurs to get it back on track. The best solution I see is some form of partnership, with not-for-profit institutions and government on one side, and experienced business people and entrepreneurs on the other. We have to find an effective convergence and alignment of interests. I'm trying to help find the way.

Marvin and Mickey were especially proud of the performing arts center they helped create in Canandaigua, which is now named in honor of Marvin.

The Sands family also has a long tradition of promoting art and culture, both in terms of our own children and in terms of the community at large. Mom and Dad helped create and sustain many important cultural institutions in our Finger Lakes region and the greater Rochester area. Richard and I and our families continue that commitment. My wife Nancy is chairman of the Rochester City Ballet, and we are both involved in the building of a new performing arts center at Rochester's Nazareth College, where my wife serves on the board of directors. For the American Crafts division of the Rochester Institute for Technology, we are funding the creation of a new addition to house their ceramics and glass studios. I am also chairman of the New York Wine & Culinary Center, an exciting new gathering place for wine tastings, cooking classes, and savoring the best of our local vineyards and cuisine. The center is located alongside Canandaigua Lake, with a lovely veranda looking out to the boats on the water. In 2006, Richard chaired a major campaign to add new energy and a welcome facelift to a wonderful 15,000-seat outdoor concert venue that Marvin set into motion 30 years ago. Today it is named the Constellation Brands Marvin Sands Performing Arts Center, CMAC, in honor of the vision and commitment of Marvin and Mickey.

As I write now, in the spring of 2008, I am pleased to report that Mickey is healthy and happy, dividing her time between her winter home in Florida and her summer sanctuary looking out onto Canandaigua Lake. I know that in the beginning she hated this little corner of western New York State, but I think now it has truly become her own "chosen spot." She loves to relax here, play some golf, and she loves going out for dinner, surrounded by her children and grandchildren and her legions of friends. Of course, too, whenever one of her flock starts to veer off into the strange or exotic, you can count on Mom to nudge them back into line.

Is she proud of what her children have accomplished? Yes, of course. But she also reminds us, by her own example, of the many virtues of being humble and kind. And if we get too big for our britches, Mom gently reminds us where it all began:

"Marvin really understood how to build confidence and strength in his sons," Mom says now. "That was something that Marvin learned from his father, and that's what he was able to do with his sons. Everybody else I know who had sons who went into their father's business, the sons were always kept down. The father wanted to be up here, on top, and the sons were obliged to do whatever the father said. That doesn't work. Marvin understood that and took a different approach. Still, what has happened since Marvin's death has been truly unbelievable. And I really think it's been a combination of both Richard and Rob. As the years have gone on, Rob has really come into his own and I know how much that would have pleased Marvin. But what the two boys have accomplished together, well, this has been beyond anything that we ever dreamed. Marvin out-shined his father, and now his sons have out-shined Marvin. I think Marvin would have been so excited and so thrilled and so proud. I know I am."

Thanks, Mom. As you know, Richard and I cherish the wealth of wisdom and guidance that you have shared with us over the years, and so do your grandchildren. We only wish that Dad were here today to share in our joy and to see what we have built on his foundation and by following his wisdom.

In closing, I want to express 10,000 thanks. I want to say "thank you" to each of our thousands of employees and partners around the world. We don't say it enough, but it's absolutely true: our success flows from your success. Our growth flows from your own professional development and your personal growth as caring and very dedicated men and women. In one way, yes, we are indeed a constellation of companies and brands, but in a much more fundamental way we're all family, working hard, growing together, supporting each other, and trying to be the best we can be. Working together as a family, yes, we can reach the stars. And the task won't be so difficult. We just need to follow the wisdom of another Zen master:

When you reach the top, keep climbing.

Mickey, seated, Richard and Rob Sands

INDEX

Acknowledgements & Photo Credits

Canandaigua Lake

Our Special Thanks

To do this book, Rob and I drew on the knowledge and talents of many exceptional people. We want to thank the men and women in our family and our company who shared with us their personal stories and recollections. Their contributions helped us to better understand and portray the history of our family and our company.

We also want to give special thanks to our mom, Mickey Sands, for sharing with us her memories, love letters, photo albums, and, above all, her illuminating insights into our family, our business, and how she and Dad raised us kids. We also want to thank our own wives, Jennifer and Nancy, and our children for their support and patience throughout this project. More than a few family nights, weekends, and holidays were consumed by work on this project; we thank each of you for your help and understanding.

Rob and I also owe a tremendous debt to the group of men and women who took our story and turned it into a beautiful book. We want to thank Mike Martin, our Vice President of Communications at Constellation Brands, for anchoring the entire project with tenacity, tact, and good humor. We thank the incomparable Milton Glaser and his design team, especially Molly Kromhout, for sharing with us their genius and elegance of taste. We thank Matthew Klein for bringing his unique photography and visual sensibility to these pages. And, finally, we also want to thank Paul Chutkow, our co-author, wordsmith, wine historian, and patient guide throughout the process. The story is ours; the final credit for this book belongs to them.

1. Page 6, Richard and Rob Sands; Photos by Matthew Klein.

2. Page 8, Mickey and Marvin Sands; Photo Courtesy of Nat Farbman/Time & Life Pictures/Getty Images.

3. Page 12, Original headquarters, Canandaigua Wine Company; Photo Courtesy of Constellation Brands.

4. Page 15, Elias Sandomirsky; Photo Courtesy of Constellation Brands.

5. Page 16, Flatbush Avenue in Brooklyn; Photo Courtesy of BrooklynPix.com.

6. Page 17, F. Scott Fitzgerald; Photo Courtesy of Princeton University Library and by permission of Harold Ober Associates, Inc.

7. Page 18, Dorothea Lange's "Migrant Mother"; Photo Courtesy of The Library of Congress.

8. Page 22, Prohibition raid in Detroit; Photo Courtesy of the Walter P. Reuther Library, Wayne State University, Detroit, MI.

9. Page 23, "Bacchus," 1596, by Michelangelo Merisi da Caravaggio, oil on canvas; Photo Courtesy of Galleria degli Uffizi, Florence, Italy/SuperStock, Inc.

10. Page 24, Persian spouted vessel, 800-600 BCE; Photo Courtesy of the Arthur M. Sackler Foundation, New York.

11. Page 25, Charles Krug Winery; Drawing Courtesy of the Charles Krug Winery, St. Helena, Ca.

12. Page 25, Father Junipero Serra; Drawing Courtesy of the San Diego Historical Society.

13. Page 26, Early California grape harvest; Photo Courtesy of the California Society of Pioneers, San Francisco, Ca.

14. Page 26, Working in California vineyard; Photo Courtesy of The Wine Institute, San Francisco, Ca.

15. Page 28, Prohibition raid, New York State; Photo Courtesy of the Albert R. Stone Negative Collection, Rochester Museum & Science Center, Rochester, N.Y.

16. Page 29, John Trumbull portrait of Thomas Jefferson; Photo Courtesy of Monticello/ Thomas Jefferson Foundation, Inc.

17. Page 30, Wine pioneer Paul Garrett; Photo Courtesy of Garrett Chapel Trust.

18. Pages 33-53, The Tools Portfolio; All photos by Matthew Klein.

19. Page 55, Sally and Mack Sands, Photo Courtesy of Constellation Brands.

20. Page 57, Marvin Sands' high school report card; Courtesy of Constellation Brands.

21. Page 58, A postcard of The Starmount Country Club; Courtesy of the Greensboro Historical Museum Archives.

22. Page 59, Marvin Sands' U.S. Navy identification card; Courtesy of Constellation Brands.

23. Page 60, U.S. Navy LSTs; Photos Courtesy of the Naval Historical Foundation, Washington D.C.

24. Page 62, U.S. fleet in San Francisco Bay; Photo Courtesy of San Francisco History Center, San Francisco Public Library.

25. Page 64, Steamboat on Canandaigua Lake; Photo Courtesy of the Ontario County Historical Society.

26. Page 66, German Surrender; Photo Courtesy of Keystone/Hulton Archive/Getty Images.

27. Page 68, Mickey and Marvin Sands; Photo Courtesy of Nat Farbman/Time & Life Pictures/Getty Images.

28. Page 71, Japanese Surrender; Photo Courtesy of Weegee/Hulton Archive/Getty Images.

29. Page 74, Marvin and Mickey Sands at Canandaigua Industries; Photo Courtesy of Nat Farbman/Time & Life Pictures/Getty Images.

30. Page 75, Canandaigua town sign; Photo Courtesy of the Ontario County Historical Society.

31. Page 76, The old Canandaigua Inn; Photo Courtesy of the Ontario County Historical Society.

32. Page 79, Mickey Sands; Photo Courtesy of Nat Farbman/Time & Life Pictures/Getty Images.

33. Page 80, The wedding of Marvin and Mickey Sands; Photo Courtesy of Mickey Sands.

34. Page 81 & 83, Marvin and Mickey Sands; Photo Courtesy of Nat Farbman/Time & Life Pictures/Getty Images.

35. Pages 85 to 103, The New York Portfolio; All Photos by Matthew Klein.

36. Page 104, Marvin and Mickey Sands outside Canandaigua Industries; Photo Courtesy of Nat Farbman/Time & Life Pictures/Getty Images.

37. Page 105, Bob Meenan; Photo Courtesy of Constellation Brands.

38. Page 106, Early magazine ad for Kleenex; © 1948 Kimberly-Clark Worldwide, Inc. Reprinted with Permission.

39. Pages 108 & 109, Gold Seal Champagne and Great Western Champagne; Drawings and Labels Courtesy of the Division of Rare and Manuscript Collections, Cornell University Library.

40. Page 112, Sheet music for Chauncey Olcott's "My Wild Irish Rose"; Photo Courtesy of the Lilly Library, Indiana University, Bloomington.

41. Page 114, Marvin Sands at the Canandaigua bottling line; Photo Courtesy of Constellation Brands.

42. Page 115, Canandaigua Industries' trucker; Rod Dutton, Constellation Wines U.S.

43. Page 117, Pilot Wink Lanier and his wife Marie; Photo Courtesy of Wink Lanier.

44. Page 119, Otto Selig and Mack Sands; Photo Courtesy of Wink Lanier.

45. Page 120, Mack Sands and Bentley contest prize; Photo Courtesy of Constellation Brands.

46. Page 124, The outdoor tank complex at Canandaigua Industries; Photo Courtesy of Constellation Brands.

47. Page 125, A staff photo at Canandaigua Industries; Photo Courtesy of Constellation Brands.

48. Page 127, Bert Silk, right; Photo Courtesy of Constellation Brands.

49. Page 129, Richard's Wild Irish Rose bus ad; Photo Courtesy of Constellation Brands.

50. Page 129, Widmer's tour guide; Photo Courtesy of Constellation Brands.

51. Page 130, Susan Read in the lab at Canandaigua Industries; Photo Courtesy of Constellation Brands.

52. Page 131, Magazine ad; Photo Courtesy of Constellation Brands.

53. Page 133, Marvin and Richard Sands; Photo Courtesy of Constellation Brands.

54. Page 134, Laurie Sands; Photo Courtesy of Constellation Brands.

55. Page 135, Rob Sands; Photo Courtesy of Constellation Brands.

56. Page 136, Richard Sands; Photo Courtesy of Constellation Brands.

57. Page 140, Richard and Marvin Sands; Photo Courtesy of Constellation Brands.

58. Page 142, California Harvest; Photo Courtesy of The Wine Institute, San Francisco, Ca.

59. Page 144, Richard Sands; Photo Courtesy of Constellation Brands.

60. Page 146, Ned Cooper; Photo Courtesy of Ned Cooper.

61. Page 149, Richard Sands; Photo Courtesy of Constellation Brands.

62. Page 151, Marvin and Richard Sands; Photo Courtesy of Constellation Brands.

63. Page 152, Ringo Starr; Photo Courtesy of Constellation Brands.

64. Page 156, Richard, Marvin & Mack Sands; Photo Courtesy of Constellation Brands.

65. Pages 159-177, The California Portfolio; All Photos by Matthew Klein.

66. Page 178, Chef Alice Waters; Photo Courtesy of Thomas Heinser.

67. Page 179, CBS newsman Morley Safer; Photo Courtesy of Carl Mydans/ Time & Life Pictures/Getty Images.

68. Page 186, The Glenmore Distillery; Photo Courtesy of Constellation Brands.

69. Page 187, Barton Bourbon; Photo Courtesy of Constellation Brands.

70. Page 189, Matthew Clark delivery truck; Photo Courtesy of Constellation Brands.

71. Pages 190 & 191, Black Velvet ads; Photos Courtesy of Constellation Brands.

72. Page 192, Thompson Health and Sands Cancer Center; Photos by Matthew Klein.

73. Page 193, Marvin Sands; Photo Courtesy of Constellation Brands.

74. Page 196, Robert Mondavi encouraging his team; Photo Courtesy of Constellation Brands.

75. Page 197, Agustin Huneeus Sr.; Photo by Matthew Klein.

76. Pages 198 & 199, Franciscan Estates; Photos by Matthew Klein.

77. Page 200, Charles Hetterich; Photo Courtesy of Constellation Brands.

78. Page 201, Agustin Huneeus and his son Agustin Francisco; Photo Courtesy of Quintessa, Rutherford, Ca.

79. Page 202, Quintessa landscape; Photo Courtesy of Quintessa.

80. Page 205, Ravenswood founder Joel Peterson and Ravenswood vineyard; Photos by Matthew Klein.

81. Page 206, Simi Winery; Photo by Matthew Klein.

82. Page 207, Thomas Hardy; Photo Courtesy of Constellation Brands.

83. Page 207, Blackstone Winery; Photo by Matthew Klein.

84. Page 210, Agustin Huneeus Sr.; Photo by Matthew Klein.

85. Page 211, Robert Mondavi; Photo Courtesy of Constellation Brands.

86. Page 212, The Robert Mondavi Winery; Photos by Matthew Klein.

87. Page 213, Robert and Margrit Mondavi; Photo Courtesy of Constellation Brands.

88. Page 214, The Culinary Institute of America, St. Helena, Ca.; Photos by Matthew Klein.

89. Page 215, Robert and Margrit Mondavi with Julia Child; Photo by MJ Wickham, Courtesy of Copia, The American Center for Wine, Food & The Arts.

90. Page 216, The Oxbow School, Napa, Ca; Photo Courtesy of The Oxbow School.

91. Page 221, Robert Mondavi; Photo Courtesy of Opus One Winery, Oakville, Ca.

92. Page 223, Hubble's Sharpest View of the Orion Nebula; Photo Courtesy of NASA, ESA, M. Robberto (Space Telescope Science Institute/ESA), the Hubble Space Telescope Orion Treasury Project Team, and Hubblesite.org.

93. Page 224, Aging barrels at Robert Mondavi; Photo by Matthew Klein.

94. Page 225, An estate of Chianti Ruffino in Tuscany; Photo Courtesy of Chianti Ruffino.

95. Page 226, Genevieve Janssens; Photo Courtesy of Constellation Brands.

96. Page 228, The Constellation Brands team rings the bell at the New York Stock Exchange; Photo Courtesy of Constellation Brands.

97. Page 230, Opus One Winery; Photos by Matthew Klein.

98. Page 231, Robert Mondavi and the Baron Philippe de Rothschild; Photo Courtesy of Opus One Winery.

99. Page 232, Baronness Philippine de Rothschild and Rob Sands; Photo Courtesy of Opus One Winery.

100. Pages 233-235, The World Portfolio; Photos Courtesy of Constellation Brands.

101. Page 236, wine bottles with maps as labels; Photo by Matthew Klein.

102. Pages 237-243, The World Portfolio; Photos Courtesy of Constellation Brands.

103. Page 244, checking the barrels at Tintara; Photo by John Myers.

104. Pages 245-249, The World Portfolio; Photos Courtesy of Constellation Brands.

105. Pages 250-251, bourbon barrels and dramatic tree; Photos by John Myers.

106. Pages 252-255, The World Portfolio; Photos Courtesy of Constellation Brands.

107. Page 257, Richard Sands in his studio; Photo by Matthew Klein.

108. Pages 233-255, in The World Portfolio, wine bottles with maps as labels